Forever I Will Sing

Metered Guitar Edition

Through-Composed Responsorial Psalms and Gospel Acclamations

November 29, 2020 – November 25, 2021

Year B

Music by Timothy R. Smith

Online Instructional Videos
Visit www.timothyrsmith.com for links to online instructional videos for each of the Responsorial Psalms and Gospel Acclamations. These are helpful in familiarizing cantors and instrumentalists with each piece.

Refrain Melodies for Assembly Worship Aids
To receive pdf of all refrain melodies at no additional charge, send copy of receipt to **forever@timothyrsmith.com**

All musical settings by Timothy R. Smith. Some settings were previously published by OCP, 5536 NE Hassalo, Portland, OR 97213-3638; as indicated, they are available at www.ocp.org

Forever I Will Sing Metered Guitar Edition
Through-Composed Responsorial Psalms and Gospel Acclamations
Year B – November 29, 2020 through November 25, 2021

Musical settings by Timothy R. Smith

www.timothyrsmith.com
ISBN 978-1-735015002

(TR TUNE, LLC)

Also available at www.timothyrsmith.com:
Forever I Will Sing 2021 Metered Keyboard Edition
Forever I Will Sing 2021 Classic Chant Edition

All musical settings by Timothy R. Smith. Some settings were previously published by OCP, 5536 NE Hassalo, Portland, OR 97213-3638; as indicated, they are available at www.ocp.org

Publisher: TR TUNE, LLC, Waterford, MI www.timothyrsmith.com
Composer: Timothy R. Smith
Editor: Barbara Bridge
Cover Art: Mary Dudek
www.marydudekart.com

We are still developing and refining this format and we welcome any feedback. Please feel free to contact me anytime if you have feedback about any aspect of this publication.
Tim Smith
tim@timothyrsmith.com

Singing the Psalm Settings

Psalm Refrains can be adapted to piano, organ, guitar accompaniment, or even SATB choir. The melodies, rhythms and harmonies are designed to embody the spirit of the text.

Verses are set for solo voice (Cantor) with keyboard or guitar accompaniment.

The mixed-meter settings of many of these Psalms was developed from extensive use of *Forever I Will Sing Classic Chant Edition* (still available for 2021). In the chant settings I became more aware of the natural rhythm of text. These settings are based on my perception of those natural rhythms.

Similar to how digital code is based on a series of *ones* and *zeros*, I believe rhythm of language can be based on syllable groupings of *twos* and *threes,* or *duples* and *triples.* In Example 1 consider the text in Psalm 105 (p. 28): *You descendants of Abraham, his servants.* I perceive the natural rhythm as this configuration of duples and triples:

Example 1

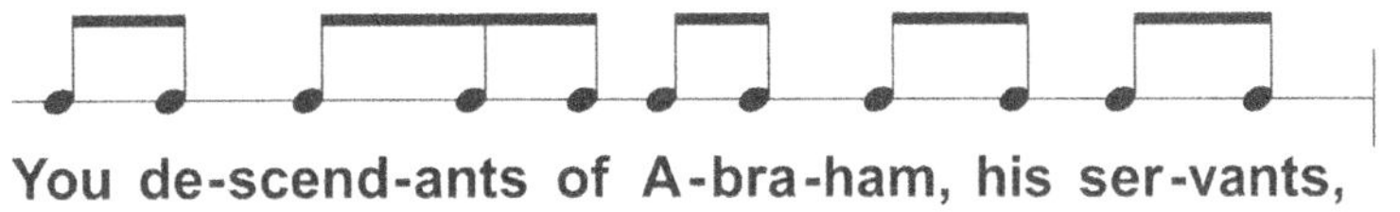
You de-scend-ants of A-bra-ham, his ser-vants,

In this instance, *descendants of* is a triple rhythm and the others are all duple. (1/8 note = 1/8 note)

Consider in Example 2 this segment of Psalm 98 (p. 12):

Example 2

he has done won-drous deeds

Why not indicate the time signature changes?

While some of these Psalms fit within traditional time signatures, many of the settings in this book are driven by the duple/triple natural language rhythm. Since there is no recurring metric structure in this mixed meter environment, we feel indicating constantly changing time signatures would add unnecessary distraction. These rhythms are implemented by following the lowest value of the duple/triple rhythmic groupings – often the 1/8 note.

Of course, there are no absolutes. In Example 3, Psalm 116 (p. 54), the natural text rhythm inspires a specific novel rhythm in which the 1/4 note is the fundamental beat.

Also note the triplet rhythm (*3*) in which 1/8 notes are not equal – but this is the exception. Keep in mind that all 1/8 notes are equal (as in Examples 1 & 2), whether beamed in twos or threes *unless* there is a triplet (*3*) indicator as seen below:

Example 3

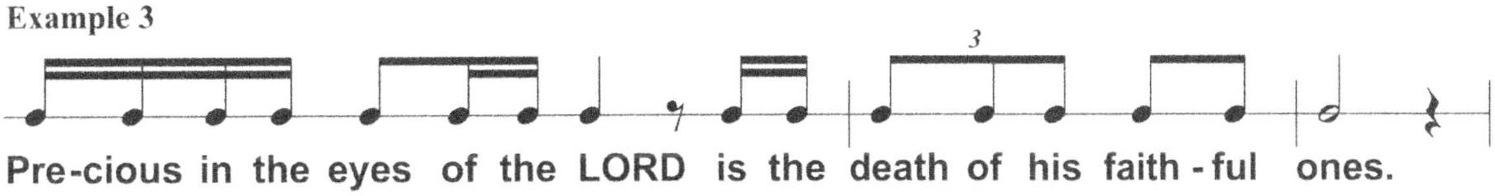
3
Pre-cious in the eyes of the LORD is the death of his faith-ful ones.

PAGE	SUNDAY	REFRAIN	PSALM REFERENCE
8	First Sunday of Advent	Lord, make us turn to you	Psalm 80:2–3, 15–16, 18–19
10	Second Sunday of Advent	Lord, let us see your kindness	Psalm 85:9–10, 11–12, 13–14
12	Immaculate Conception	Sing to the Lord a new song	Psalm 98:1, 2–3ab, 3cd–4
14	Our Lady of Guadalupe	You are the highest honor of our race	Judith 13:18bcde, 19
16	Third Sunday of Advent	My soul rejoices in my God	Luke 1:46–48, 49–50, 53–54
18	Fourth Sunday of Advent	For ever I will sing	Psalm 89:2-3, 4-5, 27, 29
20	The Nativity of the Lord (Christmas): At the Vigil Mass	Forever I will sing	Psalm 89:4-5, 16-17, 27, 29
22	The Nativity of the Lord (Christmas): At the Mass during the Night	Today is born our savior	Psalm 96:1-2, 2-3, 11-12, 13
24	The Nativity of the Lord (Christmas): At the Mass at Dawn	A light will shine on us this day	Psalm 97:1, 6, 11-12
26	The Nativity of the Lord (Christmas): At the Mass during The Day	All the ends of the earth	Psalm 98:1, 2-3, 3-4, 5-6
28	The Holy Family of Jesus, Mary and Joseph	The Lord remembers his covenant	Psalm 105:1–2, 3–4, 5–6, 8–9
30	The Holy Family of Jesus, Mary and Joseph	Blessed are those who fear the Lord	Psalm 128:1-2, 3, 4-5, 6
32	Mary, Mother of God	May God bless us in his mercy	Psalm 67:2–3, 5, 6, 8
34	The Epiphany of the Lord	Lord, every nation on earth	Psalm 72:1–2, 7–8, 10–11, 12–13
36	The Baptism of the Lord	The Lord will bless his people	Psalm 29:1-2, 3-4, 3, 9-10
40	Second Sunday in Ordinary Time	Here am I, Lord; I come to do your will	Psalm 40:2, 4, 7–8, 8–9, 10
42	Third Sunday in Ordinary Time	Teach me your ways, O Lord	Psalm 25:4–5, 6–7, 8–9
44	Fourth Sunday in Ordinary Time	If today you hear his voice	Psalm 95:1–2, 6–7, 7–9
46	Fifth Sunday in Ordinary Time	Praise the Lord, who heals	Psalm 147:1–2, 3–4, 5–6
48	Sixth Sunday in Ordinary Time	I turn to you, Lord, in time of trouble	Psalm 32:1–2, 5, 11
50	Ash Wednesday	Be merciful, O Lord,	Psalm 51:3-4, 5-6ab, 12-13, 14 & 17
52	First Sunday of Lent	Your ways, O Lord, are love and truth	Psalm 25:4–5, 6–7, 8–9
54	Second Sunday of Lent	I will walk before the Lord	Psalm 116:10, 15, 16–17, 18–19
56	Third Sunday of Lent	Lord, you have the words	Psalm 19:8, 9, 10, 11
58	RCIA Option: Third Sunday of Lent	If today you hear his voice	Psalm 95:1-2, 6-7, 8-9
60	Fourth Sunday of Lent	Let my tongue be silenced	Psalm 137:1–2, 3, 4–5, 6
62	RCIA Option: Fourth Sunday of Lent	The Lord is my shepherd	Psalm 23:1-3a, 3b-4, 5, 6
64	Fifth Sunday of Lent	Create a clean heart in me, O God	Psalm 51:3–4, 12–13, 14–15
66	RCIA Option: Fifth Sunday of Lent	With the Lord there is mercy	Psalm 130:1-2, 3-4, 5-6, 7-8
68	Palm Sunday of the Passion of the Lord	My God, my God	Psalm 22:8-9, 17-18, 19-20, 23-24
70	Thursday of the Lord's Supper: At the Evening Mass	Our blessing cup is a communion	Psalm 116:12-13, 15-16bc, 17-18
72	Friday of the Passion of the Lord (Good Friday)	Father, into your hands	Psalm 31:2, 6, 12-13, 15-16, 17, 25
74	The Easter Vigil in the Holy Night	Lord, send out your Spirit	Psalm 104:1-2, 5-6, 10, 12, 13-14, 24, 35
76	The Easter Vigil in the Holy Night	The earth is full of the goodness	Psalm 33:4-5, 6-7, 12-13, 20 & 22
78	The Easter Vigil in the Holy Night	You are my inheritance	Psalm 16:5, 8, 9-10, 11
80	The Easter Vigil in the Holy Night	Let us sing to the Lord	Exodus 15:1-2, 3-4, 5-6, 17-18
82	The Easter Vigil in the Holy Night	I will praise you Lord	Psalm 30:2, 4, 5-6, 11-12, 13
84	The Easter Vigil in the Holy Night	You will draw water	Isaiah 12:2-3, 4bcd, 5-6
86	The Easter Vigil in the Holy Night	Lord, you have the words	Psalm 19:8, 9, 10, 11
88	The Easter Vigil in the Holy Night	Like a deer	Psalm 42:3, 5; 43:3, 4
90	The Easter Vigil in the Holy Night	You will draw water	Isaiah 12:2-3, 4bcd, 5-6
92	The Easter Vigil in the Holy Night	Create a clean heart	Psalm 51:12-13, 14-15, 18-19
94	The Easter Vigil Gospel Acclamation	Alleluia	Psalm 118:1-2, 16-17, 22-23
96	Easter Sunday: Mass during the Day	This is the day	Psalm 118:1-2, 16-17, 22-23
98	Second Sunday of Easter (or Sunday of Divine Mercy)	Give thanks to the Lord	Psalm 118:2-4, 13-15, 22-24

PAGE	SUNDAY	REFRAIN	PSALM REFERENCE
102	Third Sunday of Easter	Lord, let your face shine on us	Psalm 4:2, 4, 7–8, 9
104	Fourth Sunday of Easter	The stone rejected by the builders	Psalm 118:1, 8–9, 21–23, 26, 28, 29
106	Fifth Sunday of Easter	I will praise you, Lord, in the assembly	Psalm 22:26–27, 28, 30, 31–32
108	Sixth Sunday of Easter	The Lord has revealed to the nations	Psalm 98:1, 2–3, 3–4
110	The Ascension of the Lord	God mounts his throne	Psalm 47:2-3, 6-7, 8-9
112	Seventh Sunday of Easter	The Lord has set his throne in heaven.	Psalm 103:1–2, 11–12, 19–20
114	Pentecost Sunday: Extended Vigil Mass	Blessed the people the Lord has chose	Psalm 33:10-11, 12-13, 14-15
116	Pentecost Sunday: Extended Vigil Mass	Glory and praise forever	Daniel 3:52, 53, 54, 55, 56
118	Pentecost Sunday: Extended Vigil Mass	Lord, you have the words	Psalm 19:8, 9, 10, 11
120	Pentecost Sunday: Extended Vigil Mass	Give thanks to the Lord	Psalm 107:2-3, 4-5, 6-7, 8-9
122	Pentecost Sunday: Extended Vigil Mass	Lord, send out your Spirit	Psalm 104:1-2, 24 & 35, 27-28, 29-30
124	Pentecost Sunday: At the Mass during the Day	Lord, send out your Spirit	Psalm 104:1, 24, 29-30, 31, 34
126	The Most Holy Trinity	Blessed the people the Lord has chose	Psalm 33:4–5, 6, 9, 18–19, 20, 22
128	The Most Holy Body and Blood of Christ (Corpus Christi)	I will take the cup of salvation	Psalm 116:12–13, 15–16, 17–18
130	11th Sunday in Ordinary Time	Lord, it is good to give thanks to you	Psalm 92:2–3, 13–14, 15–16
132	12th Sunday in Ordinary Time	Give thanks to the Lord	Psalm 107:23-24, 25-26, 28-29, 30-31
134	13th Sunday in Ordinary Time	I will praise you, Lord	Psalm 30:2, 4, 5–6, 11, 12, 13
136	14th Sunday in Ordinary Time	Our eyes are fixed on the Lord	Psalm 123:1–2, 2, 3–4
138	15th Sunday in Ordinary Time	Lord, let us see your kindness	Psalm 85:9–10, 11–12, 13–14
140	16th Sunday in Ordinary Time	The Lord is my shepherd	Psalm 23:1–3, 3–4, 5, 6
142	17th Sunday in Ordinary Time	The hand of the Lord feeds us	Psalm 145:10–11, 15–16, 17–18
144	18th Sunday in Ordinary Time	The Lord gave them bread from heaven	Psalm 78:3–4, 23–24, 25, 54
146	19th Sunday in Ordinary Time	Taste and see the goodness of the Lor	Psalm 34:2–3, 4–5, 6–7, 8–9
148	The Assumption of the Blessed Virgin Mary: At the Vigil Mass	Lord, go up to your place of rest	Psalm 132:6-7, 9-10, 13-14
150	The Assumption of the Blessed Virgin Mary: At the Mass during the Day	The queen stands at your right hand	Psalm 45:10, 11, 12, 16
152	21st Sunday in Ordinary Time	Taste and see the goodness of the Lor	Psalm 34:2–3, 16–17, 18–19, 20–21
154	22nd Sunday in Ordinary Time	The one who does justice	Psalm 15:2–3, 3–4, 4–5
156	23rd Sunday in Ordinary Time	Praise the Lord, my soul!	Psalm 146:6-7, 8–9, 9–10
158	24th Sunday in Ordinary Time	I will walk before the Lord	Psalm 116:1–2, 3–4, 5–6, 8–9
160	25th Sunday in Ordinary Time	The Lord upholds my life	Psalm 54:3–4, 5, 6 & 8
162	26th Sunday in Ordinary Time	The precepts of the Lord	Psalm 19:8, 10, 12–13, 14
164	27th Sunday in Ordinary Time	May the Lord bless us all the days	Psalm 128:1–2, 3, 4–5, 6
166	28th Sunday in Ordinary Time	Fill us with your love, O Lord	Psalm 90:12–13, 14–15, 16–17
168	29th Sunday in Ordinary Time	Lord, let your mercy be on us	Psalm 33:4–5, 18–19, 20, 22
170	30th Sunday in Ordinary Time	The Lord has done great things for us	Psalm 126:1–2, 2–3, 4–5, 6
174	31st Sunday in Ordinary Time	I love you, Lord, my strength	Psalm 18:2–3, 3–4, 47, 51
176	All Saints	Lord, this is the people	Psalm 24:1bc-2, 3-4ab, 5-6
178	32nd Sunday in Ordinary Time	Praise the Lord, my soul	Psalm 146:7, 8–9, 9–10
180	33rd Sunday in Ordinary Time	You are my inheritance, O Lord	Psalm 16:5, 8, 9–10, 11
182	Our Lord Jesus Christ, King of the Universe	The Lord is king; he is robed in majesty	Psalm 93:1, 1–2, 5
184	Thanksgiving Day	Blessed be the name of the Lord	Psalm 113:1-2, 3-4, 5-6, 7-8
186	Rite Of Entrance into the Order of Catechumens	Blessed the people the Lord has chose	Psalm 33:4-5, 12-13, 18-19, 20 & 22
188	Selected Psalm for Weddings	Blessed are those who fear the Lord	Psalm 128:1-2, 3, 4-5
190	Selected Psalm for Funerals	The Lord is kind and merciful	Psalm 103:8 & 10, 13-14, 15-16, 17-18
192	Selected Common (Seasonal) Psalm for Ordinary Time	The Lord is my light and my salvation	Psalm 27:1, 4, 13-14

Scriptural Index

Page	Scripture Reference
116	Daniel 3:52, 53, 54, 55, 56
80	Exodus 15:1-2, 3-4, 5-6, 17-18
84	Isaiah 12:2-3, 4bcd, 5-6
90	Isaiah 12:2-3, 4bcd, 5-6
14	Judith 13:18bcde, 19
16	Luke 1:46–48, 49–50, 53–54
154	Psalm 15:2–3, 3–4, 4–5
78	Psalm 16:5, 8, 9-10, 11
180	Psalm 16:5, 8, 9–10, 11
174	Psalm 18:2–3, 3–4, 47, 51
162	Psalm 19:8, 10, 12–13, 14
56	Psalm 19:8, 9, 10, 11
86	Psalm 19:8, 9, 10, 11
118	Psalm 19:8, 9, 10, 11
106	Psalm 22:26–27, 28, 30, 31–32
68	Psalm 22:8-9, 17-18, 19-20, 23-24
62	Psalm 23:1-3a, 3b-4, 5, 6
140	Psalm 23:1–3, 3–4, 5, 6
176	Psalm 24:1bc-2, 3-4ab, 5-6
42	Psalm 25:4–5, 6–7, 8–9
52	Psalm 25:4–5, 6–7, 8–9
192	Psalm 27:1, 4, 13-14
36	Psalm 29:1-2, 3-4, 3, 9-10
82	Psalm 30:2, 4, 5-6, 11-12, 13
134	Psalm 30:2, 4, 5–6, 11, 12, 13
72	Psalm 31:2, 6, 12-13, 15-16, 17, 25
48	Psalm 32:1–2, 5, 11
186	Psalm 33:4-5, 12-13, 18-19, 20 & 22
76	Psalm 33:4-5, 6-7, 12-13, 20 & 22
168	Psalm 33:4–5, 18–19, 20, 22
126	Psalm 33:4–5, 6, 9, 18–19, 20, 22
114	Psalm 33:10-11, 12-13, 14-15
152	Psalm 34:2–3, 16–17, 18–19, 20–21
146	Psalm 34:2–3, 4–5, 6–7, 8–9
102	Psalm 4:2, 4, 7–8, 9
40	Psalm 40:2, 4, 7–8, 8–9, 10
88	Psalm 42:3, 5; 43:3, 4
150	Psalm 45:10, 11, 12, 16
110	Psalm 47:2-3, 6-7, 8-9
92	Psalm 51:12-13, 14-15, 18-19
50	Psalm 51:3-4, 5-6ab, 12-13, 14 & 17
64	Psalm 51:3–4, 12–13, 14–15
160	Psalm 54:3–4, 5, 6 & 8
32	Psalm 67:2–3, 5, 6, 8
34	Psalm 72:1–2, 7–8, 10–11, 12–13

Page	Scripture Reference
144	Psalm 78:3–4, 23–24, 25, 54
8	Psalm 80:2–3, 15–16, 18–19
10	Psalm 85:9–10, 11–12, 13–14
138	Psalm 85:9–10, 11–12, 13–14
18	Psalm 89:2-3, 4-5, 27, 29
20	Psalm 89:4-5, 16-17, 27, 29
166	Psalm 90:12–13, 14–15, 16–17
130	Psalm 92:2–3, 13–14, 15–16
182	Psalm 93:1, 1–2, 5
58	Psalm 95:1-2, 6-7, 8-9
44	Psalm 95:1–2, 6–7, 7–9
22	Psalm 96:1-2, 2-3, 11-12, 13
24	Psalm 97:1, 6, 11-12
26	Psalm 98:1, 2-3, 3-4, 5-6
108	Psalm 98:1, 2–3, 3–4
12	Psalm 98:1, 2–3ab, 3cd–4
112	Psalm 103:1–2, 11–12, 19–20
190	Psalm 103:8 & 10, 13-14, 15-16, 17-18
122	Psalm 104:1-2, 24 & 35, 27-28, 29-30
74	Psalm 104:1-2, 5-6, 10, 12, 13-14, 24, 35
124	Psalm 104:1, 24, 29-30, 31, 34
28	Psalm 105:1–2, 3–4, 5–6, 8–9
120	Psalm 107:2-3, 4-5, 6-7, 8-9
132	Psalm 107:23-24, 25-26, 28-29, 30-31
184	Psalm 113:1-2, 3-4, 5-6, 7-8
158	Psalm 116:1–2, 3–4, 5–6, 8–9
54	Psalm 116:10, 15, 16–17, 18–19
70	Psalm 116:12-13, 15-16bc, 17-18
128	Psalm 116:12–13, 15–16, 17–18
94	Psalm 118:1-2, 16-17, 22-23
96	Psalm 118:1-2, 16-17, 22-23
104	Psalm 118:1, 8–9, 21–23, 26, 28, 29
98	Psalm 118:2-4, 13-15, 22-24
136	Psalm 123:1–2, 2, 3–4
170	Psalm 126:1–2, 2–3, 4–5, 6
188	Psalm 128:1-2, 3, 4-5
30	Psalm 128:1-2, 3, 4-5, 6
164	Psalm 128:1–2, 3, 4–5, 6
66	Psalm 130:1-2, 3-4, 5-6, 7-8
148	Psalm 132:6-7, 9-10, 13-14
60	Psalm 137:1–2, 3, 4–5, 6
142	Psalm 145:10–11, 15–16, 17–18
156	Psalm 146:6-7, 8–9, 9–10
178	Psalm 146:7, 8–9, 9–10
46	Psalm 147:1–2, 3–4, 5–6

Refrain Index

Page	Refrain
24	A light will shine on us this day
26	All the ends of the earth
94	Alleluia
50	Be merciful, O Lord,
30	Blessed are those who fear the Lord
188	Blessed are those who fear the Lord
184	Blessed be the name of the Lord
126	Blessed the people the Lord has chosen
186	Blessed the people the Lord has chosen
114	Blessed the people the Lord has chosen
92	Create a clean heart
64	Create a clean heart
72	Father, into your hands
166	Fill us with your love, O Lord
18	For ever I will sing
20	Forever I will sing
98	Give thanks to the Lord
120	Give thanks to the Lord
132	Give thanks to the Lord
116	Glory and praise forever
110	God mounts his throne
40	Here am I, Lord; I come to do your will
174	I love you, Lord, my strength
48	I turn to you, Lord, in time of trouble
82	I will praise you Lord
134	I will praise you, Lord
106	I will praise you, Lord, in the assembly
128	I will take the cup of salvation
54	I will walk before the Lord
158	I will walk before the Lord
44	If today you hear his voice
58	If today you hear his voice
60	Let my tongue be silenced
80	Let us sing to the Lord
88	Like a deer
34	Lord, every nation on earth
148	Lord, go up to your place of rest
130	Lord, it is good to give thanks to you
10	Lord, let us see your kindness
138	Lord, let us see your kindness
102	Lord, let your face shine on us
168	Lord, let your mercy be on us
8	Lord, make us turn to you
74	Lord, send out your Spirit

Page	Refrain
124	Lord, send out your Spirit
176	Lord, this is the people
56	Lord, you have the words
86	Lord, you have the words
118	Lord, you have the words
32	May God bless us in his mercy
164	May the Lord bless us all the days
68	My God, my God
16	My soul rejoices in my God
70	Our blessing cup is a communion
136	Our eyes are fixed on the Lord
178	Praise the Lord, my soul
156	Praise the Lord, my soul!
46	Praise the Lord, who heals
12	Sing to the Lord a new song
146	Taste and see the goodness of the Lord
152	Taste and see the goodness of the Lord
42	Teach me your ways, O Lord
76	The earth is full of the goodness
142	The hand of the Lord feeds us
144	The Lord gave them bread from heaven
170	The Lord has done great things for us
108	The Lord has revealed to the nations
112	The Lord has set his throne in heaven.
190	The Lord is kind and merciful
182	The Lord is king; he is robed in majesty
192	The Lord is my light and my salvation
62	The Lord is my shepherd
140	The Lord is my shepherd
28	The Lord remembers his covenant
160	The Lord upholds my life
36	The Lord will bless his people
154	The one who does justice
162	The precepts of the Lord
150	The queen stands at your right hand
104	The stone rejected by the builders
96	This is the day
22	Today is born our savior
66	With the Lord there is mercy
78	You are my inheritance
180	You are my inheritance, O Lord
14	You are the highest honor of our race
84	You will draw water
90	You will draw water

First Sunday of Advent

November 29

(M.M. ♩ = c. 60)

Psalm 80:2-3, 15-16, 18-19

REFRAIN
Em D/E Cmaj7/E D/E Am7 Bm7 Esus4
Lord, make us turn to you; let us see your face and we shall be saved.
Verse 1
Em G/D
O shep-herd of Is-ra-el, heark-en, from your throne up-on the cher-u-bim, shine
Cmaj7 D/A Asus2 C D Em
forth. Rouse your pow'r and come to save us. [Come to save us.]
to Refrain
Verse 2
Em G/D Cmaj7
Once a-gain, O LORD of hosts, look down from heav-en, and see; take
D/A Asus2 Em G/D
care of this vine, and pro-tect what your right hand has
Cmaj7 D/A Asus2 C D Em
plant-ed, the son of man whom you your-self made strong.
to Refrain

Verse 3
Em
May your help be with the man of your right hand, with the son of man whom
G/D Cmaj7 D/A Asus2 Cmaj7
you your-self made strong. Then we will no more with-draw from you; give us new
D/A Asus2 C D Em
to Refrain
life, and we will call up - on your name.

Gospel Acclamation: cf. Psalm 85:8

Acclamation: (Keyboard/SATB) NO. III

(M.M. ♩= c. 160)

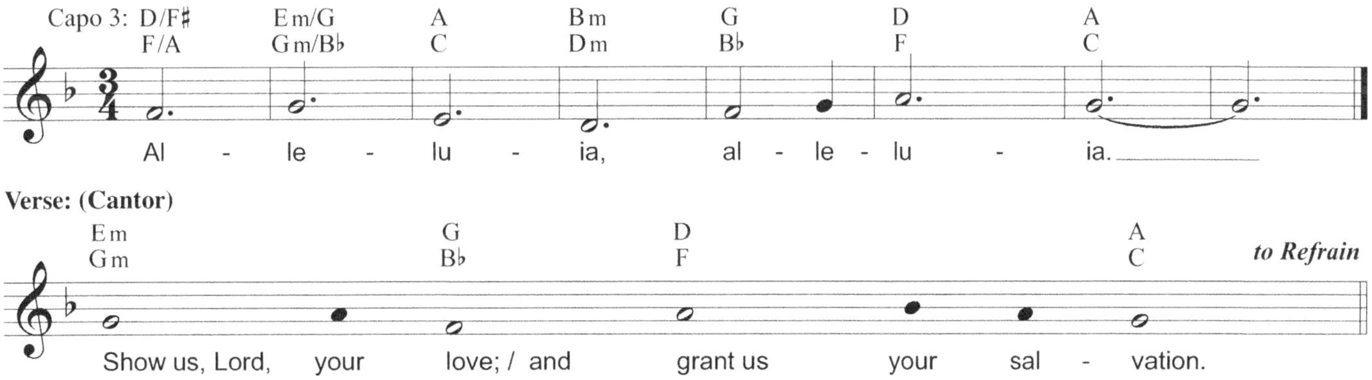
Capo 3: D/F♯ Em/G A Bm G D A
F/A Gm/B♭ C Dm B♭ F C
Al - le - lu - ia, al - le - lu - ia.
Verse: (Cantor)
Em G D A
Gm B♭ F C
to Refrain
Show us, Lord, your love; / and grant us your sal - vation.

Second Sunday of Advent

December 6

(M.M. ♩ = c. 90)

Psalm 85:9, 10, 11-12, 13-14

REFRAIN

Em G D C
Lord, let us see your kind - ness, and grant us your sal - va - tion.

Verse 1 (M.M. ♩ = c. 76)

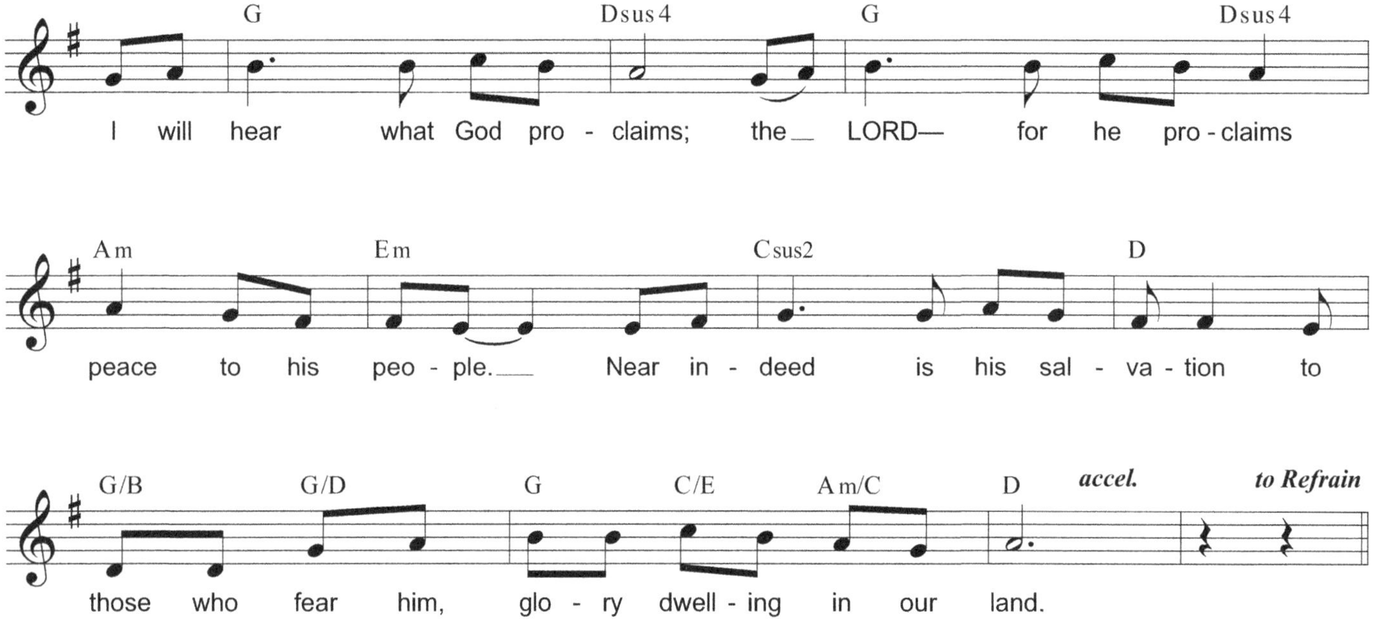
G Dsus4 G Dsus4
I will hear what God pro - claims; the LORD— for he pro - claims
Am Em Csus2 D
peace to his peo - ple. Near in - deed is his sal - va - tion to
G/B G/D G C/E Am/C D
accel.
to Refrain
those who fear him, glo - ry dwell - ing in our land.

Verse 2 (M.M. ♩ = c. 76)

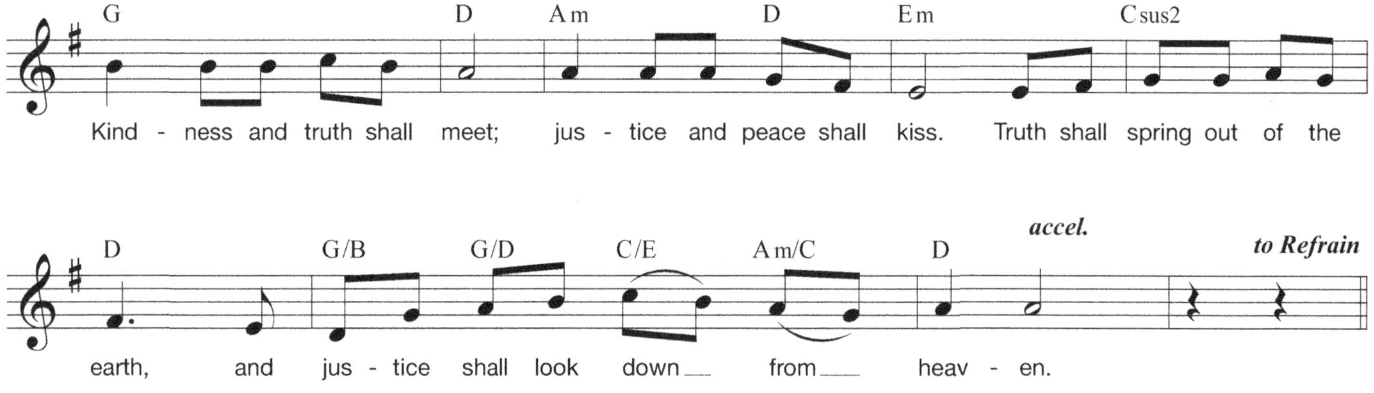
G D Am D Em Csus2
Kind - ness and truth shall meet; jus - tice and peace shall kiss. Truth shall spring out of the
D G/B G/D C/E Am/C D
accel.
to Refrain
earth, and jus - tice shall look down from heav - en.

Verse 3 (M.M. ♩ = c. 76)

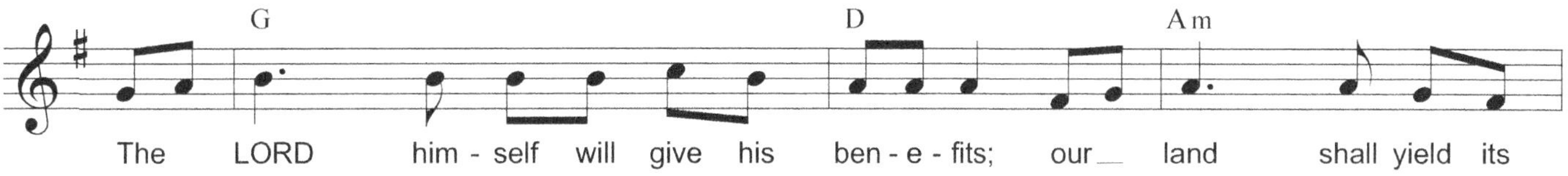
G D Am
The LORD him - self will give his ben - e - fits; our land shall yield its

Em Csus2 D
in - crease. Jus - tice shall walk be - fore him, and pre -

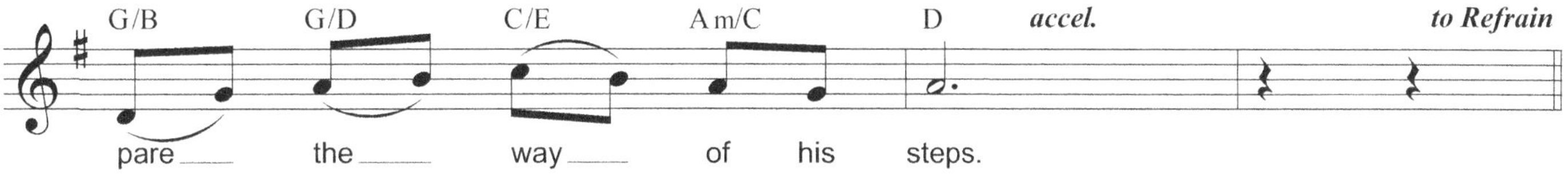
G/B G/D C/E Am/C D accel. to Refrain
pare the way of his steps.

Gospel Acclamation: Luke 3:4, 6

Acclamation: (Keyboard/SATB) NO. I

(𝅗𝅥 = c. 96)

Capo 1: D A/C♯ G/B D/A G D/F♯ D/A A Bm Em D/F♯ Gsus2
E♭ B♭/D A♭/C E♭/B♭ A♭ E♭/G E♭/B♭ B♭ Cm Fm E♭/G A♭sus2
Al - le - lu - ia, al - le - lu - ia, al - le - lu - ia.

Verse: (Cantor)

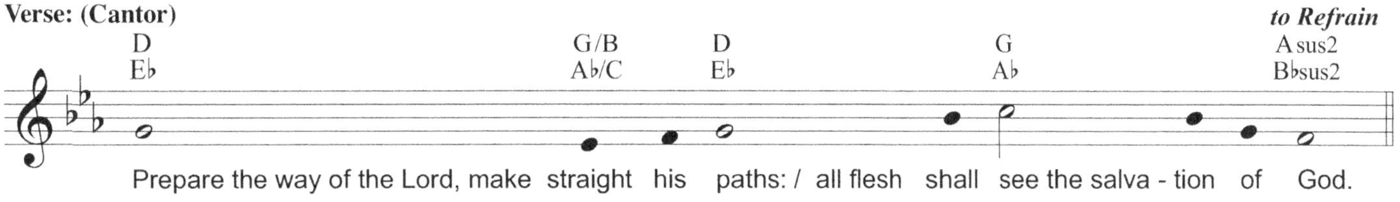
to Refrain
D G/B D G Asus2
E♭ A♭/C E♭ A♭ B♭sus2
Prepare the way of the Lord, make straight his paths: / all flesh shall see the salva - tion of God.

The Immaculate Conception of the Blessed Virgin Mary

December 8

(M.M. ♪ = c. 190)
Psalm 98:1, 2-3ab, 3cd-4
REFRAIN
Capo 5: Am C D Am7 Fmaj7 Em7 Am
Dm F G Dm7 B♭maj7 Am7 Dm
Sing to the Lord a new song, for he has done mar - vel-ous deeds.
Verse 1
Fmaj7 G Em Am Fmaj7 G Am
B♭maj7 C Am Dm B♭maj7 C Dm
Sing to the LORD a new song, for he has done won - drous deeds; His
to Refrain
Dm G/B C Am F Bdm7/D Esus4 E
Gm C/E F Dm B♭ Edm7/G Asus4 A
right hand has won vic - t'ry for him, his ho - ly arm.
Verse 2
Am Fmaj7 G Em Am Fadd2 Gsus2
Dm B♭maj7 C Am Dm B♭add2 Csus2
The LORD has made his sal - va - tion known: in the sight of the
Am Fmaj7 Gsus2 Am Dm
Dm B♭maj7 Csus2 Dm Gm
na - tions he has re - vealed his jus - tice. He has re - mem - bered his
to Refrain
G/B C Am F Bdm7/D Esus4 E
C/E F Dm B♭ Edm7/G Asus4 A
kind - ness and his faith - ful - ness toward the house of Is - ra - el.

Verse 3

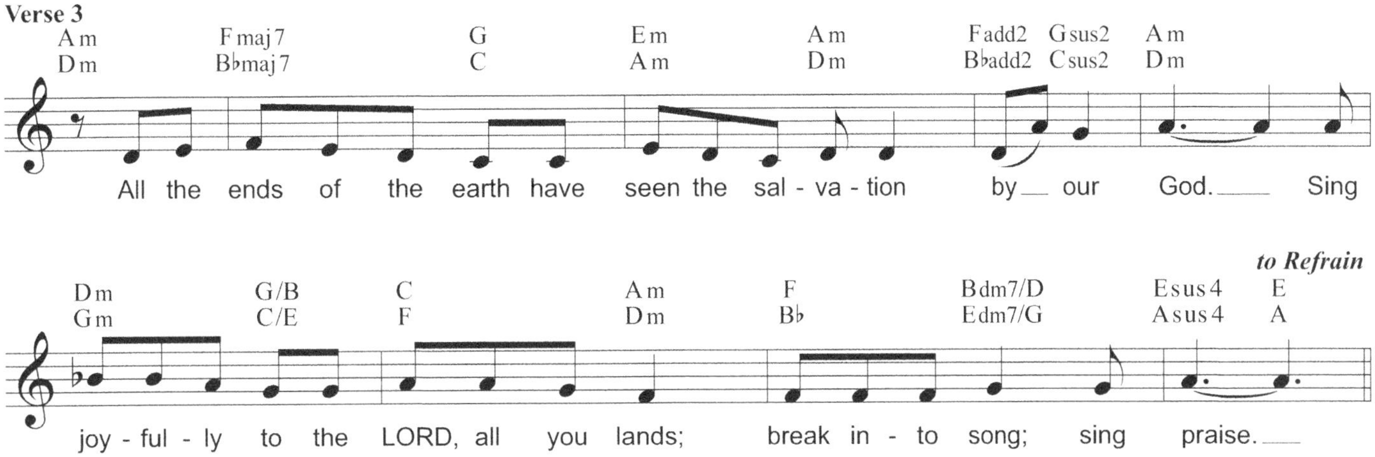
Am Fmaj7 G Em Am Fadd2 Gsus2 Am
Dm B♭maj7 C Am Dm B♭add2 Csus2 Dm
All the ends of the earth have seen the sal - va - tion by our God. Sing
to Refrain
Dm G/B C Am F Bdm7/D Esus4 E
Gm C/E F Dm B♭ Edm7/G Asus4 A
joy - ful - ly to the LORD, all you lands; break in - to song; sing praise.

Gospel Acclamation: Luke 1:28

Acclamation: (Keyboard/SATB) NO. IV

(M.M. ♩ = c. 116)

Capo 5: G Am F C Dm7
C Dm B♭ F Gm7
Al - le - lu - ia, al - le - lu - ia, al - le -
1.
2 and onward
C/E Fmaj7 Gsus4 Gsus4
F/A B♭maj7 Csus4 Csus4
lu - ia. ia.

Verse: (Cantor)

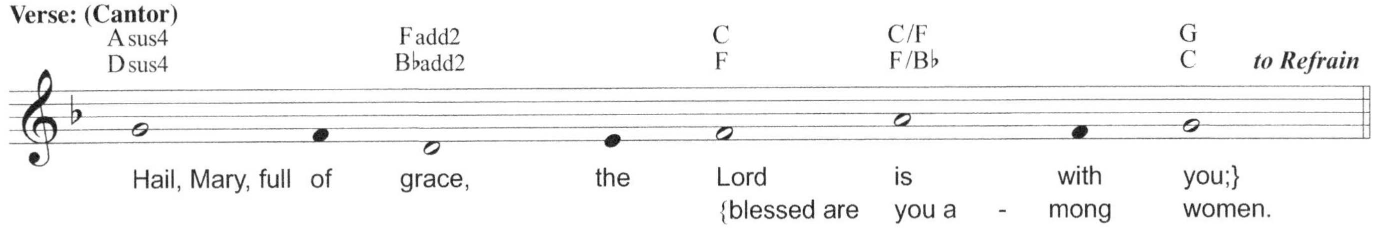
Asus4 Fadd2 C C/F G
Dsus4 B♭add2 F F/B♭ C
to Refrain
Hail, Mary, full of grace, the Lord is with you;}
{blessed are you a - mong women.

Our Lady of Guadalupe

December 12

(M.M. ♩ = c. 68)

REFRAIN
Judith 13:18bcde, 19
Capo 3: Bm Dm
F♯m/A Am/C
Gmaj7 B♭maj7
D/F♯ F/A
A C
Bm Dm
You are the high - est hon - or of our race.
Verse 1
Bless-ed are you, daugh-ter, by the Most High God, a - bove all the wom-en on
earth; and bless-ed be the LORD God, the cre - a - tor of heav - en and earth.
to Refrain
Verse 2
Your deed of hope will nev - er be for - got - ten by
those who tell of the might of God. You are the high-est hon-or of our race.
to Refrain
F♯m/B Am/D
F♯m Am
Em7 Gm7

Gospel Acclamation:

Acclamation: (Keyboard/SATB) NO. II

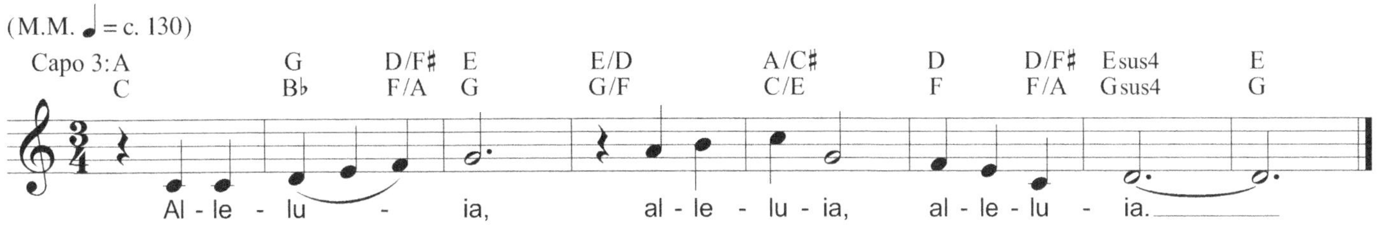
(M.M. ♩ = c. 130)
Capo 3: A G D/F♯ E E/D A/C♯ D D/F♯ Esus4 E
C B♭ F/A G G/F C/E F F/A Gsus4 G
Al - le - lu - ia, al - le - lu - ia, al - le - lu - ia.

Verse: (Cantor)

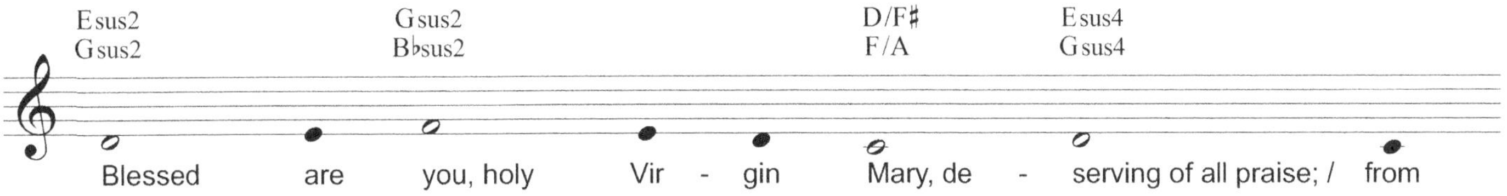
Esus2 Gsus2 D/F♯ Esus4
Gsus2 B♭sus2 F/A Gsus4
Blessed are you, holy Vir - gin Mary, de - serving of all praise; / from

A/C♯ Dsus2 E
C/E Fsus2 G
you rose the sun of justice, Christ our God.
to Refrain

Third Sunday of Advent

December 13

(M.M. ♩ = c. 66)

Luke 1:46–48, 49–50, 53–54

REFRAIN
D A/C♯ G/B D/A Em7/G A D/F♯ Bm7 G Em7 Asus4 A
My soul re-joic-es in my God. My soul re-joic-es in my God.
Verse 1
Am/C G/B D/A
My soul pro-claims the great-ness of the Lord; my spir-it re-
Dm/F Em7/G D/A D/A Fmaj7 G/B
joic-es in God my Sav-ior, for he has looked up-on his low-ly
A/C♯ Dm7 Em7 Dm/F G A
ser-vant. From this day all gen-er-a-tions will call me bless-ed:
to Refrain
Verse 2
Am/C G/B D/A
The Al-might-y has done great things for me, and
Dm/F Em7/G D/A Fmaj7 G/B
ho-ly is his Name. He has mer-cy on those who
A/C♯ Dm7 Em7 Dm/F G A
fear him in eve-ry gen-er-a-tion.
to Refrain

Verse 3
Am/C G/B D/A Dm/F
He has filled the hun - gry with good things, and the rich he has
Em7/G D/A Fmaj7 G/B
sent a - way emp - ty. He has come to the help of his ser - vant
to Refrain
A/C♯ Dm7 Em7 Dm/F G A
Is - ra - el for he has re - mem - bered his prom - ise of mer - cy,

Gospel Acclamation: Isaiah 61:1 (cited in Luke 4:18)

Acclamation: (Keyboard/SATB) NO. IV

(M.M. ♩ = c. 116)
Capo 5: G Am F C Dm7
C Dm B♭ F Gm7
Al - le - lu - ia, al - le - lu - ia, al - le -
C/E Fmaj7 Gsus4 Gsus4
F/A B♭maj7 Csus4 Csus4
1.
2 and onward
lu - ia. ia.
Verse: (Cantor)
to Refrain
Asus4 Fadd2 C C/F G
Dsus4 B♭add2 F F/B♭ C
The Spirit of the Lord is up - on me, because he has a - nointed me / to bring glad tidings to the poor.

Fourth Sunday of Advent

December 20

(M.M. ♩ = c. 90)
REFRAIN
Psalm 89:2-3, 4-5, 27, 29
Asus4 Dsus2 A/D G/D D
For ev - er I will sing the good - ness of the Lord. For
G/B D/A Gsus2 Dm/F C/E D
ev - er I will sing the good - ness of the Lord.
Verse 1 (M.M. ♩ = c. 76)
D Am Gsus2
The prom - is - es of the LORD I will sing for - ev - er; through all gen - er -
Csus2 F/B♭ Dsus2 D
a - tions my mouth shall pro - claim your faith - ful - ness. For you have said, "My
Am Em G/F Asus2
to Refrain
kind - ness is es - tab - lished for - ev - er"; in heav - en you have con - firmed your faith - ful - ness.
Verse 2 (M.M. ♩ = c. 76)
D Am Gsus2 Csus2 F/B♭ Dsus2
"I have made a cov - e - nant with my cho - sen one, I have sworn to Da - vid my ser - vant: For -
to Refrain
D Am Em G/F Asus2
ev - er will I con - firm your pos - ter - i - ty and es - tab - lish your throne for all gen - er - a - tions."

Verse 3 (M.M. ♩ = c. 76)

D Am Gsus2 Csus2 F/B♭ Dsus2
"He shall say of me, 'You are my fa - ther, my God, the Rock my sav - ior.' For-

to Refrain
D Am Em G/F Asus2
ev - er I will main - tain my kind - ness toward him, and my cov - e - nant with him stands firm."

Gospel Acclamation: Luke 1:38

Acclamation: (Keyboard/SATB) NO. II

(M.M. ♩ = c. 130)

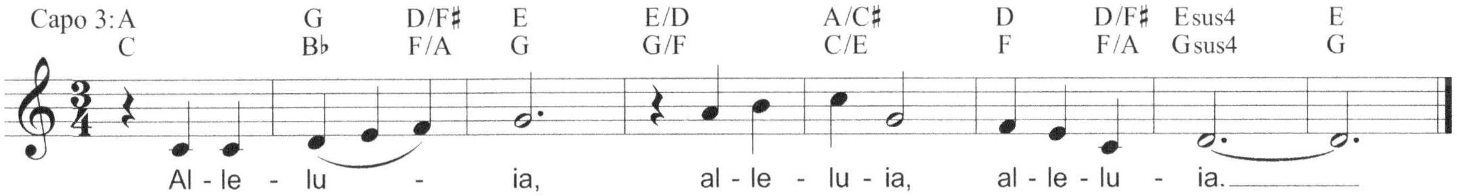
Capo 3: A G D/F♯ E E/D A/C♯ D D/F♯ Esus4 E
C B♭ F/A G G/F C/E F F/A Gsus4 G
Al - le - lu - ia, al - le - lu - ia, al - le - lu - ia.

Verse: (Cantor)

to Refrain
Esus2 Gsus2 D/F♯ A/C♯ Dsus2 E
Gsus2 B♭sus2 F/A C/E Fsus2 G
Behold, I am the handmaid of the Lord. / May it be done to me ac - cording to your word.

The Nativity of The Lord (Christmas): At the Vigil Mass

December 24

(M.M. ♩ = c. 90)
REFRAIN
Psalm 89:4-5, 16-17, 27, 29
Asus4 Dsus2 A/D G/D D
For ev - er I will sing the good - ness of the Lord. For
G/B D/A Gsus2 Dm/F C/E D
ev - er I will sing the good - ness of the Lord.
Verse 1 (M.M. ♩ = c. 76)
D Am Gsus2 Csus2 F/B♭ Dsus2
I have made a cov-e-nant with my cho-sen one, I have sworn to Da-vid my ser - vant: for-
to Refrain
D Am Em G/F Asus2
ev-er will I con - firm your pos - ter-i - ty and es-tab-lish your throne for all gen-er - a-tions.
Verse 2 (M.M. ♩ = c. 76)
D Am Gsus2 Csus2 F/B♭
Bless-ed the peo-ple who know the joy-ful shout; in the light of your coun-te-nance, O LORD; they
to Refrain
Dsus2 D Am Em G/F Asus2
walk. At your name they re - joice all the day, and through your jus-tice they are ex - alt-ed.

Verse 3 (M.M. ♩ = c. 76)

D Am Gsus2 Csus2 F/B♭ Dsus2
He shall say of me, "You are my fa - ther, my God, the rock, my sav - ior." For-

to Refrain

D Am Em G/F Asus2
ev-er I will main - tain my kind-ness toward him, and my cov-e-nant with him stands firm.

Gospel Acclamation:

Acclamation: (Keyboard/SATB) NO. V

(M.M. ♪ = c. 150)

C Dm Am Dm F/A G/B G
Al - le - lu - ia, al - le - lu - ia. Al - le - lu - ia, al - le - lu - ia.

Verse: (Cantor) *to Refrain*

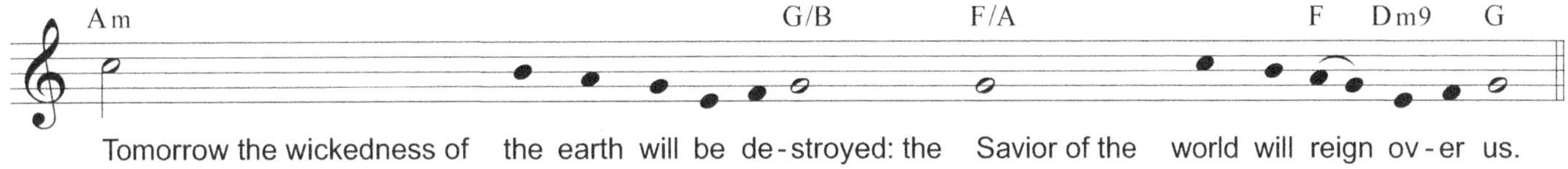
Am G/B F/A F Dm9 G
Tomorrow the wickedness of the earth will be de-stroyed: the Savior of the world will reign ov-er us.

The Nativity of the Lord (Christmas): At the Mass during the Night

December 25

(M.M. ♩ = c. 150)
REFRAIN
Psalm 96:1-2, 2-3, 11-12, 13
A D Bm F♯m G D/F♯ Em D
To - day is born our Sav - ior, Christ, the Lord, Christ the Lord. To -
C G/B G Em7/A D
day is born our Sav - ior, Christ the Lord.
Verse 1
D G D/F♯ Em D Cmaj7
Sing to the LORD a new song; sing to the
Bm7 A/C♯ Em D/F♯ Em/G Asus4 A
LORD, all you lands. Sing to the LORD; bless his name.
to Refrain
Verse 2
D G D/F♯ Em D Cmaj7 Bm7
An - nounce his sal - va - tion, day af - ter day. Tell his glo - ry a - mong the
A/C♯ Em D/F♯ Em/G Asus4 A
na - tions; a - mong all peo - ples, his won - drous deeds.
to Refrain

Verse 3

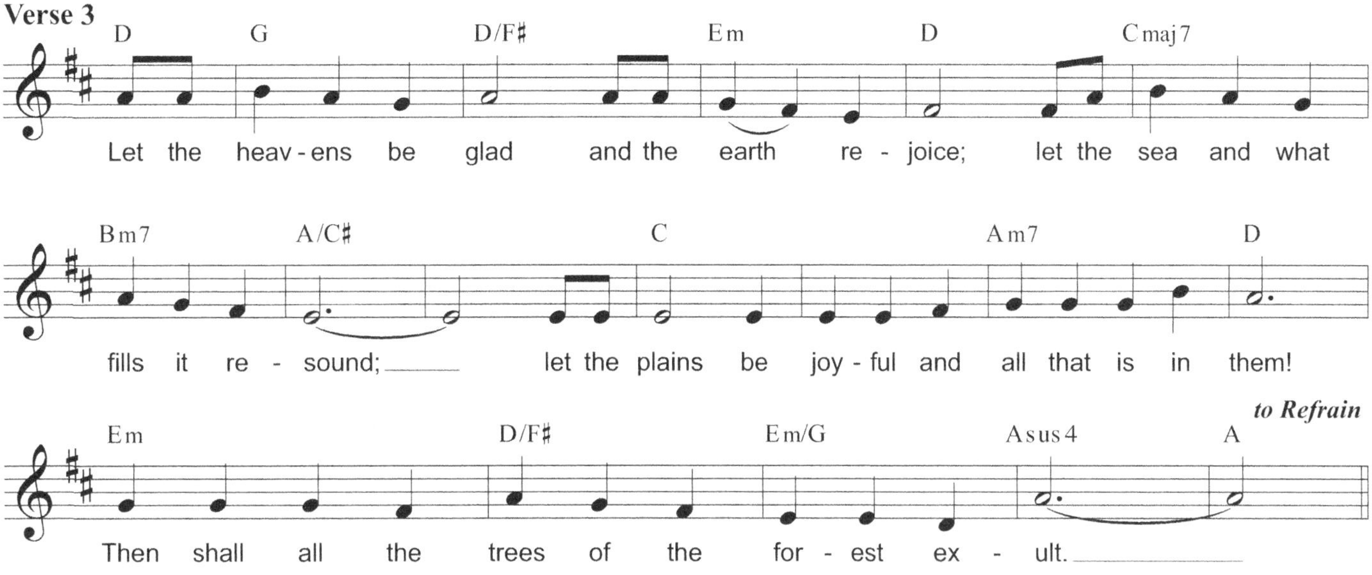
D G D/F♯ Em D Cmaj7
Let the heav - ens be glad and the earth re - joice; let the sea and what
Bm7 A/C♯ C Am7 D
fills it re - sound; let the plains be joy - ful and all that is in them!
to Refrain
Em D/F♯ Em/G Asus4 A
Then shall all the trees of the for - est ex - ult.

Verse 4

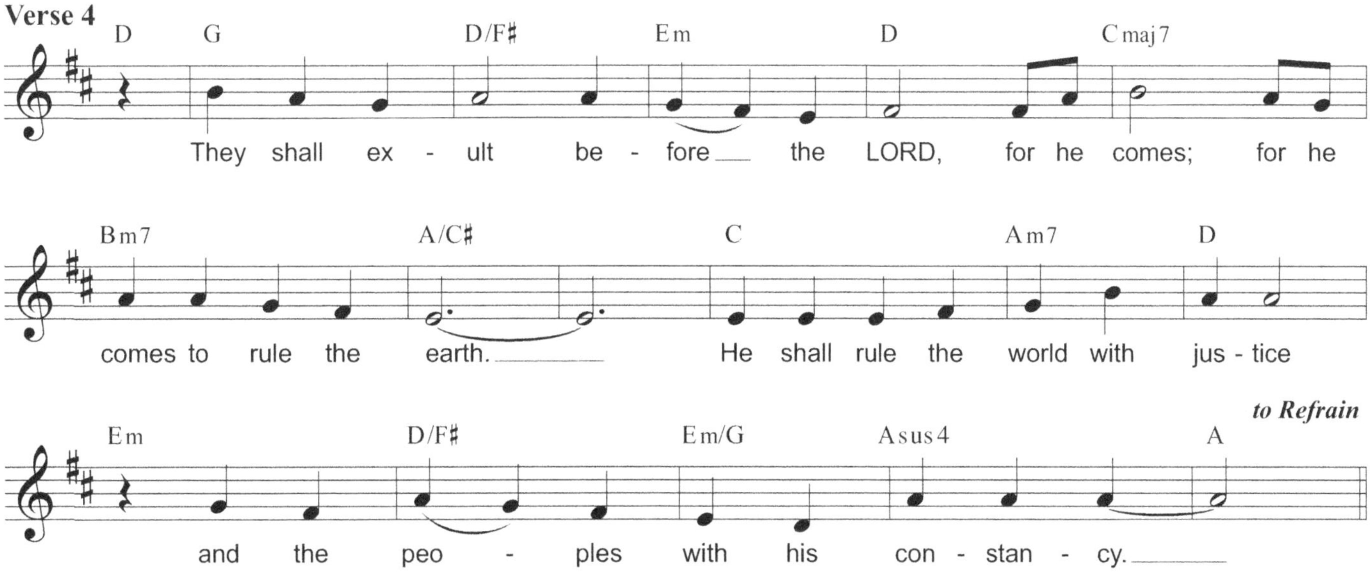
D G D/F♯ Em D Cmaj7
They shall ex - ult be - fore the LORD, for he comes; for he
Bm7 A/C♯ C Am7 D
comes to rule the earth. He shall rule the world with jus - tice
to Refrain
Em D/F♯ Em/G Asus4 A
and the peo - ples with his con - stan - cy.

Gospel Acclamation: Luke 2:10-11

Acclamation: (Keyboard/SATB) NO. V

(M.M. ♪ = c. 150)

C Dm Am Dm F/A G/B G
Al - le - lu - ia, al - le - lu - ia. Al - le - lu - ia, al - le - lu - ia.

Verse: (Cantor)

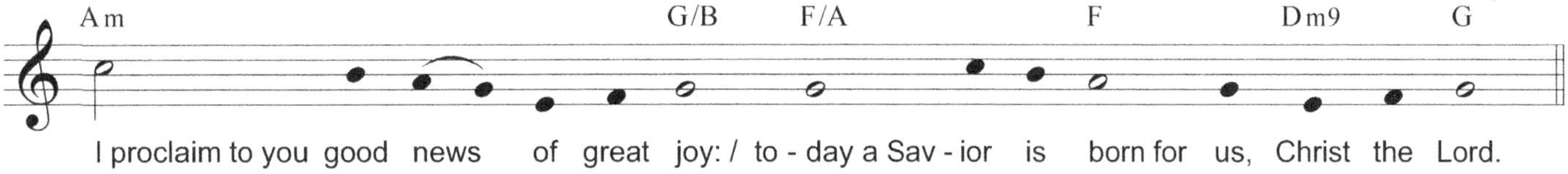
to Refrain
Am G/B F/A F Dm9 G
I proclaim to you good news of great joy: / to - day a Sav - ior is born for us, Christ the Lord.

The Nativity of the Lord (Christmas): At the Mass at Dawn

(M.M. ♩ = c. 63)

December 25

Psalm 97:1, 6, 11-12

REFRAIN
Capo 1: Bm D Em Bm/D G D/A A F♯m7 Bm
Cm E♭ Fm Cm/E♭ A♭ E♭/B♭ B♭ Gm7 Cm
A light will shine on us this day: the Lord is born for us, born for us.
Verse 1
Bm D G/D A5
Cm E♭ A♭/E♭ B♭5
The LORD is king; let earth re - joice; let the man - y isles be glad. The
D G D Bm Gmaj7 B5
E♭ A♭ E♭ Cm A♭maj7 C5
to Refrain
heav - ens pro - claim his jus - tice, and all peo - ples see his glo - ry.
Verse 2
Bm D G/D A5
Cm E♭ A♭/E♭ B♭5
Light dawns for the just; and glad - ness, for the up - right of heart. Be
D G/D Bm Gmaj7 B5
E♭ A♭/E♭ Cm A♭maj7 C5
to Refrain
glad in the LORD, you just, and give thanks to his ho - ly name.

Gospel Acclamation: Luke 2:14

Acclamation: (Keyboard/SATB) NO. V

(M.M. ♪ = c. 150)

C
Dm
Am
Dm
F/A
G/B
G
Al - le - lu - ia, al - le - lu - ia. Al - le - lu - ia, al - le - lu - ia.

Verse: (Cantor) *to Refrain*

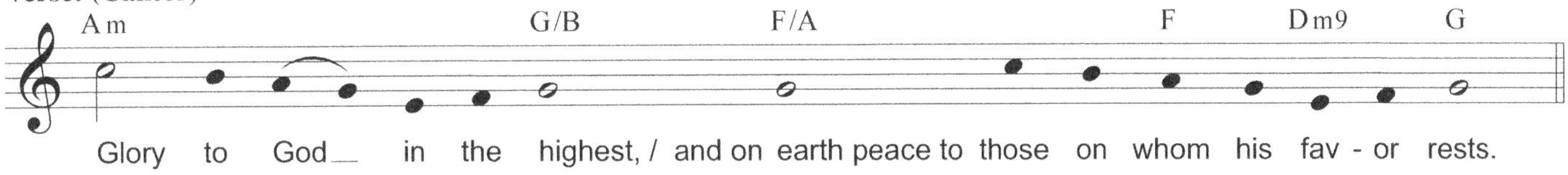
Am
G/B
F/A
F
Dm9
G
Glory to God in the highest, / and on earth peace to those on whom his fav - or rests.

The Nativity of the Lord (Christmas): At the Mass during the Day

December 25

(M.M. ♩ = c. 78)

Psalm 98:1, 2-3, 3-4, 5-6

REFRAIN

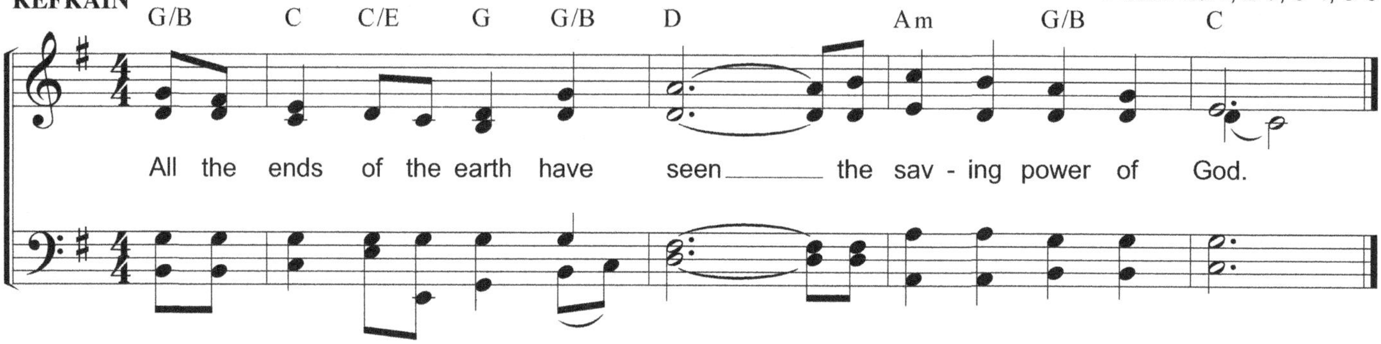
G/B C C/E G G/B D Am G/B C
All the ends of the earth have seen___ the sav - ing power of God.

Verse 1 (M.M. ♩ = c. 71)

Em Bm/D C G/B Am/C D
Sing to the LORD a new song, for he has done won - drous deeds; his
Am G/B C G/D D
to Refrain
right hand has won vic - t'ry for him, his ho - ly arm.

Verse 2 (M.M. ♩ = c. 71)

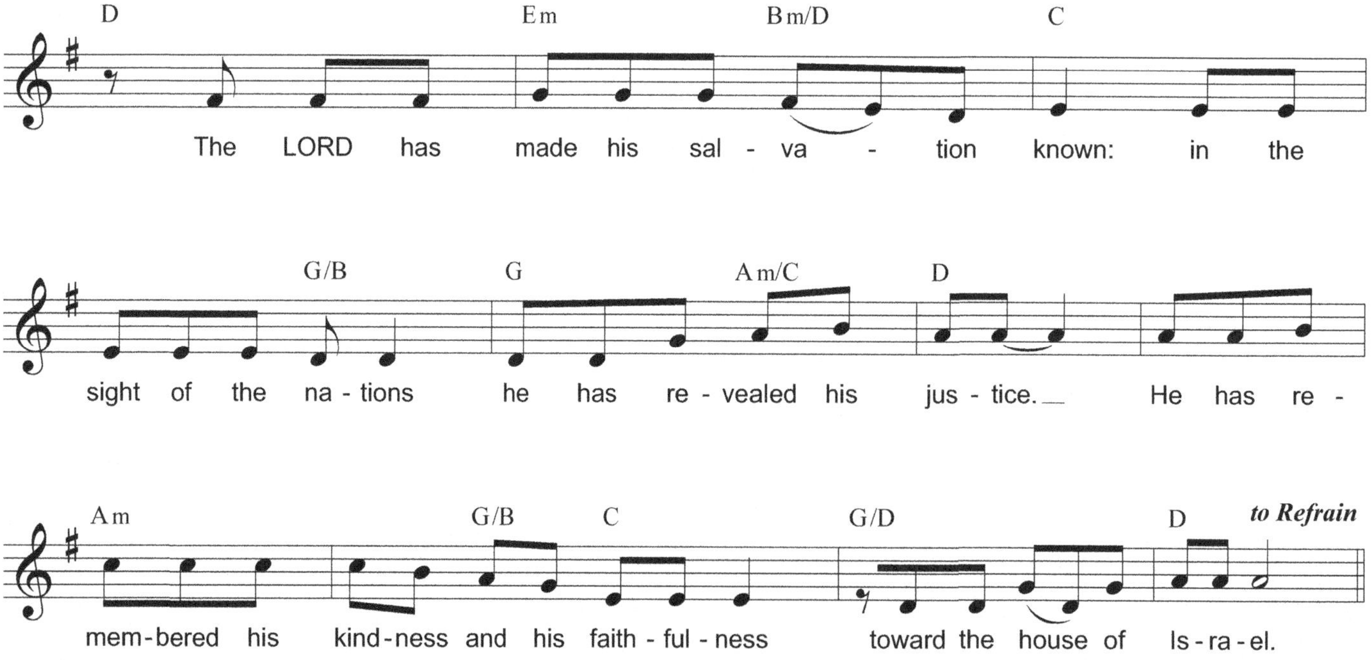
D Em Bm/D C
The LORD has made his sal - va - tion known: in the
G/B G Am/C D
sight of the na - tions he has re - vealed his jus - tice.__ He has re -
Am G/B C G/D D
to Refrain
mem-bered his kind-ness and his faith - ful - ness toward the house of Is - ra - el.

Verse 3 (M.M. ♩ = c. 71)

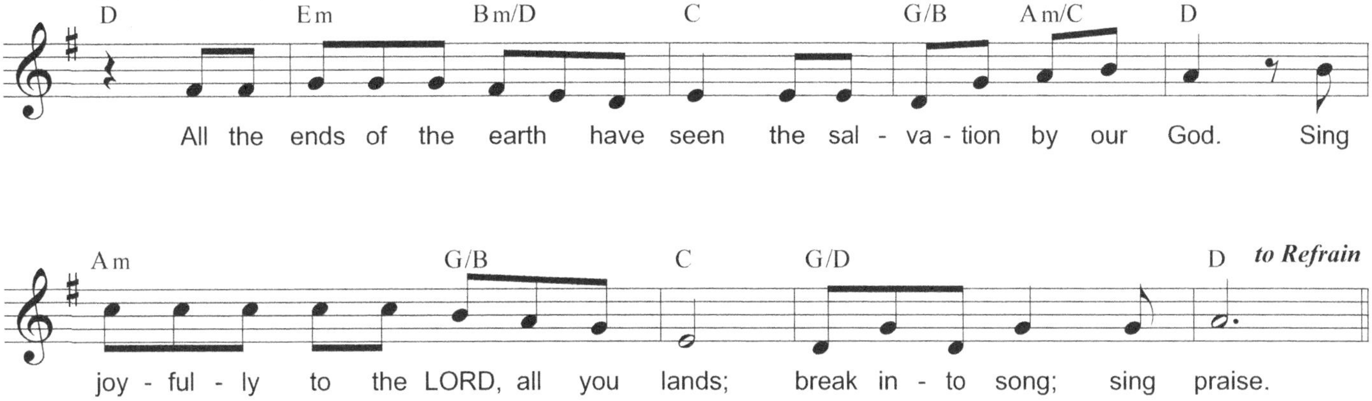
D Em Bm/D C G/B Am/C D
All the ends of the earth have seen the sal - va - tion by our God. Sing
Am G/B C G/D D to Refrain
joy - ful - ly to the LORD, all you lands; break in - to song; sing praise.

Verse 4 (M.M. ♩ = c. 71)

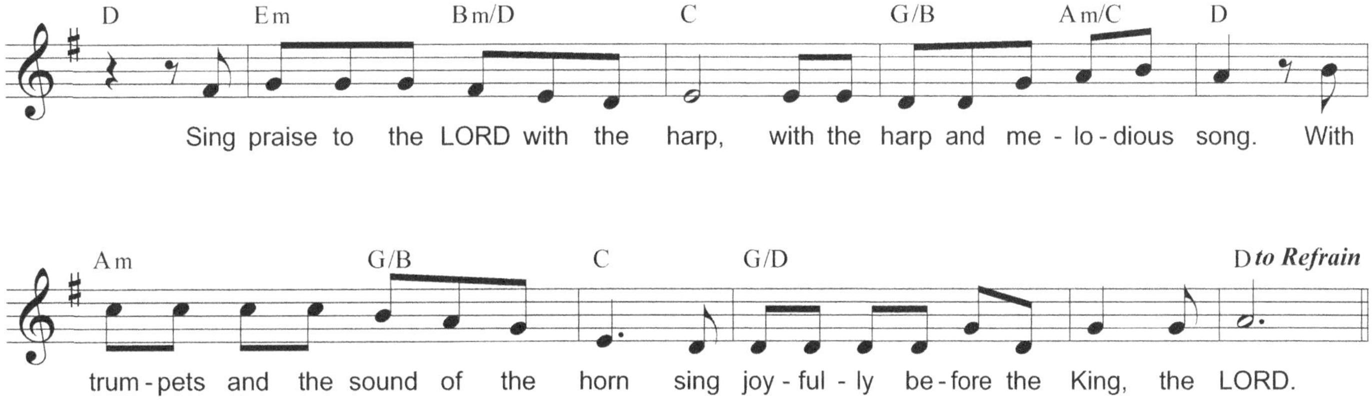
D Em Bm/D C G/B Am/C D
Sing praise to the LORD with the harp, with the harp and me - lo - dious song. With
Am G/B C G/D D to Refrain
trum - pets and the sound of the horn sing joy - ful - ly be - fore the King, the LORD.

Gospel Acclamation:

Acclamation: (Keyboard/SATB) NO. V

(M.M. ♪ = c. 150)

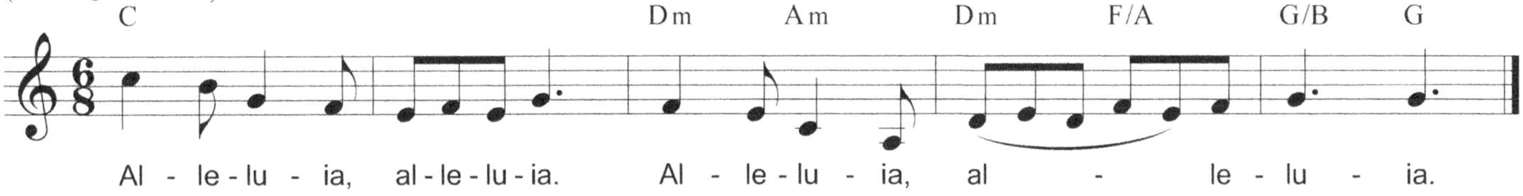
C Dm Am Dm F/A G/B G
Al - le - lu - ia, al - le - lu - ia. Al - le - lu - ia, al - le - lu - ia.

Verse: (Cantor)

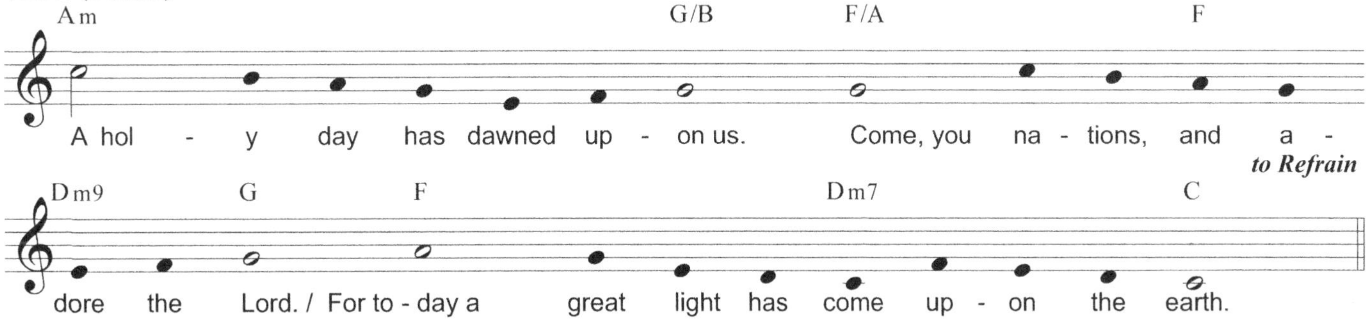
Am G/B F/A F
A hol - y day has dawned up - on us. Come, you na - tions, and a -
to Refrain
Dm9 G F Dm7 C
dore the Lord. / For to - day a great light has come up - on the earth.

The Holy Family of Jesus, Mary and Joseph

(M.M. ♩ = c. 66)

Optional Year B
December 27

Psalm 105:1–2, 3–4, 5–6, 8–9

REFRAIN
Capo 3: D F
D/F♯ F/A
G B♭
Bm Dm
G/D B♭/F
The Lord re - mem - bers his cov - e - nant for ev - er.
Verse 1
G/D B♭/F
D F
D/F♯ F/A
Gsus2 B♭sus2
Bm Dm
C/E E♭/G
C E♭
Give thanks to the LORD, in - voke his name; make known a - mong the na - tions his
G/D B♭/F
D F
G/D B♭/F
D/C F/E♭
C/E E♭/G
D F
to Refrain
deeds. Sing to him, sing his praise, pro - claim all his won - drous deeds.
Verse 2
D F
D/F♯ F/A
Gsus2 B♭sus2
Bm Dm
C/E E♭/G
C E♭
G/D B♭/F
Glo - ry in his ho - ly name; re - joice, O hearts that seek the LORD! Look to the
D F
G/D B♭/F
D/C F/E♭
C/E E♭/G
D F
to Refrain
LORD in his strength; con - stant - ly seek his face.
Verse 3
G/D B♭/F
D F
D/F♯ F/A
Gsus2 B♭sus2
You de - scend - ants of A - bra - ham, his ser - vants, sons of
Bm Dm
C/E E♭/G
C E♭
G/D B♭/F
Bm Dm
C/E E♭/G
C E♭
Ja - cob, his cho - sen ones! He, the LORD, is our

G/D B♭/F D F G/D B♭/F D/C F/E♭ C/E E♭/G D F
to Refrain
God; through - out the earth his judg - ments pre - vail.
Verse 4
G/D B♭/F D F D/F♯ F/A Gsus2 B♭sus2 Csus2 E♭sus2
He re - mem - bers for - ev - er his cov - e - nant which he made
Bm Dm C/E E♭/G C E♭ G/D B♭/F
bind - ing for a thou - sand gen - er - a - tions which he en - tered
D F G/D B♭/F D/C F/E♭ C/E E♭/G D F
to Refrain
in - to with A - bra - ham and by his oath to I - saac.

Gospel Acclamation: Hebrew 1:1-2

Acclamation: (Keyboard/SATB) NO. III

(M.M. ♩ = c. 160)

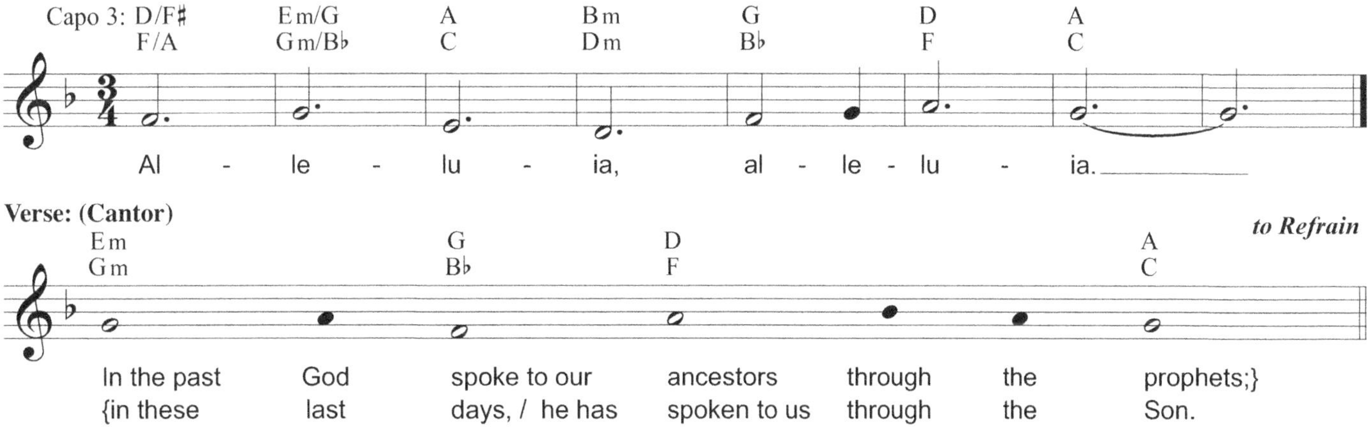
Capo 3: D/F♯ F/A Em/G Gm/B♭ A C Bm Dm G B♭ D F A C
Al - le - lu - ia, al - le - lu - ia.
Verse: (Cantor)
to Refrain
Em Gm G B♭ D F A C
In the past God spoke to our ancestors through the prophets;}
{in these last days, / he has spoken to us through the Son.

The Holy Family of Jesus, Mary and Joseph

Psalm for Years ABC
December 27

(M.M. ♩ = c. 78)

Psalm 128:1-2, 3, 4-5, 6

REFRAIN

Capo 1: A7sus4 D A/D D D/F♯ Asus4 A
B♭7sus4 E♭ B♭/E♭ E♭ E♭/G B♭sus4 B♭
Bless-ed are those who fear the Lord, and walk in his ways.

Verse 1 (M.M. ♩ = c. 67)

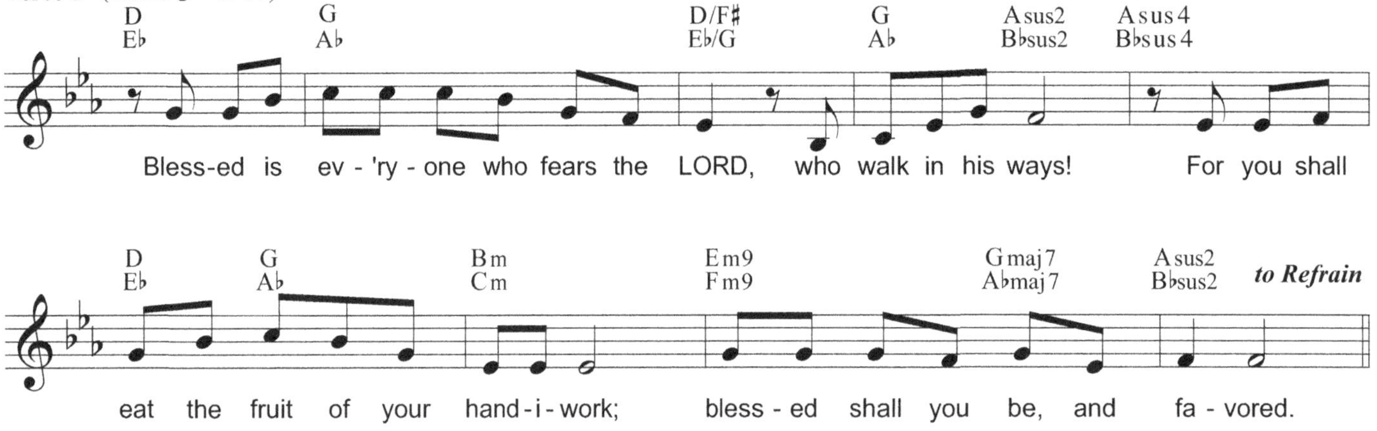

D G D/F♯ G Asus2 Asus4
E♭ A♭ E♭/G A♭ B♭sus2 B♭sus4
Bless-ed is ev - 'ry - one who fears the LORD, who walk in his ways! For you shall
D G Bm Em9 Gmaj7 Asus2
E♭ A♭ Cm Fm9 A♭maj7 B♭sus2
to Refrain
eat the fruit of your hand - i - work; bless - ed shall you be, and fa - vored.

Verse 2 (M.M. ♩ = c. 67)

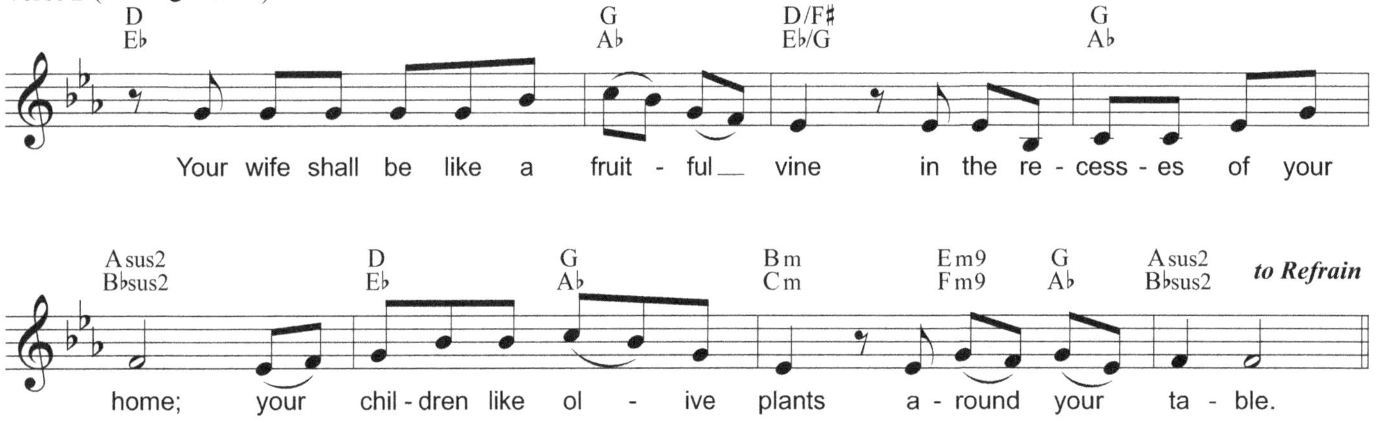

D G D/F♯ G
E♭ A♭ E♭/G A♭
Your wife shall be like a fruit - ful__ vine in the re - cess - es of your
Asus2 D G Bm Em9 G Asus2
B♭sus2 E♭ A♭ Cm Fm9 A♭ B♭sus2
to Refrain
home; your chil - dren like ol - ive plants a - round your ta - ble.

Verse 3 (M.M. ♩ = c. 67)

D G D/F♯ G Asus2 D
E♭ A♭ E♭/G A♭ B♭sus2 E♭
Be - hold, thus is the man bless-ed who fears the LORD. The LORD

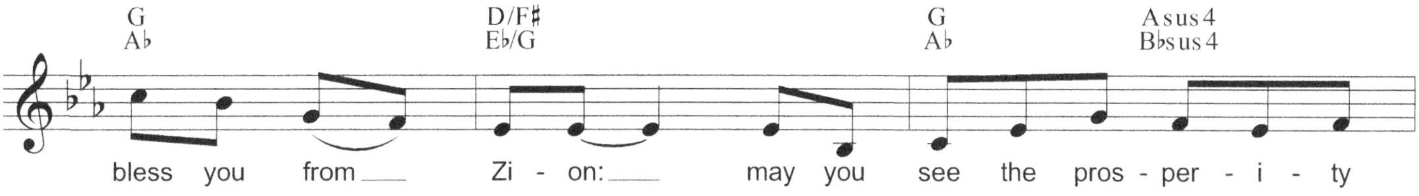
G
A♭
D/F♯
E♭/G
G
A♭
Asus4
B♭sus4
bless you from Zi - on: may you see the pros - per - i - ty

D
E♭
G
A♭
Bm
Cm
Em9
Fm9
Gmaj7
A♭maj7
Asus2
B♭sus2
to Refrain
of Je - ru - sa - lem all the days of your life.

Gospel Acclamation: Col 3: 15A, 16A

Acclamation: (Keyboard/SATB) NO. III

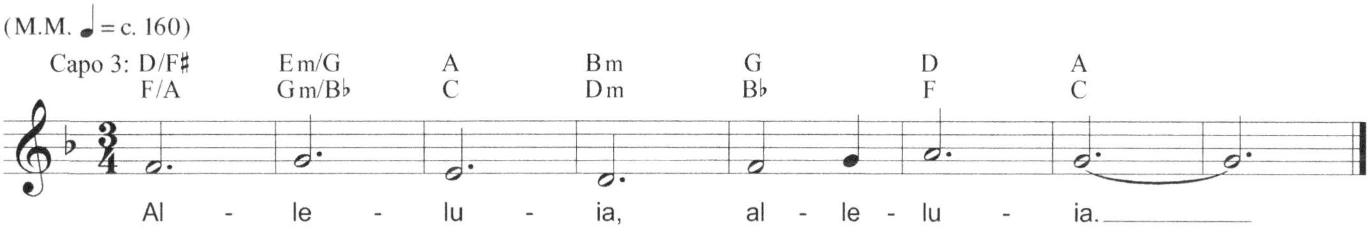
(M.M. ♩= c. 160)
Capo 3: D/F♯ Em/G A Bm G D A
F/A Gm/B♭ C Dm B♭ F C
Al - le - lu - ia, al - le - lu - ia.

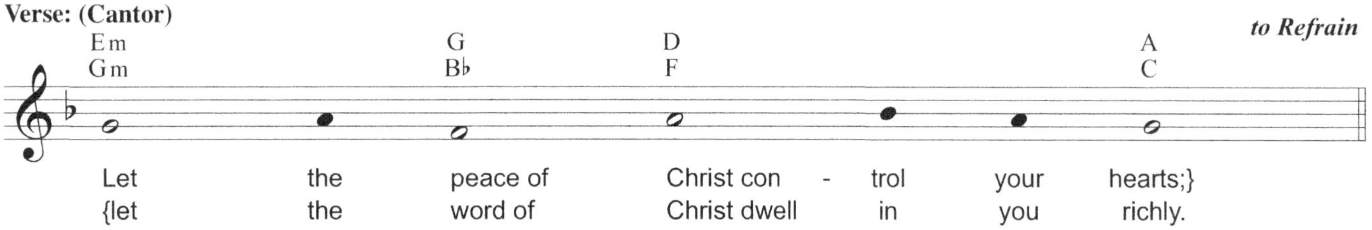
Verse: (Cantor)
Em
Gm
G
B♭
D
F
A
C
to Refrain
Let the peace of Christ con - trol your hearts;}
{let the word of Christ dwell in you richly.

For alternate **Responsorial Psalm** and **Gospel Acclamation Verse,** see *Lectionary for the Mass, Second Typical Edition* #17, ABC.

Solemnity of Mary, the Holy Mother of God

January 1

(M.M. ♩ = c. 78)

REFRAIN

Psalm 67:2-3, 5, 6, 8

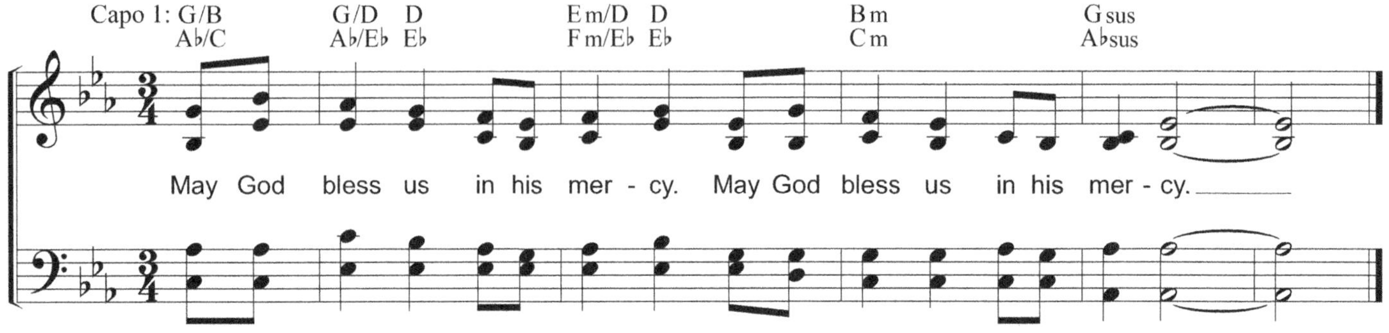
Capo 1: G/B G/D D Em/D D Bm Gsus
A♭/C A♭/E♭ E♭ Fm/E♭ E♭ Cm A♭sus
May God bless us in his mer - cy. May God bless us in his mer - cy.

Verse 1 (M.M. ♩ = c. 70)

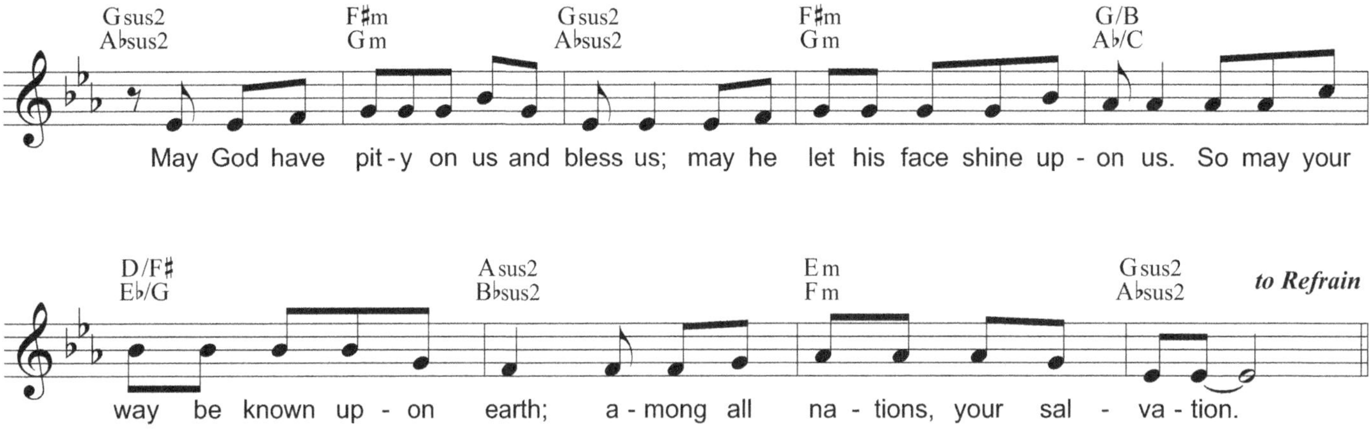
Gsus2 F♯m Gsus2 F♯m G/B
A♭sus2 Gm A♭sus2 Gm A♭/C
May God have pit - y on us and bless us; may he let his face shine up - on us. So may your
D/F♯ Asus2 Em Gsus2
E♭/G B♭sus2 Fm A♭sus2
way be known up - on earth; a - mong all na - tions, your sal - va - tion.
to Refrain

Verse 2 (M.M. ♩ = c. 70)

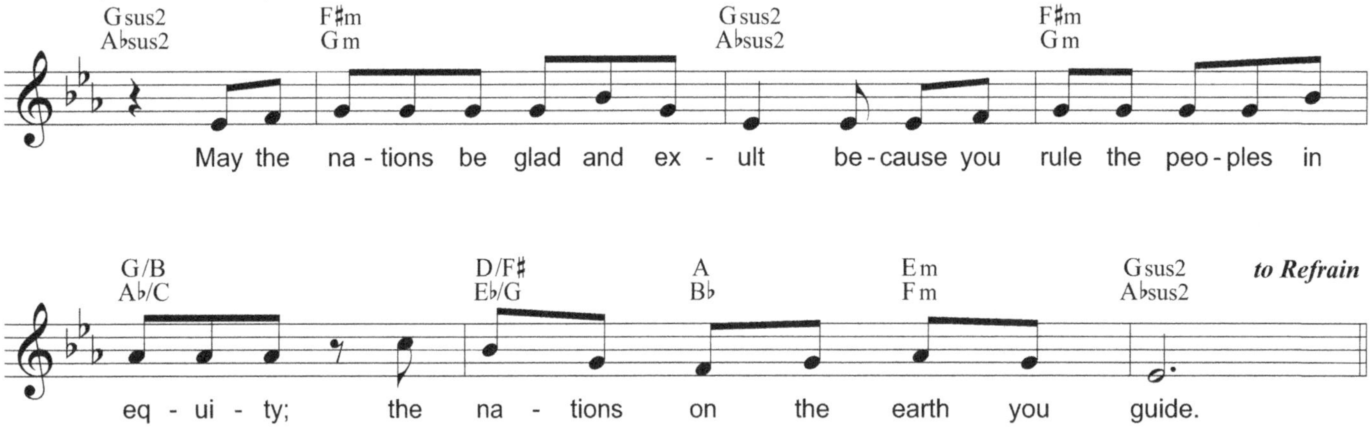
Gsus2 F♯m Gsus2 F♯m
A♭sus2 Gm A♭sus2 Gm
May the na - tions be glad and ex - ult be - cause you rule the peo - ples in
G/B D/F♯ A Em Gsus2
A♭/C E♭/G B♭ Fm A♭sus2
eq - ui - ty; the na - tions on the earth you guide.
to Refrain

Verse 3 (M.M. ♩ = c. 70)

Gsus2 F♯m Gsus2 F♯m G/B
A♭sus2 Gm A♭sus2 Gm A♭/C
May the peo - ples praise you, O God; may all the peo - ples praise you!

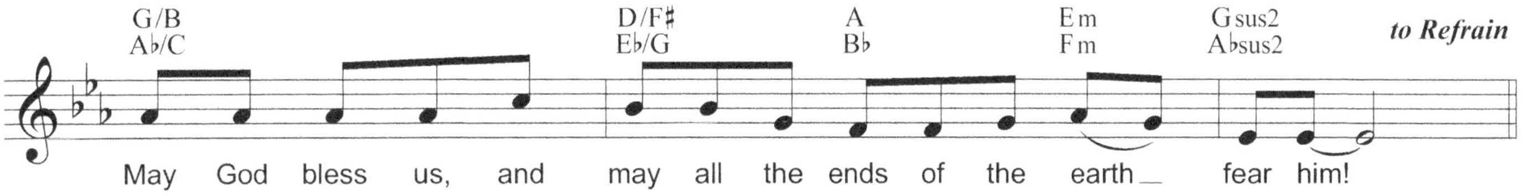
G/B
A♭/C
D/F♯
E♭/G
A
B♭
Em
Fm
Gsus2
A♭sus2
to Refrain
May God bless us, and may all the ends of the earth fear him!

Gospel Acclamation: Hebrews 1:1-2

Acclamation: (Keyboard/SATB) NO. I

(= c. 96)
Capo 1: D
E♭
A/C♯
B♭/D
G/B
A♭/C
D/A
E♭/B♭
G
A♭
D/F♯
E♭/G
D/A
E♭/B♭
A
B♭
Bm
Cm
Em
Fm
D/F♯
E♭/G
Gsus2
A♭sus2
Al - le - lu - ia, al - le - lu - ia, al - le - lu - ia.

Verse: (Cantor)

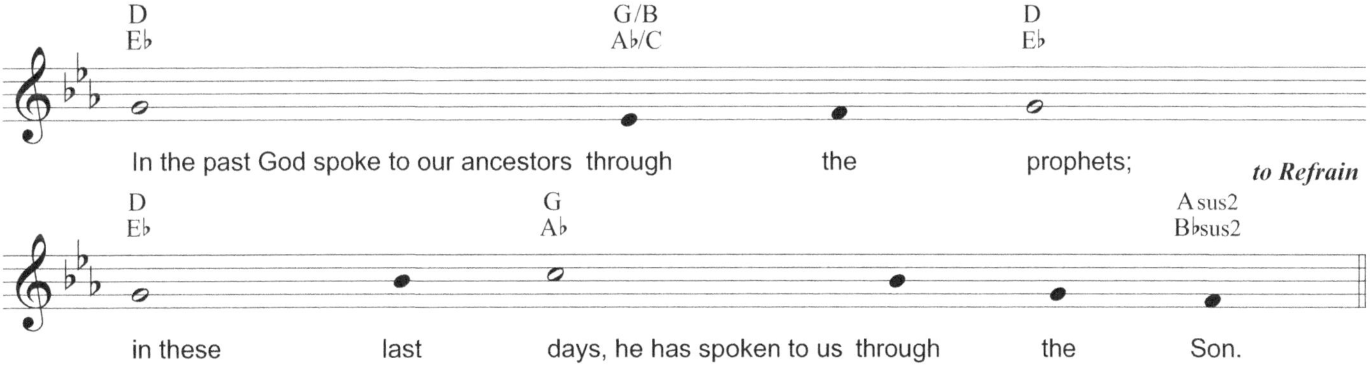
D
E♭
G/B
A♭/C
D
E♭
In the past God spoke to our ancestors through the prophets;
to Refrain
D
E♭
G
A♭
Asus2
B♭sus2
in these last days, he has spoken to us through the Son.

The Epiphany of the Lord,

January 3

(M.M. ♩= c. 126)

Psalm 72:1-2, 7-8, 10-11, 12-13

REFRAIN
Capo 3: D F
Am/C Cm/E♭
G/B B♭/D
Gmaj7 B♭maj7
D/A F/C
A C
Lord, ev - 'ry na - tion on earth will a - dore you.
Verse 1
A C / Em Gm / Bm/D Dm/F / C E♭ / G/B B♭/D / A C
O God, with your judg-ment en-dow the king, and with your jus-tice, the king's son;
to Refrain
Em Gm / Bm/D Dm/F / A/C♯ C/E / G/B B♭/D / Asus4 Csus4 / A C
he shall gov-ern your peo-ple with jus-tice and your af - flict-ed ones with judg-ment.
Verse 2
A C / Em Gm / Bm/D Dm/F / C E♭ / G/B B♭/D / G B♭
Jus-tice shall flow-er in his days, and pro-found peace, till the moon be no
to Refrain
A C / Em Gm / Bm/D Dm/F / A/C♯ C/E / G/B B♭/D / G B♭ / Asus4 Csus4 / A C
more. May he rule from sea to sea, and from the Riv-er to the ends of the earth.
Verse 3
A C / Em Gm / Bm/D Dm/F / C E♭
The kings of Tar - shish and the Isles shall of - fer gifts; the
G/B B♭/D / G B♭ / A C
kings of A - ra - bia and Se - ba shall bring trib - ute. All

to Refrain
Em Gm
Bm/D Dm/F
A/C♯ C/E
G/B B♭/D
Asus4 Csus4
A C
kings shall pay him hom - age, all na - tions shall serve him.

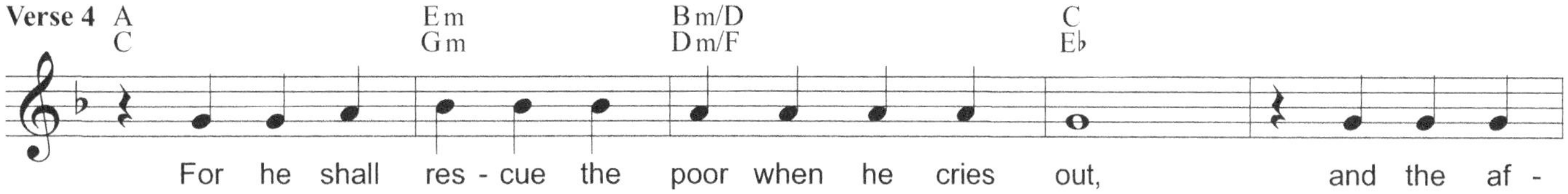
Verse 4
A C
Em Gm
Bm/D Dm/F
C E♭
For he shall res - cue the poor when he cries out, and the af -

G/B B♭/D
G B♭
A C
Em Gm
flict - ed when he has no one to help him. He shall have pit - y for the

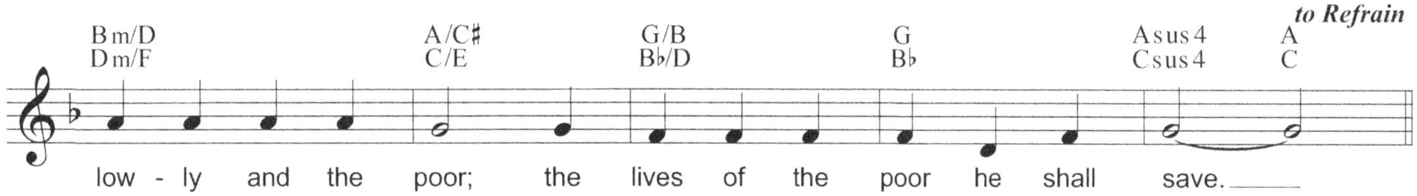
to Refrain
Bm/D Dm/F
A/C♯ C/E
G/B B♭/D
G B♭
Asus4 Csus4
A C
low - ly and the poor; the lives of the poor he shall save.

Gospel Acclamation: Matthew 2:2

Acclamation: (Keyboard/SATB) NO. II

(M.M. ♩ = c. 130)

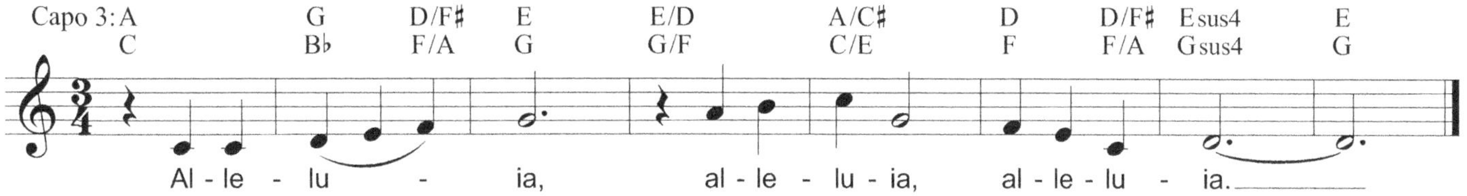
Capo 3: A C
G B♭
D/F♯ F/A
E G
E/D G/F
A/C♯ C/E
D F
D/F♯ F/A
Esus4 Gsus4
E G
Al - le - lu - ia, al - le - lu - ia, al - le - lu - ia.

Verse: (Cantor)

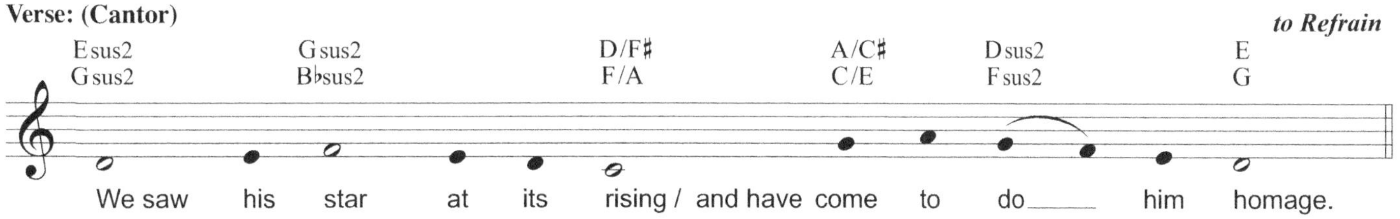
to Refrain
Esus2 Gsus2
Gsus2 B♭sus2
D/F♯ F/A
A/C♯ C/E
Dsus2 Fsus2
E G
We saw his star at its rising / and have come to do him homage.

The Baptism of the Lord

January 10
Psalm for Years ABC.
(Psalm for Optional Year B on p.137)

Psalm 29:1-2, 3-4, 3, 9-10

(M.M. ♩ = c. 98)

REFRAIN

Capo 3:
The Lord will bless his peo - ple, the Lord will bless his peo - ple with peace.
Verse 1
Give to the LORD, you sons of God, give to the LORD glo - ry and praise, give to the LORD the glo - ry due his name; a - dore the LORD in ho - ly at - tire.
to Refrain
Verse 2
The voice of the LORD is ov - er the wat - ers, the LORD, ov - er vast wat - ers. The voice of the LORD is

Through composed octavo Ed. 21019, available at www.ocp.org.

Gmaj7 A sus4 C maj7 G/B E m7
B♭maj7 C sus4 E♭maj7 B♭/D G m7
to Refrain
migh - ty; the voice of the LORD is ma - jest - ic.
Verse 3
Dsus2 F♯m7 B m7 Gmaj7 A sus4
F sus2 A m7 D m7 B♭maj7 C sus4
The God of glo - ry thun - ders, and
F♯m7 B m7 Gmaj7 D/A A sus4 G
A m7 D m7 B♭maj7 F/C C sus4 B♭
in his tem - ple all say, "Glo - ry!" The LORD is en -
D F♯m7 Gsus2 Cmaj7
F A m7 B♭sus2 E♭maj7
throned ab - ove the flood; the LORD is en -
Bsus4 Bm G D/F♯ E m7
Dsus4 Dm B♭ F/A G m7
to Refrain
throned as king for - ev - er.

Gospel Acclamation

Acclamation: (Keyboard/SATB) NO. IV

(M.M. ♩ = c. 116)

Capo 5: G C
Am Dm
F B♭
C F
Dm7 Gm7
Al - le - lu - ia, al - le - lu - ia, al - le -

C/E F/A
Fmaj7 B♭maj7
1.
Gsus4 Csus4
2 and onward
Gsus4 Csus4
lu - ia. ia.

Verse with Responsorial Psalm on p. 36 (Years ABC) cf. Mark 9:7

Verse: (Cantor)

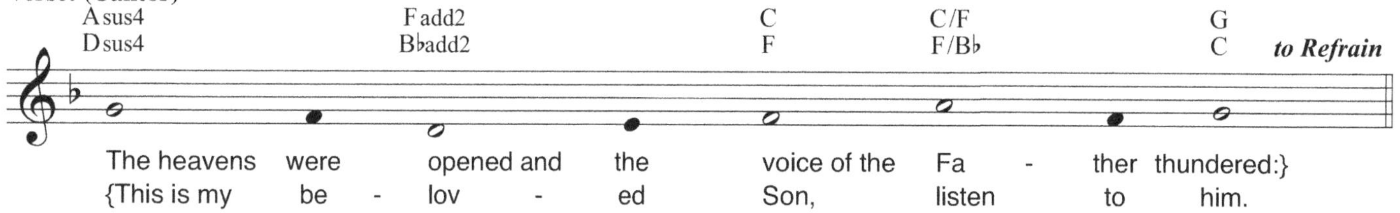
Asus4 Dsus4
Fadd2 B♭add2
C F
C/F F/B♭
G C
to Refrain
The heavens were opened and the voice of the Fa - ther thundered:}
{This is my be - lov - ed Son, listen to him.

Verse with Responsorial Psalm on p. 84 (Optional Year B) cf. John 1:29

Verse: (Cantor)

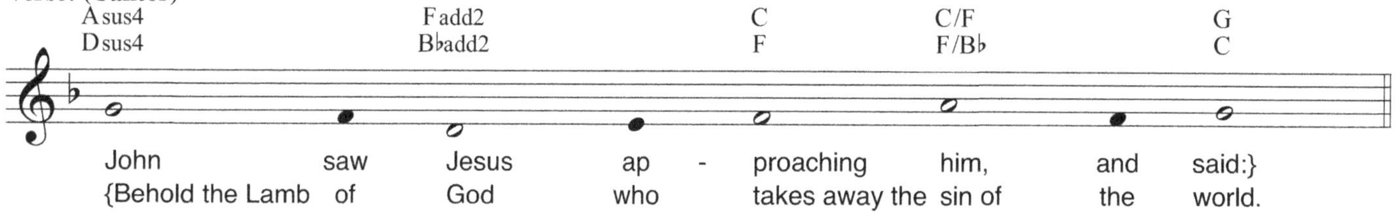
Asus4 Dsus4
Fadd2 B♭add2
C F
C/F F/B♭
G C
John saw Jesus ap - proaching him, and said:}
{Behold the Lamb of God who takes away the sin of the world.

Second Sunday in Ordinary Time

January 17

(M.M. ♩ = c. 128)

Psalm 40:2, 4, 7-8, 8-9, 10

REFRAIN
Capo 2: D E | Bm7 C♯m7 | Csus2 Dsus2 | D/A E/B | Bm C♯m | C/G D/A
Here am I, Lord; I come to do your will.
Verse 1
C/G D/A | D E | C/D D/E | D E
I have wait-ed, wait-ed for the LORD, and he stooped toward me and
C/D D/E | C D | Bm7 C♯m7 | G/D A/E
heard my cry. And he put a new song in-to my
C/E D/F♯ | C D | Am7 Bm7 | D E
mouth, a hymn, [a hymn] to our God.
to Refrain
Verse 2
C/G D/A | D E | C/D D/E | C D
Sac-ri-fice or of-fer-ing you wished not, but ears o-pen to o-
Bm7 C♯m7 | C D | C/E D/F♯ | D E | D E | C/D D/E | C D
be-di-ence you gave me. Hol-o-causts or sin-of-fer-ings you sought
Bm7 C♯m7 | G/D A/E | C/E D/F♯ | C D | Am7 Bm7 | D E
not, [you sought not;] then said I, "Be-hold I come."
to Refrain

www.timothyrsmith.com

Verse 3
C/G D/A D E C/D D/E D E Bm7 C#m7
"In the writ-ten scroll it is pre-scribed for me, to do your will, O my
D/A E/B C D C/E D/F# C D Am7 Bm7 D E
to Refrain
God, is my de-light, and your law is with-in my heart!"
Verse 4
C/G D/A D E C/D D/E C D
I an-nounced your jus-tice in the vast as-sem-bly; I did not re-
Bm7 C#m7 C/E D/F# C D Am7 Bm7 D E
to Refrain
strain my lips, as you, O LORD, know.

Gospel Acclamation: John 1:41, 17b

Acclamation: (Keyboard/SATB) NO. V

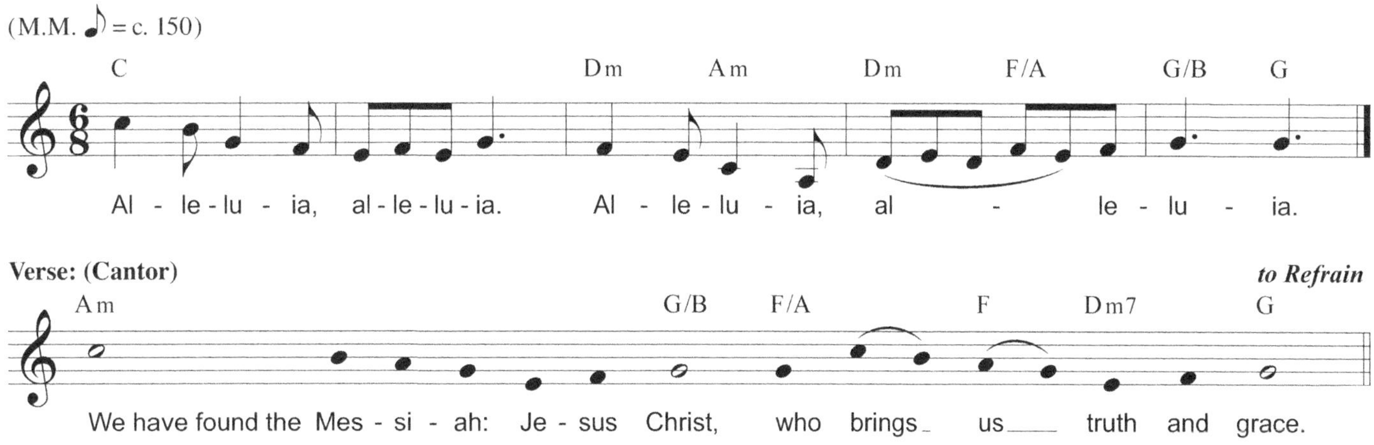
(M.M. ♪ = c. 150)
C Dm Am Dm F/A G/B G
Al-le-lu-ia, al-le-lu-ia. Al-le-lu-ia, al-le-lu-ia.
Verse: (Cantor)
to Refrain
Am G/B F/A F Dm7 G
We have found the Mes-si-ah: Je-sus Christ, who brings us truth and grace.

Third Sunday in Ordinary Time

January 24

Psalm 25:4–5, 6–7, 8–9

(♩= c. 70)

REFRAIN

Capo 3: D G/B C Em Bm7 Gsus2 Em7 Asus4 A
F B♭/D E♭ Gm Dm7 B♭sus2 Gm7 Csus4 C
Teach me your ways, teach me your ways, O Lord.

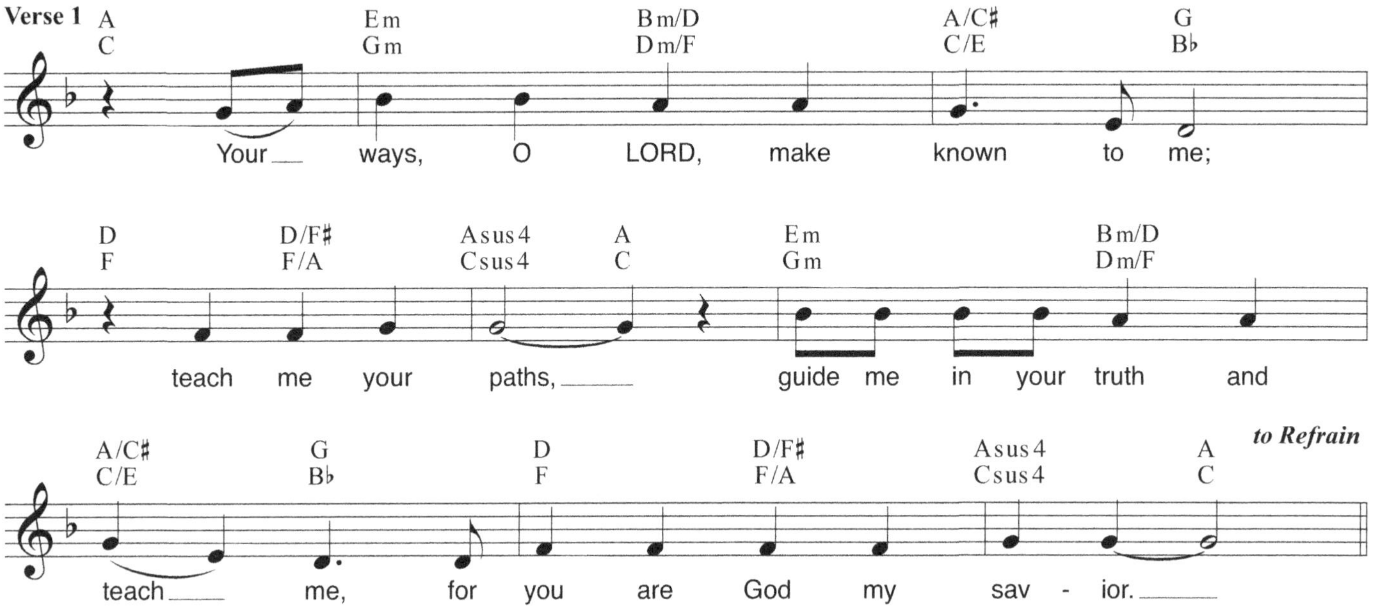
Verse 1
A Em Bm/D A/C♯ G
C Gm Dm/F C/E B♭
Your ways, O LORD, make known to me;
D D/F♯ Asus4 A Em Bm/D
F F/A Csus4 C Gm Dm/F
teach me your paths, guide me in your truth and
A/C♯ G D D/F♯ Asus4 A
C/E B♭ F F/A Csus4 C
teach me, for you are God my sav - ior.
to Refrain

Verse 2
A Em Bm/D A/C♯ G
C Gm Dm/F C/E B♭
Re - mem - ber that your com - pas - sion, O LORD, and your
D D/F♯ Asus4 A Em Bm/D
F F/A Csus4 C Gm Dm/F
love are from of old. In your kind - ness re -
A/C♯ G D D/F♯ Asus4 A
C/E B♭ F F/A Csus4 C
mem - ber me, be - cause of your good - ness, O LORD.
to Refrain

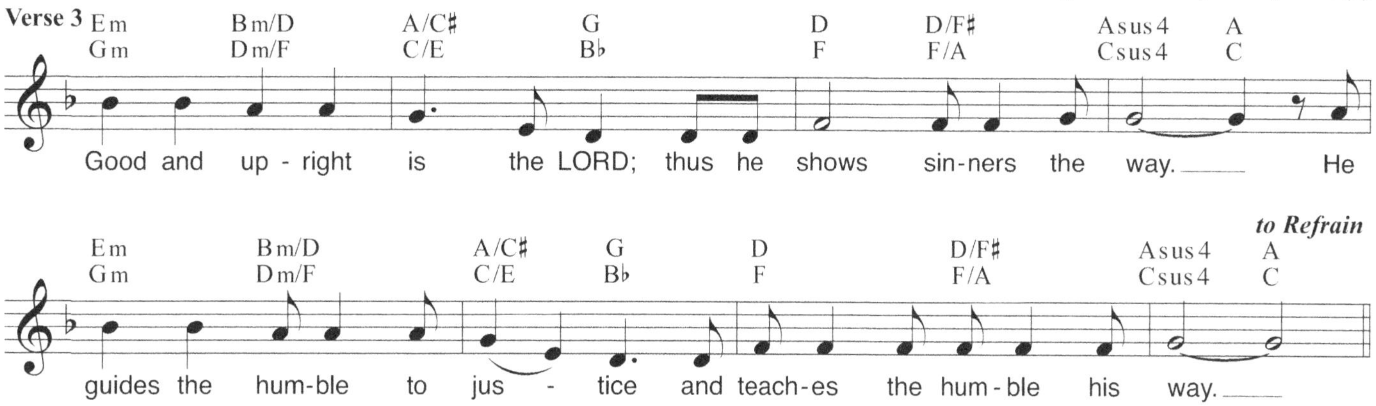
Verse 3
Em Bm/D A/C♯ G D D/F♯ Asus4 A
Gm Dm/F C/E B♭ F F/A Csus4 C
Good and up - right is the LORD; thus he shows sin-ners the way. He
to Refrain
Em Bm/D A/C♯ G D D/F♯ Asus4 A
Gm Dm/F C/E B♭ F F/A Csus4 C
guides the hum-ble to jus - tice and teach-es the hum-ble his way.

Gospel Acclamation: Mark 1:15

Acclamation: (Keyboard/SATB) NO. III

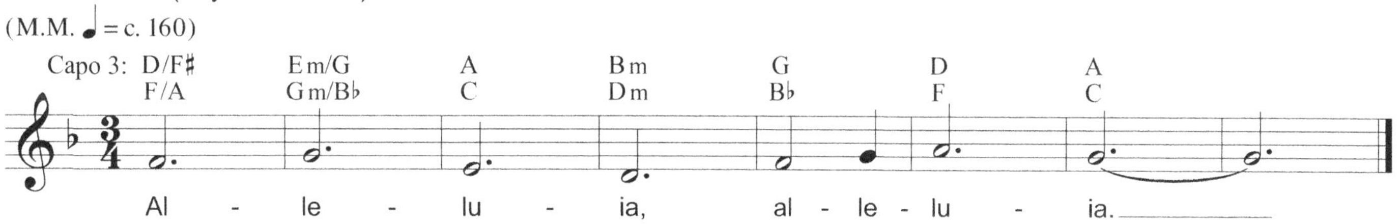
(M.M. ♩= c. 160)
Capo 3: D/F♯ Em/G A Bm G D A
F/A Gm/B♭ C Dm B♭ F C
Al - le - lu - ia, al - le - lu - ia.

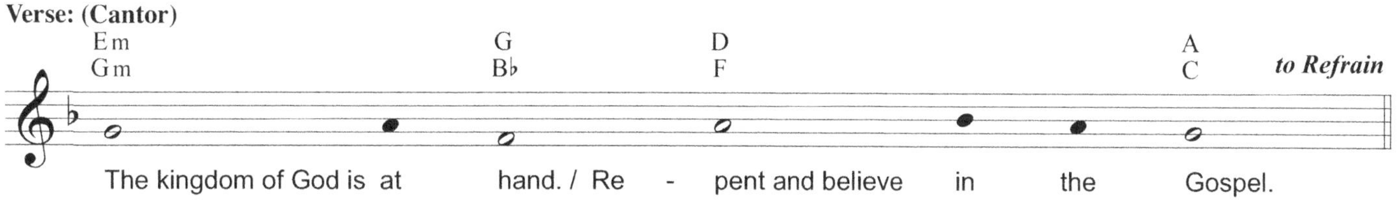
Verse: (Cantor)
Em G D A
Gm B♭ F C
to Refrain
The kingdom of God is at hand. / Re - pent and believe in the Gospel.

Fourth Sunday in Ordinary Time

January 31

(M.M. ♩ = c. 100)

Psalm 95:1-2, 6-7, 7-9

REFRAIN
C/D D Dsus4 D Am7 Gmaj7 D C/D D C/D
If to-day you hear his voice, hard - en not your hearts.
Verse 1
D Am7 D
Come, let us sing joy-ful-ly to the LORD; let us ac-
Am7 D Em D/F♯
claim the rock of our sal-va-tion. Let us come in-to his pre-sence with thanks-
G Am7 D
giv-ing; let us joy-ful-ly sing psalms to him.
to Refrain
Verse 2
C/D D C/D
Come, let us bow down in wor-ship; let us kneel be-fore the LORD who
D Em D/F♯ G
made us. For he is our God, and we are the peop-le he
Am C D
shep-herds, the flock he guides.
to Refrain
Verse 3
D Am D
Oh, that to-day you would hear his voice:

Through composed octavo Ed. 30115859 available at www.ocp.org.

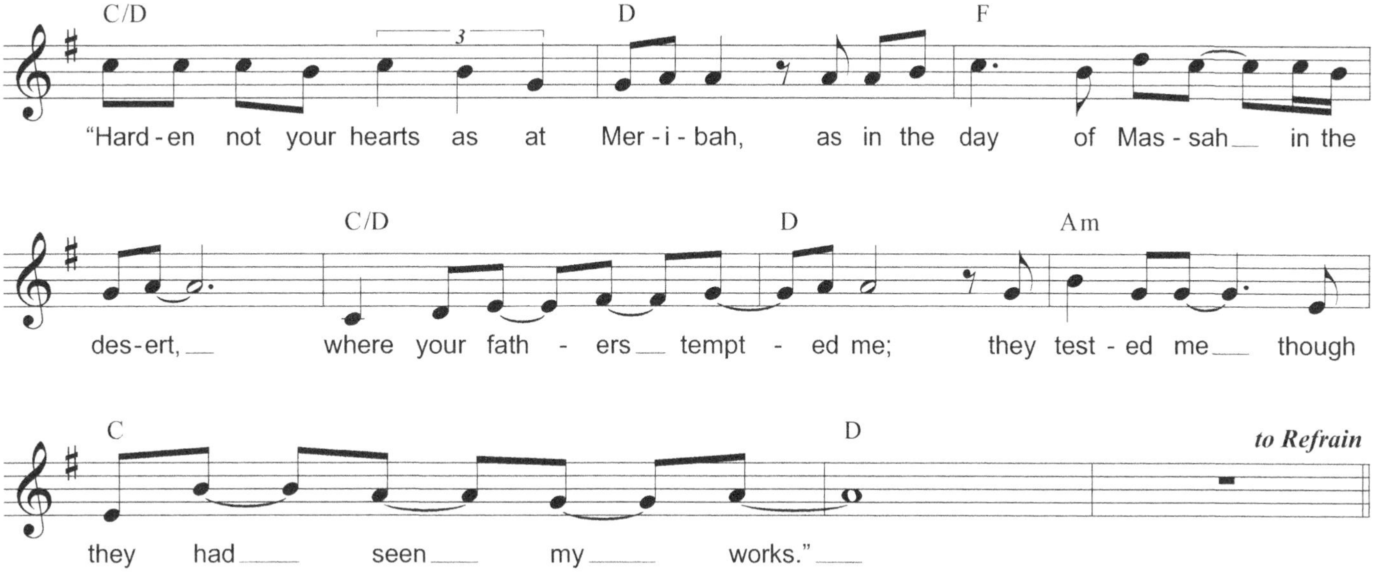
C/D D F
"Hard-en not your hearts as at Mer-i-bah, as in the day of Mas-sah__ in the
C/D D Am
des-ert,__ where your fath - ers__ tempt - ed me; they test-ed me__ though
C D
they had__ seen__ my__ works."__
to Refrain

Gospel Acclamation: Matthew 4:16

Acclamation: (Keyboard/SATB) NO. IV

(M.M. ♩ = c. 116)

Capo 5: G C
Am Dm
F B♭
C F
Dm7 Gm7
Al - le - lu - ia,__ al - le - lu - ia,__ al - le -
C/E F/A
F maj7 B♭maj7
1.
Gsus4 Csus4
2 and onward
Gsus4 Csus4
lu - ia. ia.

Verse: (Cantor)

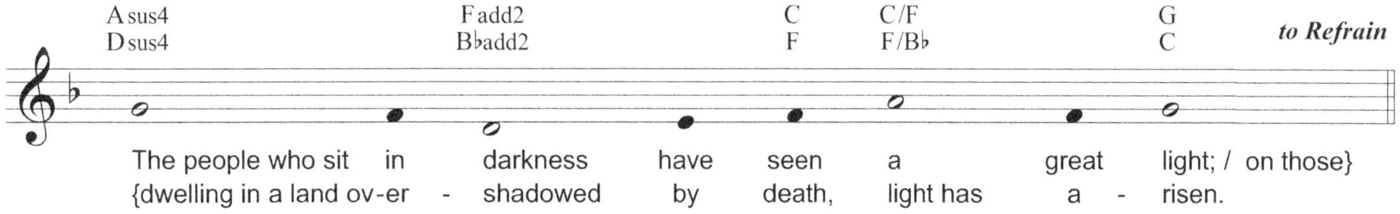
Asus4 Dsus4
Fadd2 B♭add2
C F
C/F F/B♭
G C
to Refrain
The people who sit in darkness have seen a great light; / on those}
{dwelling in a land ov-er - shadowed by death, light has a - risen.

Fifth Sunday in Ordinary Time

(M.M. ♩ = c. 94)

February 7

Psalm 147:1–2, 3–4, 5–6

REFRAIN [or: Alleluia]

Capo 3: D F
C Eb
Cmaj7 Ebmaj7
D F
Praise the Lord. Praise the Lord, who heals the bro-ken-heart-ed.
Verse 1
Em Gm
Bm/D Dm/F
Cmaj7 Ebmaj7
Am7 Cm7
Praise the LORD, for he is good; sing praise to our God, for he is
Bm7 Dm7
Am7 Cm7
Dsus2 Fsus2
G/B Bb/D
gra-cious; it is fit-ting to praise him. The LORD re-builds Je-
C Eb
Am7 Cm7
Cmaj7 Ebmaj7
C/E Eb/G
D F
to Refrain
ru-sa-lem; the dis-persed of Is-ra-el he gath-ers.
Verse 2
D F
Em Gm
Bm/D Dm/F
C Eb
Am7 Cm7
Bm7 Dm7
He heals the bro-ken-heart-ed and binds up their wounds. He
G/B Bb/D
C Eb
Am7 Cm7
C Eb
C/E Eb/G
D F
to Refrain
tells the num-ber of the stars; he calls each by name.
Verse 3
Em Gm
Bm/D Dm/F
C Eb
Am7 Cm7
Bm7 Dm7
Great is our LORD and might-y in pow'er; to his wis-dom there is no lim-it. The

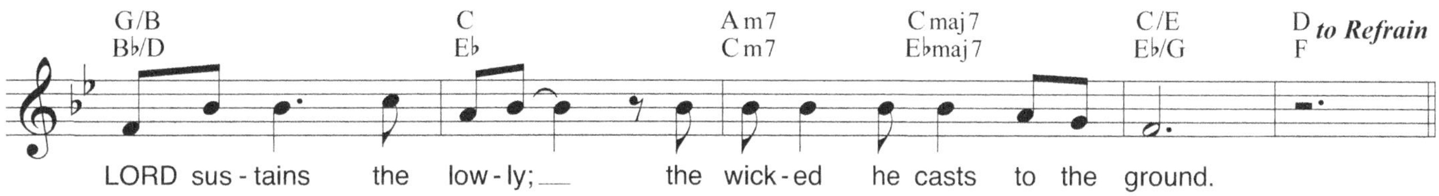
G/B Bb/D
C Eb
Am7 Cm7
Cmaj7 Ebmaj7
C/E Eb/G
D F
to Refrain
LORD sus - tains the low - ly; the wick - ed he casts to the ground.

Gospel Acclamation: Matthew 8:17

Acclamation: (Keyboard/SATB) NO. I

(𝅗𝅥 = c. 96)
Capo 1: D Eb
A/C♯ Bb/D
G/B Ab/C
D/A Eb/Bb
G Ab
D/F♯ Eb/G
D/A Eb/Bb
A Bb
Bm Cm
Em Fm
D/F♯ Eb/G
Gsus2 Absus2
Al - le - lu - ia, al - le - lu - ia, al - le - lu - ia.

Verse: (Cantor)

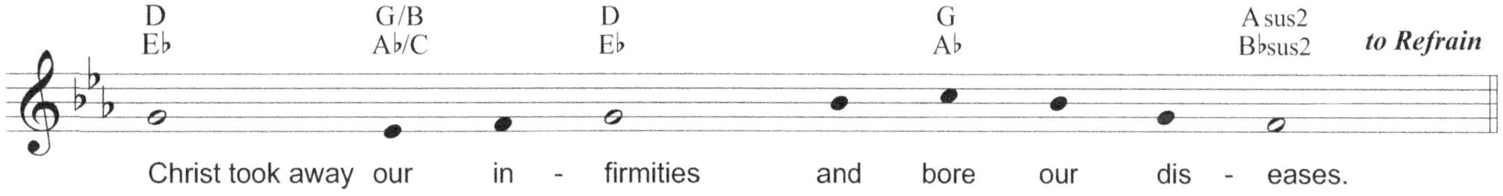
D Eb
G/B Ab/C
D Eb
G Ab
Asus2 Bbsus2
to Refrain
Christ took away our in - firmities and bore our dis - eases.

Sixth Sunday in Ordinary Time

February 14

Psalm 32:1-2, 5, 11

(M.M. ♩= c. 68)
REFRAIN
Em Cmaj7 D Bm C Am G/B C D Bm Em
I turn to you, Lord, in time of trou-ble, and you fill me with the joy of sal-va-tion.
Verse 1
C D/C Csus2 D/A
Bless - ed is he whose fault is tak - en a - way, whose sin is cov - ered.
C/G D/G C/G D/A Am C D Em
to Refrain
Bless-ed the man to whom the LORD im-putes not guilt, in whose spir-it there is no guile.
Verse 2
C D/C C D/A C/G D/G
Then I ac-knowl-edged my sin to you, my guilt I cov-ered not. I said, "I con-fess my
C/G D/G Am G/B C Em
to Refrain
faults to the LORD," and you took a - way the guilt of my sin.
Verse 3
C D/C C D/A C/G
Be glad in the LORD and re - joice, you just; ex - ult, all you up-right of
D/G Am C D Em
to Refrain
heart. [Ex - ult, all you up - right of heart.]

Gospel Acclamation: Luke 7:16

Acclamation: (Keyboard/SATB) NO. III

(M.M. ♩ = c. 160)

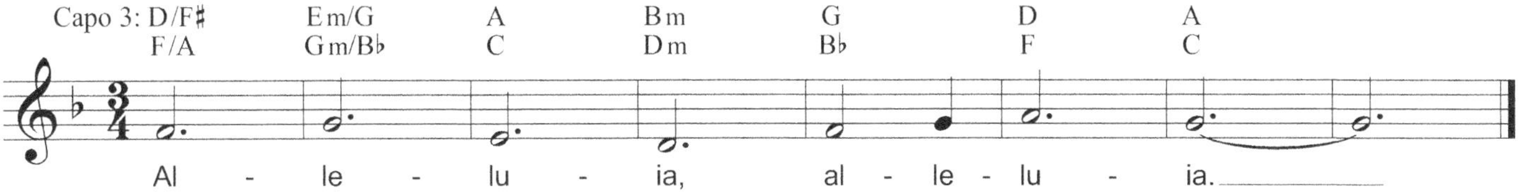
Capo 3: D/F♯ Em/G A Bm G D A
F/A Gm/B♭ C Dm B♭ F C
Al - le - lu - ia, al - le - lu - ia.

Verse: (Cantor)

Em G D A
Gm B♭ F C
to Refrain
A great prophet has arisen in our midst, God has visited his people.

Ash Wednesday

February 17

Psalm 51:3-4, 5-6ab, 12-13, 14 & 17

(M.M. ♩ = c. 118)
REFRAIN
Capo 3: E/G♯ Am E/G♯ G
G/B Cm G/B B♭
Be mer - ci - ful, O Lord, for we have
Am Dm Am/C Dm/F E/G♯
Cm Fm Cm/E♭ Fm/A♭ G/B
sinned. Be mer - ci - ful, O Lord, for we have sinned.
Verse 1 (M.M. ♩ = c. 125)
Gsus2 G/B F/A Dm Am Dm
B♭sus2 B♭/D A♭/C Fm Cm Fm
Have mer - cy on me, O God, in your good - ness; in the great - ness of
Am C Gsus2 Dm Am
Cm E♭ B♭sus2 Fm Cm
your com - pas - sion wipe out my of - fense. Thor - ough - ly wash me from my guilt and
F C/E G to Refrain
A♭ E♭/G B♭
of my sin cleanse me.
Verse 2 (M.M. ♩ = c. 125)
G G/B F/A Dm
B♭ B♭/D A♭/C Fm
For I ac - knowl - edge my of -
Am Dm Am/C G/B G
Cm Fm Cm/E♭ B♭/D B♭
fense, and my sin is be - fore me al - ways: "A - gainst
Dm Am F C/E G to Refrain
Fm Cm A♭ E♭/G B♭
you on - ly have I sinned, and done what is e - vil in your sight."

www.timothyrsmith.com

Verse 3 (M.M. ♩ = c. 125)

Gsus2 Bbsus2 G/B Bb/D F/A Ab/C Dm Fm Am Cm Am/C Cm/Eb Dm Fm
A clean heart cre - ate for me, O God, and a stead-fast spir - it re -
Am/C Cm/Eb G/B Bb/D G Bb Dm Fm Am Cm
new with - in me. Cast me not out from your pres-ence, and your Ho - ly
Verse 4 (M.M. ♩ = c. 125)
F Ab C/E Eb/G G Bb to Refrain G/B Bb/D F/A Ab/C Dm Fm Am Cm
Spir - it take not from me. Give me back the joy of your sal - va - tion,
Dm Fm Am/C Cm/Eb G/B Bb/D Gsus2 Bbsus2
and a will - ing spir - it sus - tain in me. O Lord,
Dm Fm Am Cm F Ab C/E Eb/G G Bb to Refrain
o - pen my lips, and my mouth shall pro - claim your praise.

Gospel Acclamation: See Psalm 95:8

Acclamation: (Keyboard/SATB) NO. VII

(♩ = c. 90)

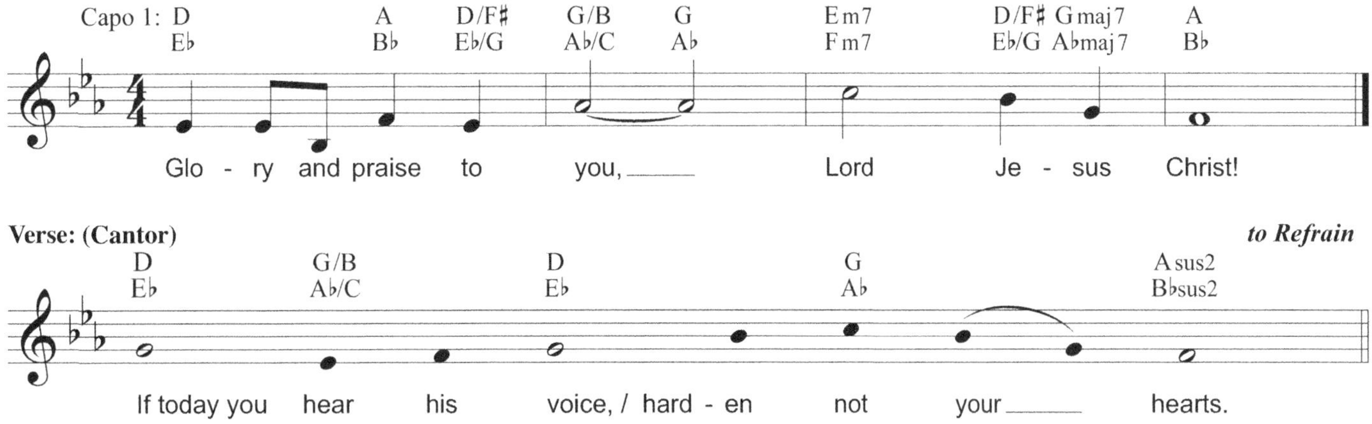
Capo 1: D Eb A Bb D/F♯ Eb/G G/B Ab/C G Ab Em7 Fm7 D/F♯ Eb/G Gmaj7 Abmaj7 A Bb
Glo - ry and praise to you, Lord Je - sus Christ!
Verse: (Cantor)
to Refrain
D Eb G/B Ab/C D Eb G Ab Asus2 Bbsus2
If today you hear his voice, / hard - en not your hearts.

First Sunday of Lent

February 21

Psalm 25:4–5, 6–7, 8–9

(M.M. ♩ = c. 93)

REFRAIN

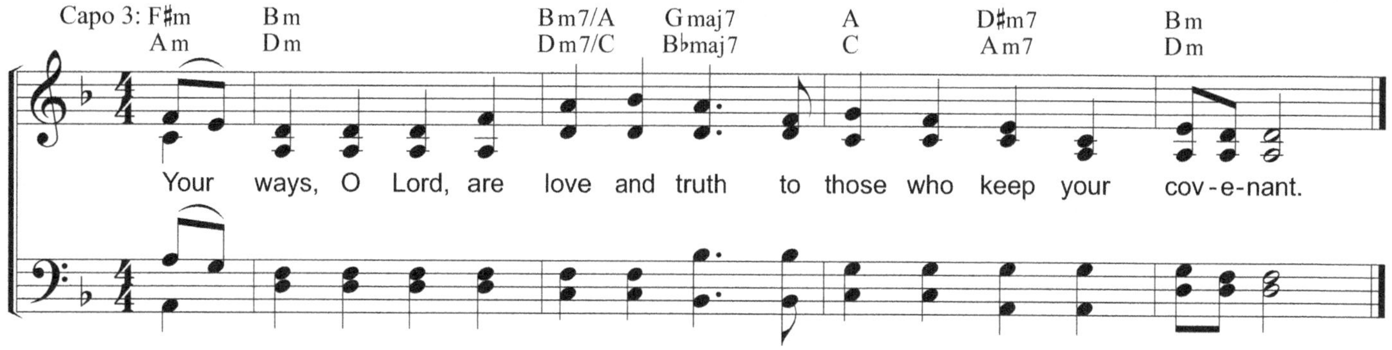
Capo 3: F♯m
Am
Bm Dm
Bm7/A Dm7/C
Gmaj7 B♭maj7
A C
D♯m7 Am7
Bm Dm
Your ways, O Lord, are love and truth to those who keep your cov-e-nant.

Verse 1

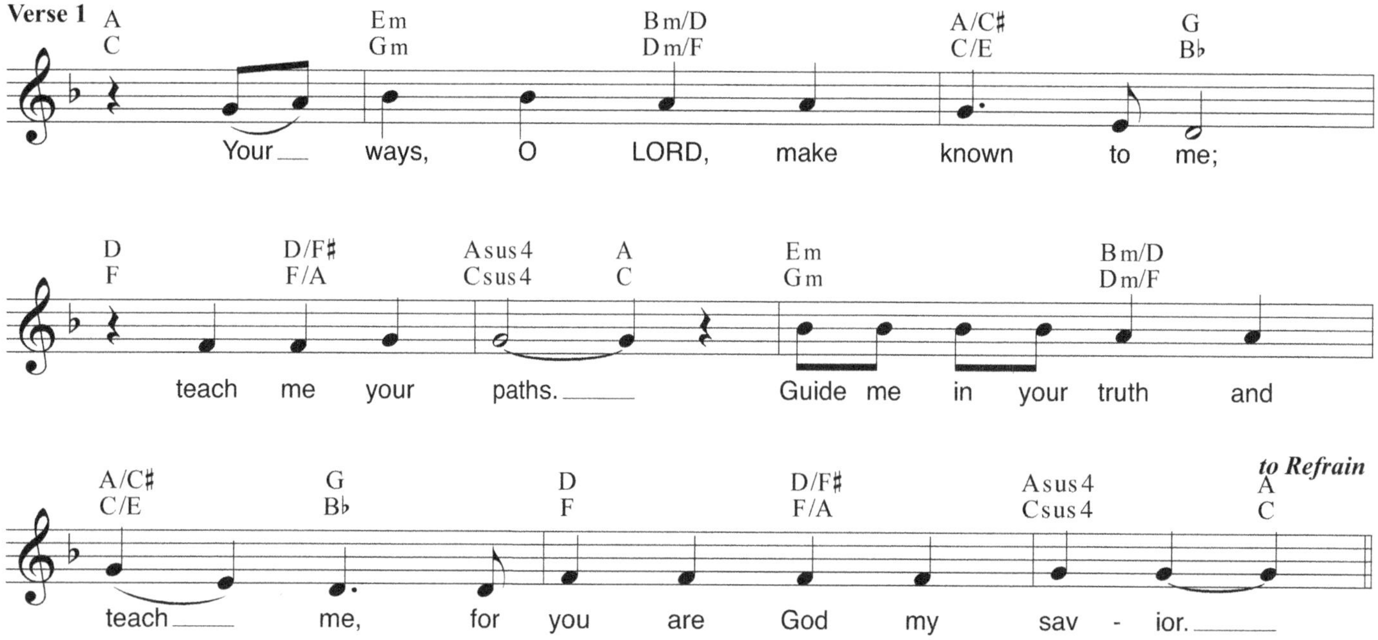
A C
Em Gm
Bm/D Dm/F
A/C♯ C/E
G B♭
Your ways, O LORD, make known to me;
D F
D/F♯ F/A
Asus4 Csus4
A C
Em Gm
Bm/D Dm/F
teach me your paths. Guide me in your truth and
A/C♯ C/E
G B♭
D F
D/F♯ F/A
Asus4 Csus4
to Refrain
A C
teach me, for you are God my sav - ior.

Verse 2

A C
Em Gm
Bm/D Dm/F
A/C♯ C/E
G B♭
Re - mem - ber that your com - pas - sion, O LORD, and your
D F
D/F♯ F/A
Asus4 Csus4
A C
Em Gm
Bm/D Dm/F
love are from of old. In your kind - ness re -
A/C♯ C/E
G B♭
D F
D/F♯ F/A
Asus4 Csus4
to Refrain
A C
mem - ber me, be - cause of your good - ness, O LORD.

Verse 3
A C
Em Gm
Bm/D Dm/F
A/C♯ C/E
G B♭
D F
D/F♯ F/A
Asus4 Csus4
A C
Good and up - right is the LORD, thus he shows sin-ners the way. He

to Refrain
Em Gm
Bm/D Dm/F
A/C♯ C/E
G B♭
D F
D/F♯ F/A
Asus4 Csus4
A C
guides the hum-ble to jus - tice and he teach-es the hum-ble his way.

Gospel Acclamation: Matthew 4:4b

Acclamation: (Keyboard/SATB) NO. VI

(M.M. ♩ = c. 104)

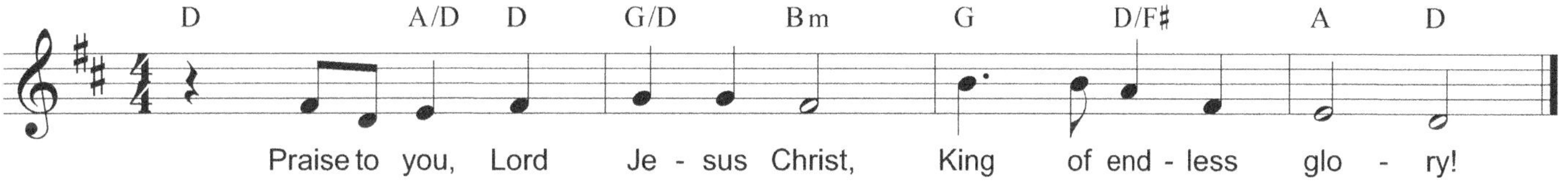
D
A/D
D
G/D
Bm
G
D/F♯
A
D
Praise to you, Lord Je - sus Christ, King of end - less glo - ry!

Verse: (Cantor)

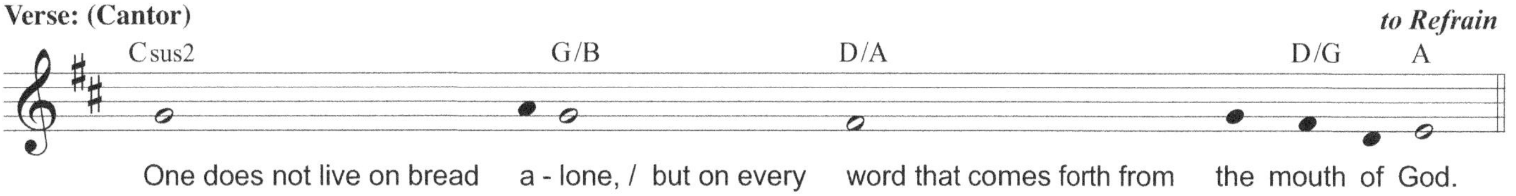
to Refrain
Csus2
G/B
D/A
D/G
A
One does not live on bread a - lone, / but on every word that comes forth from the mouth of God.

Second Sunday of Lent

February 28

(M.M. ♩ = c. 72)

Psalm 116:10, 15, 16–17, 18–19

REFRAIN
A Em7 Em/G A F Em G/B A
I will walk be-fore the Lord, in the land of the liv - ing.
Verse 1
Asus2 Em7 G/B A C/G Bm7
I be - lieved, e - ven when I said, "I am great - ly af - flict - ed."
Asus2 C/G Fmaj7 Esus4
to Refrain
Pre-cious in the eyes of the LORD is the death of his faith - ful ones.
Verse 2
Asus2 Em7 G/B A C/G
O LORD, I am your ser - vant; I am your ser - vant, the son of your
Bm7 Csus2 G/B Gm6/B♭ Asus2
poco rit.
a tempo
hand - maid; you have loosed my bonds. To you will I of - fer sac - ri - fice of thanks -
C/G Fmaj7 Esus4
to Refrain
giv - ing, and I will call up - on the name of the LORD.
Verse 3
Asus2 Em7 G/B A C/G Bm7
My vows to the LORD I will pay in the pres-ence of all his peo - ple, In the

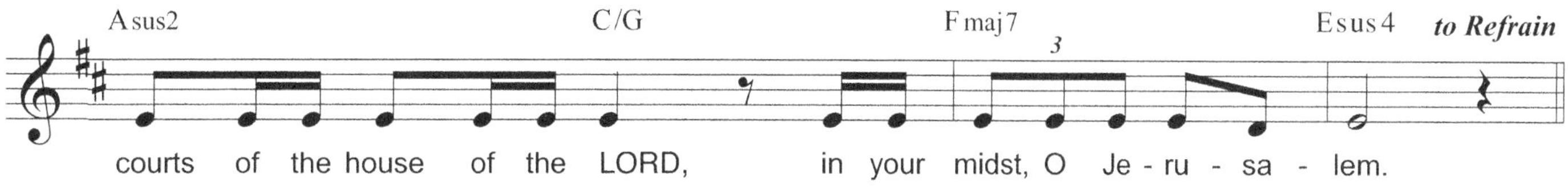
Asus2
C/G
Fmaj7
3
Esus4
to Refrain
courts of the house of the LORD, in your midst, O Je - ru - sa - lem.

Second Sunday of Lent, cont. (2)

Gospel Acclamation: Matthew 17:5

Acclamation: (Keyboard/SATB) NO. VII

(♩ = c. 90)

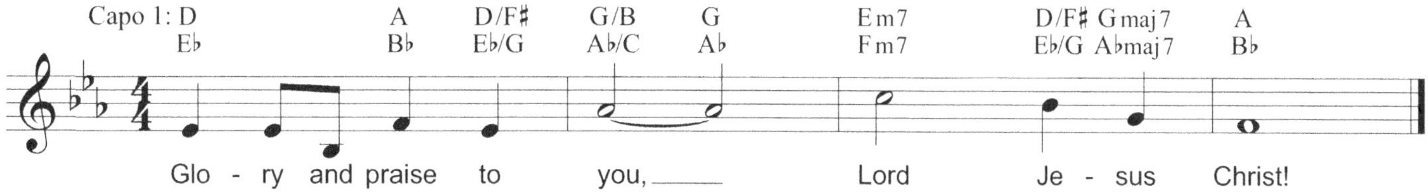
Capo 1: D
E♭
A
B♭
D/F♯
E♭/G
G/B
A♭/C
G
A♭
Em7
Fm7
D/F♯ Gmaj7
E♭/G A♭maj7
A
B♭
Glo - ry and praise to you, Lord Je - sus Christ!

Verse: (Cantor)

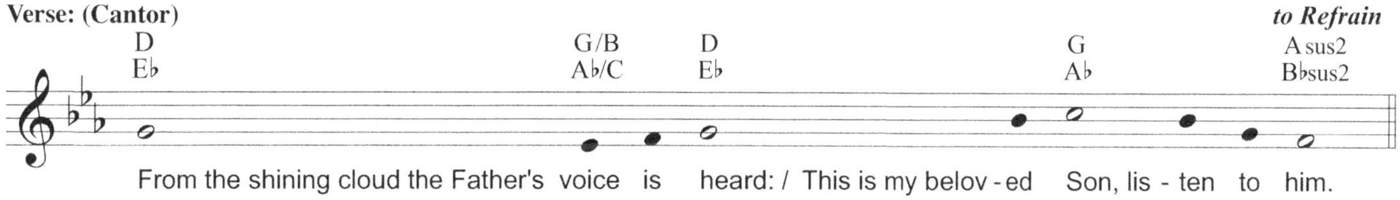
to Refrain
D
E♭
G/B
A♭/C
D
E♭
G
A♭
Asus2
B♭sus2
From the shining cloud the Father's voice is heard: / This is my belov - ed Son, lis - ten to him.

Third Sunday of Lent

March 7

Psalm 19:8, 9, 10, 11

(M.M. ♩ = c. 124)
REFRAIN
A/C♯ D D/F♯ Gsus2 D/F♯ G Dmaj7/F♯
Lord, you have the words, Lord, you have the words,
Em7 D/F♯ Gsus2 D/A A Bm Asus2
you have the words of ev - er - last - ing life.
(Keyboard)
Verse 1
D/C G/B G Dmaj7/F♯
The law of the LORD is per - fect, re - fresh - ing the soul; the de-
D/C G/B Em7 D/F♯ G A7sus4
cree of the LORD is trust - wor - thy, giv - ing wis - dom to the sim - ple.
to Refrain
Verse 2
D/C G/B G Dmaj7/F♯
The pre - cepts of the LORD are right, re - joic - ing the heart; the com-
D/C Bm7 Em7 D/F♯ Em7/G A7sus4
mand of the LORD is clear, en - light - en - ing the eye.
to Refrain
Verse 3
D/C G/B G Dmaj7/F♯
The fear of the LORD is pure, en - dur - ing for - ev - er; the

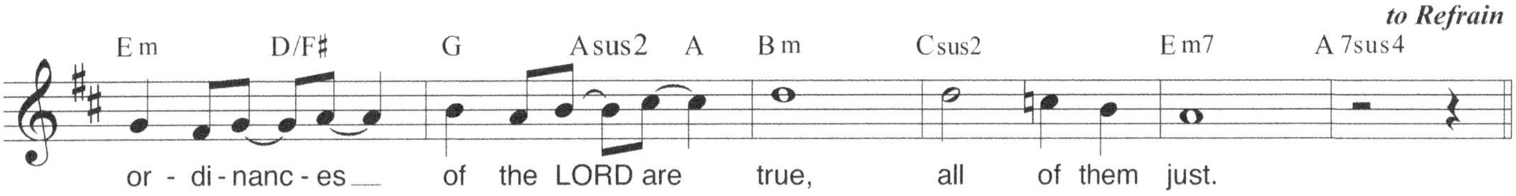
to Refrain
Em D/F♯ G Asus2 A Bm Csus2 Em7 A7sus4
or - di - nanc - es of the LORD are true, all of them just.

Verse 4

F Dsus2 Fsus2 F D
They are more pre - cious than gold, than a heap of pur - est gold;

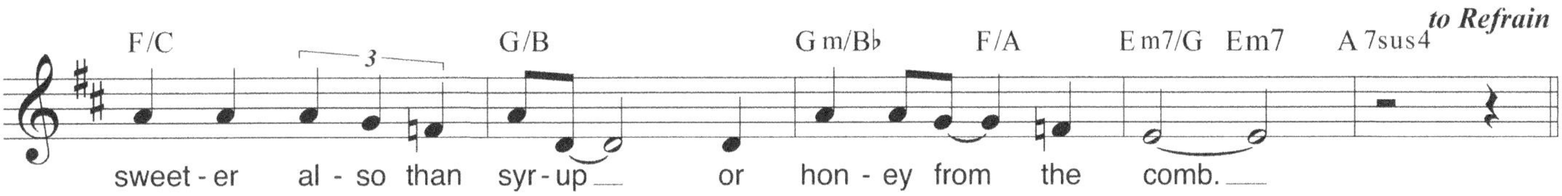
to Refrain
F/C G/B Gm/B♭ F/A Em7/G Em7 A7sus4
sweet - er al - so than syr - up or hon - ey from the comb.

Gospel Acclamation: John 3:16
Acclamation: (Keyboard/SATB) NO. VI
(M.M. ♩ = c. 104)

D A/D D G/D Bm G D/F♯ A D
Praise to you, Lord, Je - sus Christ, King of end - less glo - ry!

Verse: (Cantor)

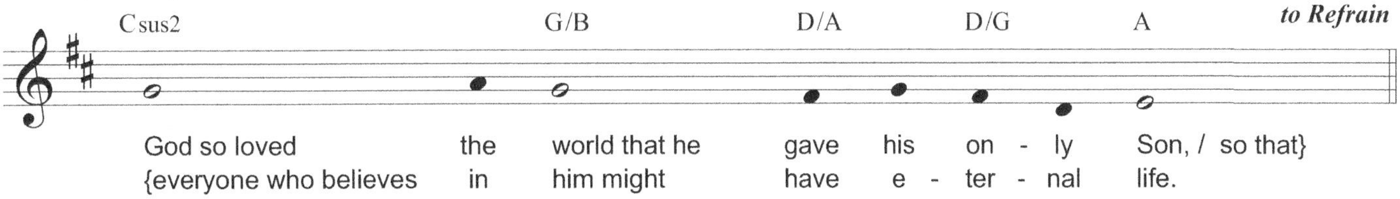
to Refrain
Csus2 G/B D/A D/G A
God so loved the world that he gave his on - ly Son, / so that}
{everyone who believes in him might have e - ter - nal life.

RCIA Option: Third Sunday of Lent

January 31

(M.M. ♩ = c. 100)

Psalm 95:1-2, 6-7, 7-9

REFRAIN

If to-day you hear his voice, hard - en not your hearts.
Verse 1
Come, let us sing joy-ful-ly to the LORD; let us ac-claim the rock of our sal-va-tion. Let us come in-to his pre-sence with thanks-giv-ing; let us joy-ful-ly sing psalms to him.
to Refrain
Verse 2
Come, let us bow down in wor-ship; let us kneel be-fore the LORD who made us. For he is our God, and we are the peop-le he shep-herds, the flock he guides.
to Refrain
Verse 3
Oh, that to-day you would hear his voice:

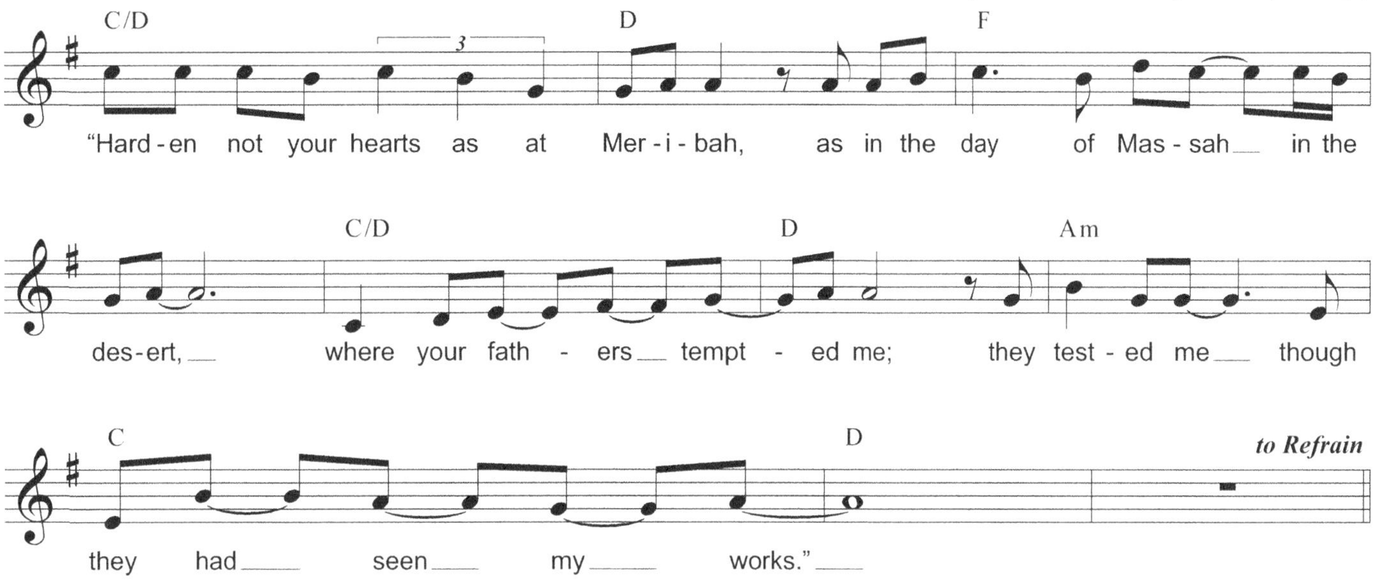
C/D D F
"Hard-en not your hearts as at Mer-i-bah, as in the day of Mas-sah in the
C/D D Am
des-ert, where your fath - ers tempt - ed me; they test-ed me though
C D
they had seen my works."
to Refrain

Gospel Acclamation: cf. John 4:42, 15

Acclamation: (Keyboard/SATB) NO. VI

(M.M. ♩ = c. 104)

D A/D D G/D Bm G D/F♯ A D
Praise to you, Lord Je - sus Christ, King of end - less glo - ry!

Verse: (Cantor)

to Refrain
Csus2 G/B D/A D/G A
Lord, you are truly the Sav - ior of the world;}
{give me liv - ing water, / that I may nev - er thirst a - gain.

Fourth Sunday of Lent

(M.M. ♩ = c. 124)

March 14

Psalm 137:1–2, 3, 4–5, 6

REFRAIN

Capo 1: Bm Cm
Em/B Bm Fm/C Cm
G A♭
D/A A E♭/B♭ B♭
Let my tongue be si - lenced, if I ev - er for - get you,
C/E D♭/F
Bm Cm
A B♭
F♯m/A Gm/B♭
A/G B♭/A♭
G A♭
ev - er for - get you!
(Keyboard)
Verse 1
C E♭
Am7 Cm7
C E♭
C/E E♭/G
By the streams of Bab - y - lon we sat and wept when we re - mem-bered
G B♭
Dm Fm
C/E E♭/G
F A♭
C/G E♭/B♭
G B♭
to Refrain
Zi - on. On the as - pens of that land we hung up our harps.
Verse 2
C E♭
Am7 Cm7
C E♭
G B♭
For there our cap - tors asked of us the lyr - ics of our songs, And our de - spoil - ers
Dm Fm
C/E E♭/G
F A♭
C/G E♭/B♭
G B♭
to Refrain
urged us to be joy - ous: "Sing for us the songs of Zi - on!"
Verse 3
C E♭
Am7 Cm7
C E♭
C E♭
G B♭
G/B B♭/D
How could we sing a song of the LORD in a for - eign land? If I for -

Dm Fm
C/E E♭/G
F A♭
C/G E♭/B♭
G B♭
to Refrain
get___ you, Je - ru - sa - lem, may my right hand be for - got - ten!
Verse 4
C E♭
Am7 Cm7
C E♭
G B♭
May my tongue cleave to my pal - ate if I re - mem - ber you not,
G/B B♭/D
Dm Fm
C/E E♭/G
F A♭
C/G E♭/B♭
G B♭
to Refrain
if I place not Je - ru - sa - lem a - head of my joy.

Gospel Acclamation: John 3:16

Acclamation: (Keyboard/SATB) NO. VII

(♩ = c. 90)

Capo 1: D E♭
A B♭
D/F♯ E♭/G
G/B A♭/C
G A♭
Em7 Fm7
D/F♯ E♭/G
Gmaj7 A♭maj7
A B♭
Glo - ry and praise to you, Lord Je - sus Christ!
Verse: (Cantor)
to Refrain
D E♭
G/B A♭/C
D E♭
G A♭
A/C♯ B♭/D
God so loved the world that gave his on - ly Son, / so}
{everyone who be - lieves in him might have e - ter - nal life.

RCIA Option: Fourth Sunday of Lent

(M.M. ♩ = c. 114)

March 14

Psalm 23:1-3a, 3b-4, 5, 6

REFRAIN

Capo 3: C/G Fmaj7 Em7 Dm7 Fmaj7/C
E♭/B♭ A♭maj7 Gm7 Fm7 A♭maj7/E♭
The Lord is my shep - herd; there is noth - ing I shall want.
Verse 1
F G/F Em Am F
A♭ B♭/A♭ Gm Cm A♭
The LORD is my shep-herd; I shall not want. In ver - dant pas - tures
G A/E Em Bm/D A/C♯
B♭ C/G Gm Dm/F C/E
3
he gives me re - pose; be - side rest - ful wa - ters he leads me;
A/E C/G F Gsus4 G
C/G E♭/B♭ A♭ B♭sus4 B♭
to Refrain
he re - fresh - es my soul.
Verse 2
F G/F Em Am F
A♭ B♭/A♭ Gm Cm A♭
He guides me in right paths for his name's sake. E - ven though I
G A/E Em Bm/D Cmaj7
B♭ C/G Gm Dm/F E♭maj7
walk in the dark val - ley I fear no e - vil; for you are at my
A/E C/G F Gsus4 G
C/G E♭/B♭ A♭ B♭sus4 B♭
to Refrain
side with your rod and your staff that give me cour - age.
Verse 3
F G/F Em
A♭ B♭/A♭ Gm
You spread the ta - ble be - fore me in the sight of my

 Through composed version in *With the Lord* songbook Ed. 10581 available at www.ocp.org.

Am Cm
F A♭
G B♭
A/E C/G
foes; you a - noint my head with oil;
C/G E♭/B♭
F A♭
Gsus4 B♭sus4
G B♭
to Refrain
my cup o - ver - flows.
Verse 4
F A♭
G/F B♭/A♭
Em Gm
Am Cm
3
On-ly good-ness and kind - ness fol-low me all the days of my life; and I shall
to Refrain
F A♭
G B♭
A/E C/G
C/G E♭/B♭
F A♭
Gsus4 B♭sus4
G B♭
dwell in the house of the LORD for years to come.

Gospel Acclamation: John 8:12

Acclamation: (Keyboard/SATB) NO. VI

(M.M. ♩ = c. 104)

D
A/D
D
G/D
Bm
G
D/F♯
A
D
Praise to you, Lord Je - sus Christ, King of end - less glo - ry!
Verse: (Cantor)
to Refrain
Csus2
G/B
D/A
D/G
A
I am the light of the world, says the Lord; / whoever follows me will have the light of life.

Fifth Sunday of Lent

March 21

Psalm 51:3–4, 12–13, 14–15

(M.M. ♩ = c. 77)
REFRAIN
G Bsus4 Bsus4/A Em7 F♯m7 D/F♯ Gmaj7
Cre - ate a clean heart, a clean heart in me, O God.
Verse 1 (M.M. ♩ = c. 69)
Asus2 Em Bsus4 Bm
Have mer - cy on me, O God, in your good - ness; in the
Em Bm D D/F♯ Asus2
great - ness of your com - pas - sion wipe out my of - fense. Thor - ough - ly
Em7 Bm G D/F♯ Asus2
wash me from my guilt and of my sin cleanse me.
to Refrain
G
Verse 2 (M.M. ♩ = c. 69)
Asus2 Em Bsus4 Bm
A clean heart cre - ate for me, O God, and a stead - fast
Em Bm Asus2 Em7
spir - it re - new with - in me. Cast me not out from your
Bm Bm Bm/A G D/F♯ Asus2
pres - ence, and your Ho - ly Spir - it take not from me.
to Refrain
G

Verse 3 (M.M. ♩ = c. 69)

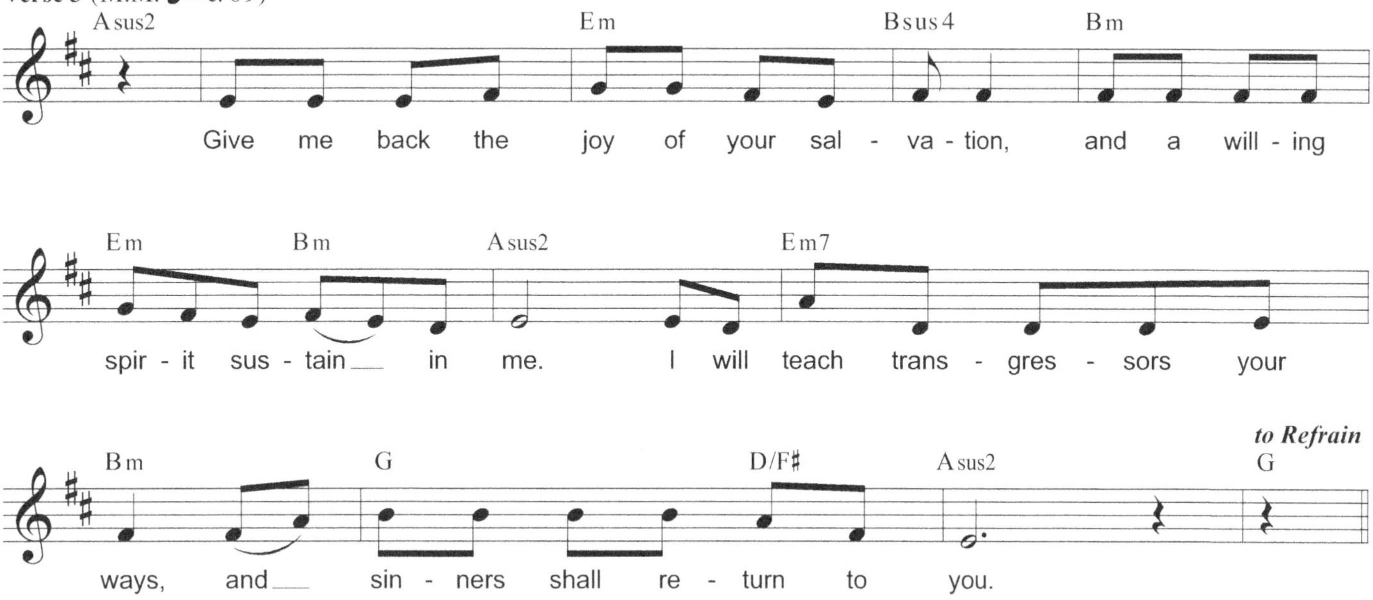
Asus2 Em Bsus4 Bm
Give me back the joy of your sal - va - tion, and a will - ing
Em Bm Asus2 Em7
spir - it sus - tain in me. I will teach trans - gres - sors your
to Refrain
Bm G D/F♯ Asus2 G
ways, and sin - ners shall re - turn to you.

Gospel Acclamation: John 12:26

Acclamation: (Keyboard/SATB) NO. VI

(M.M. ♩ = c. 104)

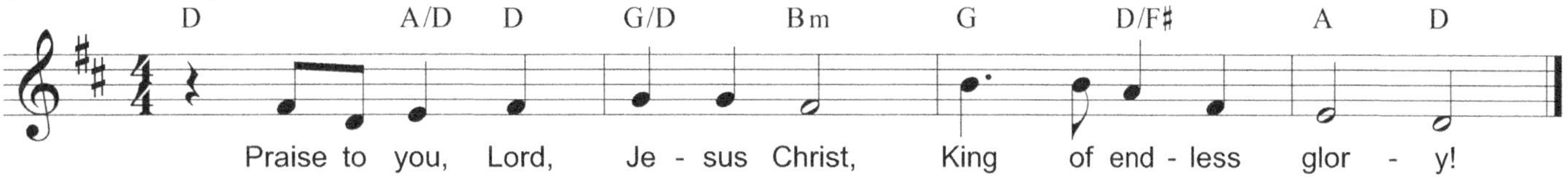
D A/D D G/D Bm G D/F♯ A D
Praise to you, Lord, Je - sus Christ, King of end - less glor - y!

Verse: (Cantor)

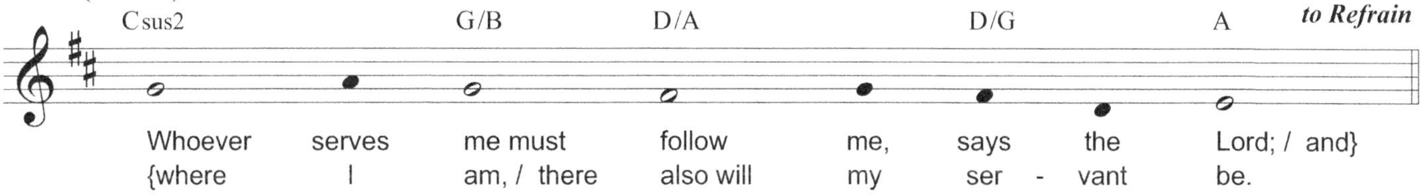
Csus2 G/B D/A D/G A
to Refrain
Whoever serves me must follow me, says the Lord; / and}
{where I am, / there also will my ser - vant be.

RCIA Option: Fifth Sunday of Lent

March 21

(M.M. ♩ = c. 80)

Psalm 130:1-2, 3-4, 5-6, 7-8

REFRAIN
With the Lord there is mer-cy and full-ness of ___ re-demp-tion.
(Keyboard)
Verse 1
Out of the depths I cry to you, O LORD; LORD, hear my voice!
to Refrain
Let your ears be at-ten-tive to my voice in sup-pli-ca-tion.
Verse 2
If you, O LORD, mark in-iq-ui-ties, LORD, who can stand?
to Refrain
But with you is for-give-ness, that you may be re-vered.
Verse 3
I trust in the LORD; my soul trusts in his word. More than
to Refrain
sen-ti-nels wait for the dawn, let Is-ra-el wait for the LORD.
Verse 4
For with the LORD is kind-ness and with him

Through composed version in *With the Lord* songbook Ed. 92562 available at www.ocp.org.

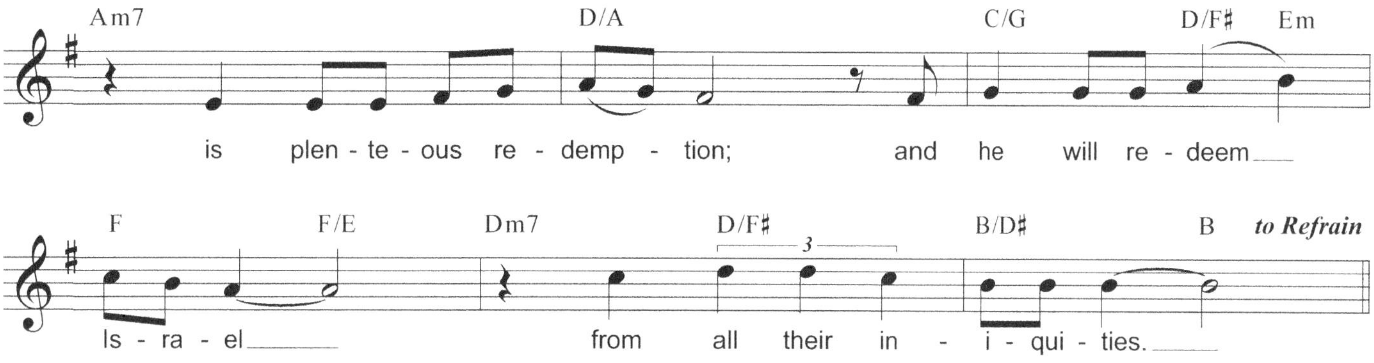
Am7 D/A C/G D/F♯ Em
is plen - te - ous re - demp - tion; and he will re - deem
F F/E Dm7 D/F♯ B/D♯ B
to Refrain
Is - ra - el from all their in - i - qui - ties.

Gospel Acclamation: John 11:25a, 26

Acclamation: (Keyboard/SATB) NO. VI

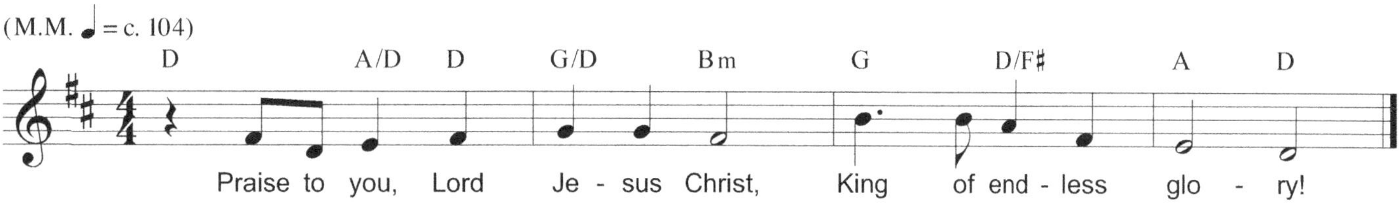
(M.M. ♩ = c. 104)
D A/D D G/D Bm G D/F♯ A D
Praise to you, Lord Je - sus Christ, King of end - less glo - ry!

Verse: (Cantor)

to Refrain
Csus2 G/B D/A D/G A
I am the resurrection and the life, says the Lord; / whoever be - lieves in me,}
{even if he dies, will nev - er die.

Palm Sunday of the Passion of the Lord

March 28

(M.M. ♩ = c. 89)

Psalm 22:8-9, 17-18, 19-20, 23-24

REFRAIN
Capo 3: Bm Dm F♯m/A Am/C Gmaj7 B♭maj7 F♯m7 Am7 Em7 Gm7 Bm Dm
1st time
My God, my God, why have you a - ban - doned me?
Verse 1
All who see me scoff at me; they mock me with part - ed lips, they wag their heads: "He re - lied on the LORD; let him de - liv - er him, let him res - cue him, if he loves him."
to Refrain
Verse 2
In - deed, man-y dogs sur - round me, a pack of ev-il-do-ers clos-es in u - pon me; they have pierced my hands and my feet, I can count all my bones.
to Refrain
Verse 3
They div - ide my gar - ments a - mong them, and for my vest - ure they cast lots. But you, O LORD, be not far from me; O my help, hast - en to aid me.
to Refrain

Verse 4
Bm G A/G G A/G
Dm B♭ C/B♭ B♭ C/B♭
I will pro - claim your name to my breth - ren; in the
D E/D D C D/C
F G/F F E♭ F/E♭
midst of the as - sem - bly I will praise you: "You who fear the LORD,
C Bm F♯m/A G D/F♯ Em7
E♭ Dm Am/C B♭ F/A Gm7
praise him; all you des - cen - dants of Jac - ob, give glo - ry to
Bm Bm F♯m/A Em7 Bm
Dm Dm Am/C Gm7 Dm
him; re - vere him, all you des - cen - dants of Is - ra - el!"

Gospel Acclamation: Philippians 2:8-9

Acclamation: (Keyboard/SATB) NO. VII

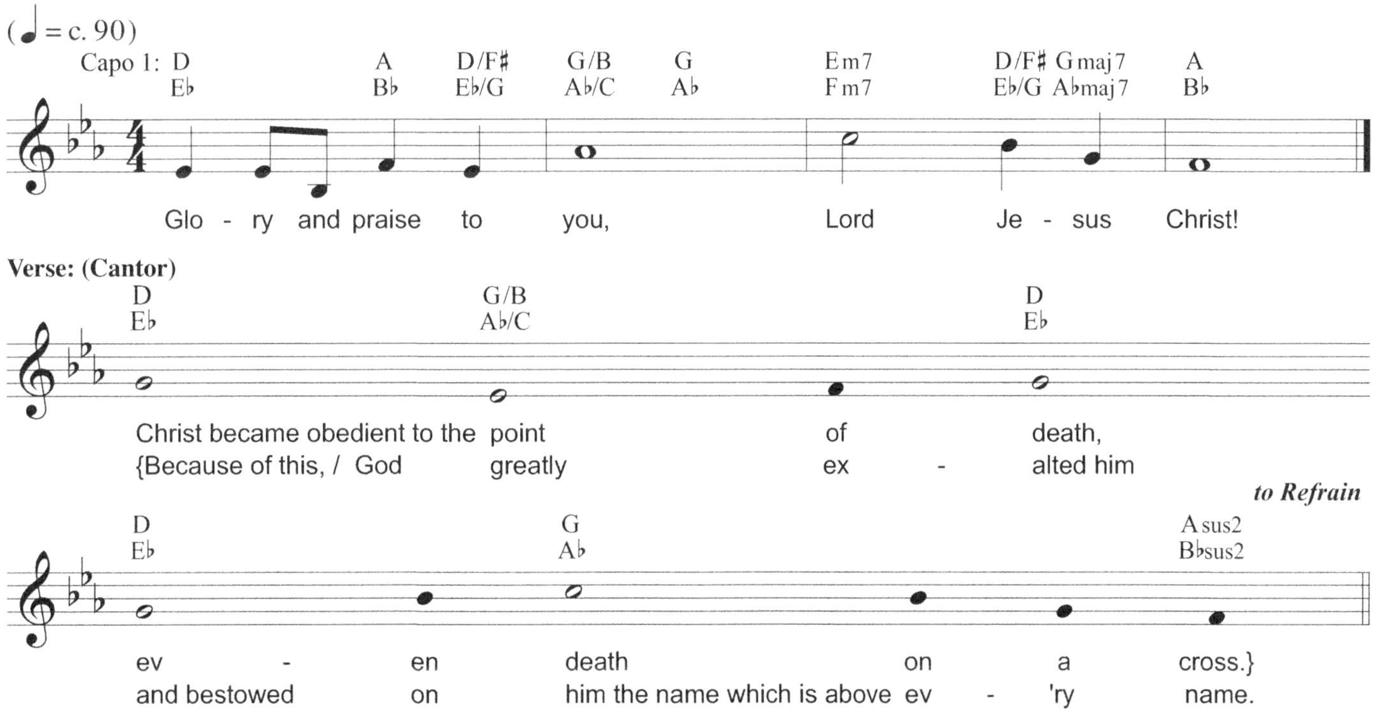
(♩ = c. 90)
Capo 1: D A D/F♯ G/B G Em7 D/F♯ Gmaj7 A
E♭ B♭ E♭/G A♭/C A♭ Fm7 E♭/G A♭maj7 B♭
Glo - ry and praise to you, Lord Je - sus Christ!
Verse: (Cantor)
D G/B D
E♭ A♭/C E♭
Christ became obedient to the point of death,
{Because of this, / God greatly ex - alted him
to Refrain
D G Asus2
E♭ A♭ B♭sus2
ev - en death on a cross.}
and bestowed on him the name which is above ev - 'ry name.

Thursday of the Lord's Supper (Holy Thursday):

At the Evening Mass

(M.M. ♩ = c. 79)

April 1

Psalm 116:12-13,15-16bc, 17-18

REFRAIN

Capo 3: D/A F/C A C F♯m Am G B♭ D/F♯ F/A Em Gm D/F♯ F/A A C
Our bless-ing - cup___ is a com-mun-ion with the Blood of Christ.
Verse 1
A C Em Gm Bm/D Dm/F G/B B♭/D A C G B♭ D F A C
How shall I make a re-turn to the LORD for all the good he has done for me? The
Em Gm Bm/D Dm/F G/B B♭/D A C G B♭ D F
to Refrain
A C
cup of sal-va-tion I will take up, and I will call up-on the name of the LORD.
Verse 2
A C Em Gm G/B B♭/D A C G B♭ D F A C
Pre-cious in the eyes of the LORD is the death of his faith-ful ones.
Em Gm Bm/D Dm/F G/B B♭/D A C G B♭ D F
to Refrain
A C
I am your ser-vant, the son of your hand-maid; you have loosed my bonds.
Verse 3
A C Em Gm Bm/D Dm/F G/B B♭/D A C
To you will I of-fer sac-ri-fice of thanks-giv-ing,___ and I will
G B♭ D F A C Em Gm Bm/D Dm/F
call up-on the name of the LORD. My vows to the LORD___

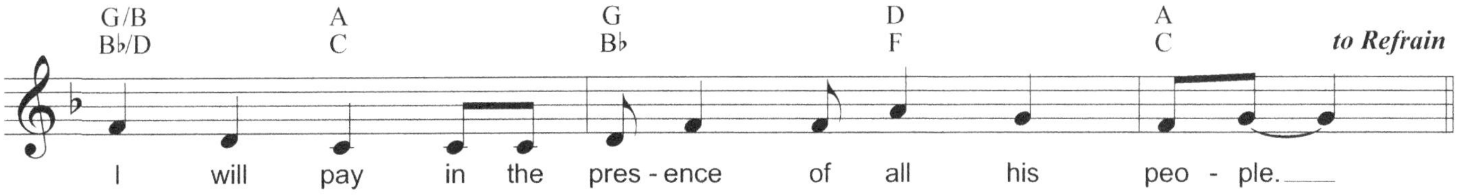
G/B
B♭/D
A
C
G
B♭
D
F
A
C
to Refrain
I will pay in the pres - ence of all his peo - ple.

Gospel Acclamation: John 13:34

Acclamation: (Keyboard/SATB) NO. VII

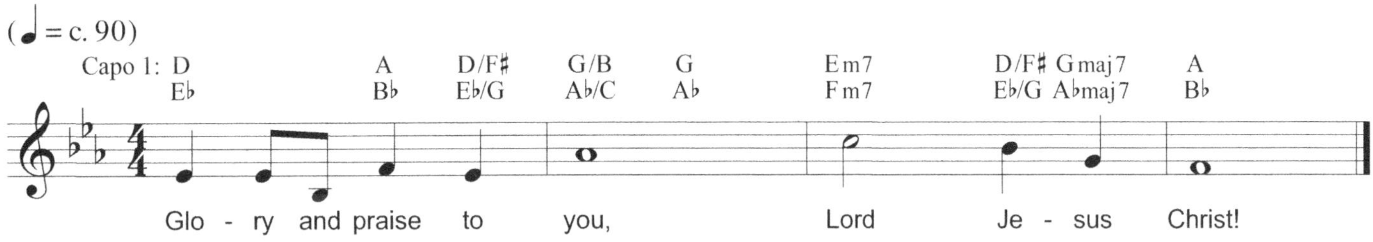
(♩= c. 90)
Capo 1: D
E♭
A
B♭
D/F♯
E♭/G
G/B
A♭/C
G
A♭
Em7
Fm7
D/F♯ Gmaj7
E♭/G A♭maj7
A
B♭
Glo - ry and praise to you, Lord Je - sus Christ!

Verse: (Cantor)

to Refrain
D
E♭
G/B
A♭/C
D
E♭
G
A♭
Asus2
B♭sus2
I give you a new commandment, says the Lord: / love one an - other as I have loved you.

Friday of the Passion of the Lord (Good Friday)

(M.M. ♩ = c. 120)

April 19

Psalm 31:2, 6, 12-13, 15-16, 17, 25

REFRAIN
Capo 3: Asus4 Am F/A F Dm7 Dm/F A5
Csus4 Cm Ab/C Ab Fm7 Fm/Ab C5
Fa - ther, in - to your hands I com - mend my spir - it.
Verse 1
Am E7/A Dm/F Dm7
Cm G7/C Fm/Ab Fm7
In you, O LORD, I take ref - uge; let me nev - er be put to
Am F G/F C/E G
Cm Ab Bb/Ab Eb/G Bb
shame. In your jus - tice res - cue me. In - to your hands I com - mend my
Am F/A Dm/F Esus4 E
Cm Ab/C Fm/Ab Gsus4 G
spir - it; you will re - deem me, O LORD, O faith - ful God.
to Refrain
Verse 2
Am E7/A Dm/F Dm7 Am
Cm G7/C Fm/Ab Fm7 Cm
For all my foes I am an ob - ject of re - proach, a
F G/F C/E G
Ab Bb/Ab Eb/G Bb
laugh - ing - stock to my neigh - bors, and a dread to my friends;
F G/F C/E
Ab Bb/Ab Eb/G
they who see me a - broad flee from me. I am for - got - ten like the
G Am F/A Dm/F Esus4 E
Bb Cm Ab/C Fm/Ab Gsus4 G
un - re - mem - bered dead; I am like a dish that is bro - ken.
to Refrain
Verse 3
Am E7/A Dm/F Dm7 Am
Cm G7/C Fm/Ab Fm7 Cm
But my trust is in you, O LORD; I say, “You are my God. In your

F Ab G/F Bb/Ab C/E Eb/G G Bb
hands is my des - ti - ny; res - cue me from the clutch - es of my
Am Cm F/A Ab/C Dm/F Fm/Ab Esus4 Gsus4 E G
to Refrain
en - e - mies and my per - se - cu - tors."
Verse 4
Am Cm E7/A G7/C Dm/F Fm/Ab Dm7 Fm7 Am Cm
Let your face shine up - on your ser - vant; save me in your kind - ness.
F Ab G/F Bb/Ab C/E Eb/G
Take cour - age and be stout - heart - ed, all you who
G Bb Am Cm F/A Ab/C Dm/F Fm/Ab Esus4 Gsus4 E G
to Refrain
hope in the LORD, [all you who hope in the LORD.

Gospel Acclamation: Philippians 2:8-9

Acclamation: (Keyboard/SATB) NO. VII

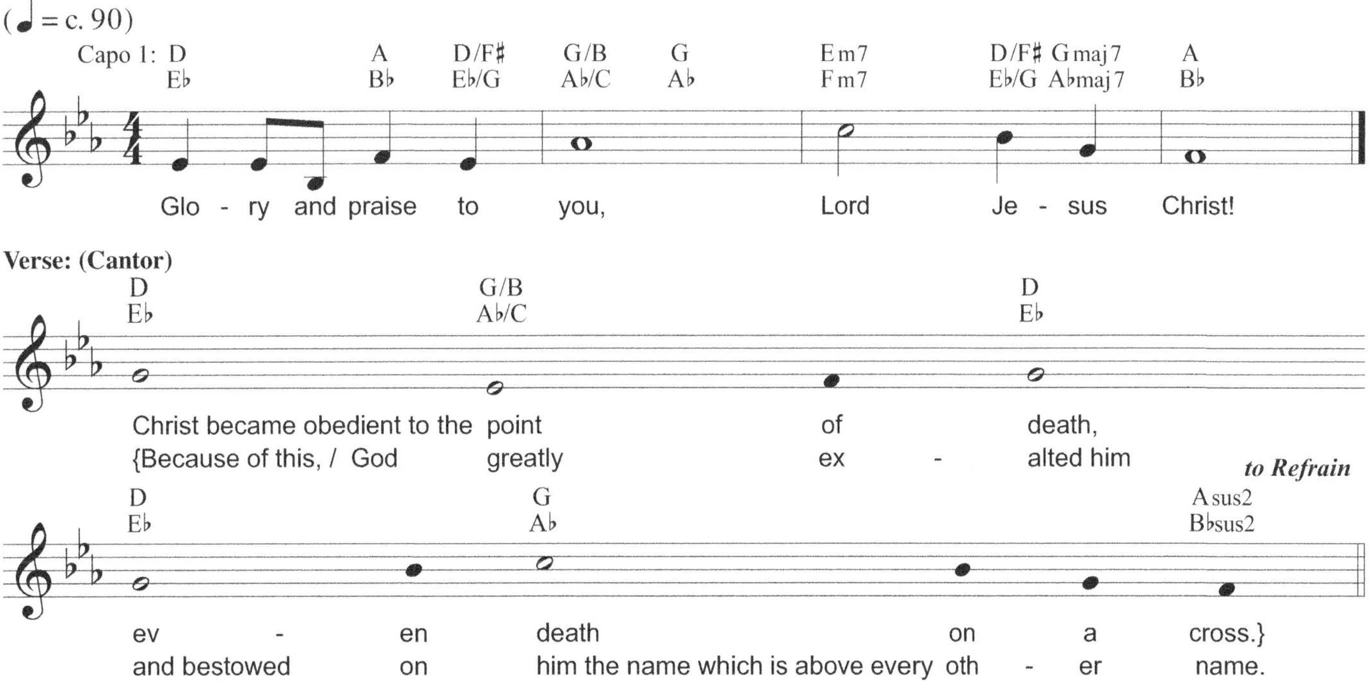
(♩ = c. 90)
Capo 1: D Eb A Bb D/F♯ Eb/G G/B Ab/C G Ab Em7 Fm7 D/F♯ Eb/G Gmaj7 Abmaj7 A Bb
Glo - ry and praise to you, Lord Je - sus Christ!
Verse: (Cantor)
D Eb G/B Ab/C D Eb
Christ became obedient to the point of death,
{Because of this, / God greatly ex - alted him
to Refrain
D Eb G Ab Asus2 Bbsus2
ev - en death on a cross.}
and bestowed on him the name which is above every oth - er name.

The Easter Vigil in the Holy Night

Responsorial Psalm (following first reading) *April 3*

(M.M. ♩ = c. 116)

Psalm 104:1-2, 5-6, 10, 12, 13-14, 24, 35

REFRAIN

D C/D D Bm7 C D
Lord, send out your Spir - it, and re-new the face of the earth.
Verse 1
D C/D G/D D
Bless the LORD, O my soul! O LORD, my God, you are great in - deed! You are
Bm7 C G C/E Gsus2
clothed with maj - es - ty and glo - ry, robed in light as with a cloak.
Gsus4 G
to Refrain
Verse 2
D C/D
You fixed the earth up - on its foun - da - tion, not to be
G/D D Bm7 C
moved for - ev - er; with the o - cean, as with a gar - ment, you
Gsus2 C/E Gsus2 Gsus4 G
cov - ered it; a - bove the moun - tains the wa - ters stood.
to Refrain
Verse 3
D C/D G/D
You send forth springs in - to the wa - ter - cours - es that wind a - mong the

D Bm7 C
moun - tains. Be - side them the birds of heav - en
to Refrain
Gsus2 C/G Gsus2 Gsus4 G
dwell; from a - mong the branch - es they send forth their song.
Verse 4
D C/D G/D
You wa - ter the moun - tains from your pal - ace; the earth is re - plete with the fruit of your
D Bm7 C C/G
works. You raise grass for the cat - tle, and veg - e - ta - tion for man's
to Refrain
Gsus2 C/E Gsus2 Gsus4 G
use, pro - duc - ing bread from the earth.
Verse 5
D C/D G/D D
How man - i - fold are your works, O LORD! In
Bm7 C G C/G G
wis - dom you have wrought them all— the earth is full of your crea - tures. Bless the
to Refrain
C/E Gsus2
LORD, O my soul! Al - le - lu - ia.

Alternate Responsorial Psalm (following first reading)

Psalm 33:4-5, 6-7, 12-13, 20 & 22

(M.M. ♩ = c. 61)
REFRAIN
D G Em7 A7sus4 D
The earth is full of the good - ness of the Lord.
Verse 1
Dsus2 A/C♯ Bm Gsus2 Em7
Up - right is the word of the LORD, and all his works are trust - wor - thy. He
Dsus2 A/C♯ Bm Em7 D/F♯ Gsus2 to Refrain
loves jus - tice and right; of the kind - ness of the LORD the earth is full.
Verse 2
Dsus2 A/C♯ Bm
By the word of the LORD the heav - ens were made; by the
Gsus2 Em7 Dsus2
breath of his mouth all their host. He gath - ers the wa - ters of the
A/C♯ Bm Em7 D/F♯ Gsus2 to Refrain
sea as in a flask; in cel - lars he con - fines the deep.
Verse 3
Dsus2 A/C♯ Bm
Bless - ed the na - tion whose God is the LORD, the

Gsus2
Em7
peo - ple he has cho - sen for his own in - her - it - ance. From
D A/C♯ Bm Em7 D/F♯ Gsus2
to Refrain
heav - en the LORD looks down; he sees all man - kind.
Verse 4
D A/C♯ Bm Gsus2 Em7
Our soul waits for the LORD, who is our help and our shield. May your
D A/C♯ Bm Esus4 D/F♯ Gsus2
to Refrain
kind - ness, O LORD, be up - on us who have put our hope in you.

Responsorial Psalm (following second reading)

Psalm 16:5, 8, 9-10, 11

(M.M. ♩ = c. 106)

REFRAIN

Capo 1: B m7 F♯m7 G B m7 F♯m7
C m7 G m7 A♭ C m7 G m7
You are my in - her - i - tance, you are my in - her -
(her-)
Gmaj7 A sus4 C/E Cmaj7 D
A♭maj7 B♭sus4 D♭/F D♭maj7 E♭
- i - tance, O Lord.
(her-)

Verse 1
D G D/A Gsus2
E♭ A♭ E♭/B♭ A♭sus2
O LORD, my al - lot - ted por - tion and my cup, you it is who
G/B D/A C/E D C G/D
A♭/C E♭/B♭ D♭/F E♭ D♭ A♭/E♭
hold fast my lot. I set the LORD ev - er be - fore me; with
G/B A/C♯ D Gmaj7 A sus4 A
A♭/C B♭/D E♭ A♭maj7 B♭sus4 B♭
to Refrain
him at my right hand I shall not be dis - turbed.
Verse 2
G sus2 D/A G sus2 D G sus2
A♭sus2 E♭/B♭ A♭sus2 E♭ A♭sus2
There-fore my heart is glad and my soul re - joic - es, my bod-y, too, a - bides in

D/A Eb/Bb D Eb C/E Db/F C Db G/D Ab/Eb
con - fi - dence; because you will not a-ban - don my soul to the neth-er-world,
G/B Ab/C A/C♯ Bb/D D Eb Gmaj7 Abmaj7 A sus4 Bbsus4 A Bb
to Refrain
nor will you suf-fer your faith-ful one to un-der-go cor-rup-tion.
Verse 3
Dsus2 Ebsus2 D Eb Gadd9/B Abadd9/C Gmaj7 Abmaj7 A Bb Bm7 Cm7 Bm9/A Cm9/Bb
You will [show me,] show me the path to life,
G Ab D/F♯ Eb/G C/E Db/F G/D Ab/Eb Csus2 Dbsus2
full-ness of joys in your pres-ence, the de-lights at your right hand [for-
G/D Ab/Eb G/B Ab/C G Ab D Eb
to Refrain
ev - er,] for - ev - er.

The Easter Vigil in the Holy Night, cont. (7)

Responsorial Psalm (following third reading)

(M.M. ♩ = c. 92)

Exodus 15:1-2, 3-4, 5-6, 17-18

REFRAIN

Capo 3:
Let us sing to the Lord; he has cov-ered him-self in glo - ry.
Verse 1
I will sing to the LORD, for he is glo-ri-ous-ly tri-um-phant; horse and
char-iot he has cast in-to the sea. My strength and my cour-age
is the LORD, and he has been my sav-ior. He is my God, I
praise him; the God of my fa-ther, I ex-tol him.
to Refrain
Verse 2
The LORD is a war-rior, LORD is his name! Phar-aoh's
char-iots and ar-my he hurled in-to the sea; the e-lite of his

Dm/F G Em Asus4
Fm/A♭ B♭ Gm Csus4
to Refrain
of - fic - ers were sub - merged in the Red Sea.
Verse 3
Asus2 G/A D/A
Csus2 B♭/C F/C
The flood wa - ters cov - ered them, they sank in - to the depths like a
Asus2 Am A/C G/D D/A Asus2
Csus2 Cm C/E♭ B♭/F F/C Csus2
stone. Your right hand, O LORD, mag - nif - i - cent in pow'r, your
Dm Dm/F G Em7 Asus4
Fm Fm/A♭ B♭ Gm7 Csus4
to Refrain
right hand, O LORD, has shat - tered the en - e - my.
Verse 4
Asus2
Csus2
You brought in the peo - ple you re - deemed and plant - ed them on the
G/A D/A Asus4 Am/C
B♭/C F/C Csus4 Cm/E♭
moun - tain of your in - her - it - ance— the place where you made your
G/D A/E G/D A/E A/C♯
B♭/F C/G B♭/F C/G C/E
seat, O LORD, the sanc - tu - ar - y, LORD, which your hands es - tab - lished. The
Dm Dm/F G Em7 Asus4
Fm Fm/A♭ B♭ Gm7 Csus4
to Refrain
LORD shall reign for - ev - er and ev - er.

Responsorial Psalm (following fourth reading)

(M.M. ♩ = c. 118)

Psalm 30:2, 4, 5-6, 11-12, 13

REFRAIN

Bm Gmaj7 A F♯m7 G
I will praise you, Lord, for you have res - cued me.

Verse 1

D/A G D/A G/B A/C♯ Em D/F♯
I will ex - tol you, O LORD, for you drew me clear and did not let my en-e-mies re -
Asus2 G D/F♯ Em G/B
joice o - ver me. O LORD, you brought me up from the neth - er - world; you pre -
D/A G/B Em7 D/F♯ G Asus2
served me from a - mong those go - ing down in - to the pit.
to Refrain

Verse 2

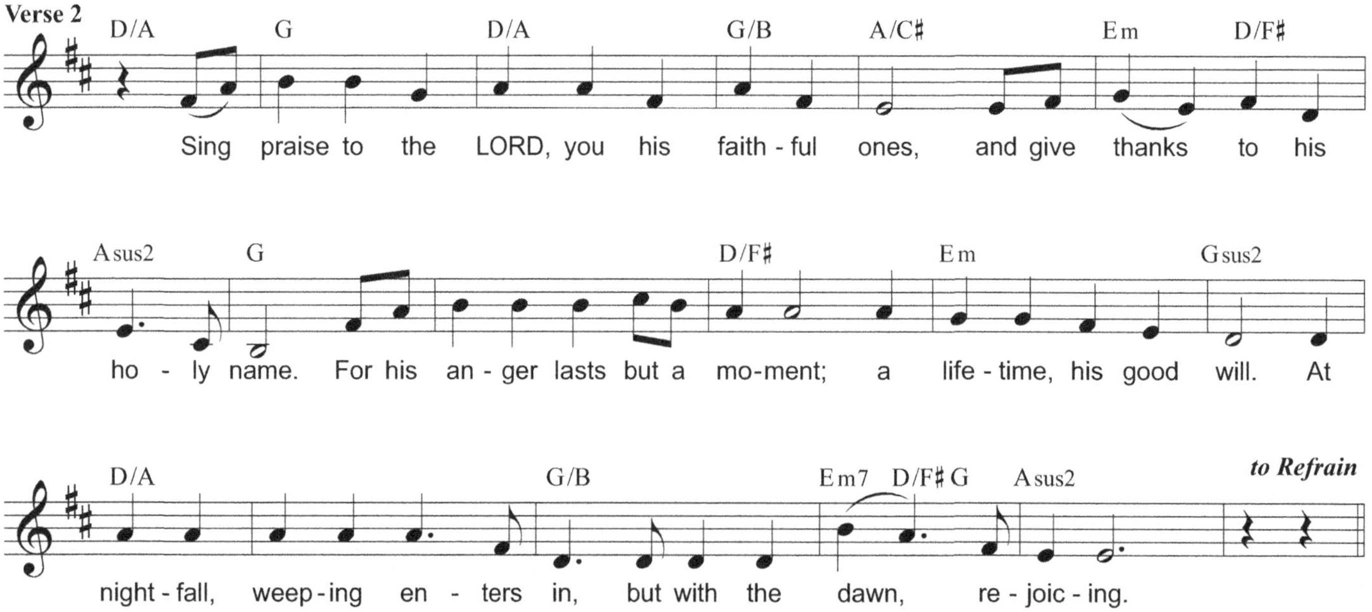
D/A G D/A G/B A/C♯ Em D/F♯
Sing praise to the LORD, you his faith - ful ones, and give thanks to his
Asus2 G D/F♯ Em Gsus2
ho - ly name. For his an - ger lasts but a mo-ment; a life - time, his good will. At
D/A G/B Em7 D/F♯ G Asus2
night - fall, weep - ing en - ters in, but with the dawn, re - joic - ing.
to Refrain

Verse 3
D/A G D/A G/B A/C♯ D/F♯ A
Hear, O LORD, and have pit - y [have pit - y] on me; O LORD, be my
G D/F♯ Em
help - er. You changed my mourn-ing in - to danc-ing; O LORD, my
G/B D/A G/B Em7 D/F♯ G Asus2
to Refrain
God, for - ev - er will I give you thanks.

The Easter Vigil in the Holy Night, cont. (11)
Responsorial Psalm (following fifth reading)
Isaiah 12:2-3, 4bcd, 5-6

(M.M. ♩ = c. 120)
REFRAIN

Capo 2: D C/D D C/D D/A D/F♯ Gsus2 Asus4
E D/E E D/E E/B E/G♯ Asus2 Bsus4
You will draw wat-er joy-ful-ly from the springs of sal-va-tion.
Verse 1
Asus4 Csus2 Bm7 D/F♯ Gsus2
Bsus4 Dsus2 C♯m7 E/G♯ Asus2
God in-deed is my sav-ior; I am con-fi-dent and un-a-
Asus4 Em Bm/D Asus4
Bsus4 F♯m C♯m/E Bsus4
fraid. My strength and my cour-age is the LORD, and
D/F♯ Gsus2 Asus4 D/F♯ Gsus2 Asus4
E/G♯ Asus2 Bsus4 E/G♯ Asus2 Bsus4
he has been my sav-ior. With
C/E Bm/D C Asus4
D/F♯ C♯m/E D Bsus4
joy you will draw wa-ter at the foun-tain of sal-va-tion.
to Refrain
Verse 2
Asus4 D C/D D
Bsus4 E D/E E
Give thanks to the LORD, ac-claim his name; a-mong the
D/F♯ Gsus2 Asus4 Em
E/G♯ Asus2 Bsus4 F♯m
na-tions make known his deeds, pro-claim how ex-

Bm/D C G/B Asus4
C♯m/E D A/C♯ Bsus4
to Refrain
alt - ed is his name.
Verse 3
Asus4 D C/D D
Bsus4 E D/E E
Sing praise to the LORD for his glo - rious a - chieve - ment; let this be
D/F♯ Gsus2 Asus4 Em Bm/D
E/G♯ Asus2 Bsus4 F♯m C♯m/E
known through-out all the earth. Shout with ex - ul - ta - tion, O cit - y of Zi - on, for
G/B C C D C/E G/B Asus4
A/C♯ D D E D/F♯ A/C♯ Bsus4
to Refrain
great in your midst is the Ho - ly One of Is - ra - el!

Responsorial Psalm (following sixth reading)

(M.M. ♩ = c. 124)

Psalm 19:8, 9, 10, 11

REFRAIN
A/C♯ D D/F♯ Gsus2 D/F♯ G Dmaj7/F♯
Lord, you have the words, Lord, you have the words,
Em7 D/F♯ Gsus2 D/A A Bm Asus2
you have the words of ev - er - last - ing life.
(Keyboard)
Verse 1
D/C G/B G Dmaj7/F♯
The law of the LORD is per - fect, re - fresh - ing the soul; the de-
to Refrain
D/C G/B Em7 D/F♯ G A7sus4
cree of the LORD is trust - wor - thy, giv - ing wis - dom to the sim - ple.
Verse 2
D/C G/B G Dmaj7/F♯
The pre - cepts of the LORD are right, re - joic - ing the heart; the com-
to Refrain
D/C Bm7 Em7 D/F♯ Em7/G A7sus4
mand of the LORD is clear, en - light - en - ing the eye.
Verse 3
D/C G/B G Dmaj7/F♯
The fear of the LORD is pure, en - dur - ing for - ev - er; the

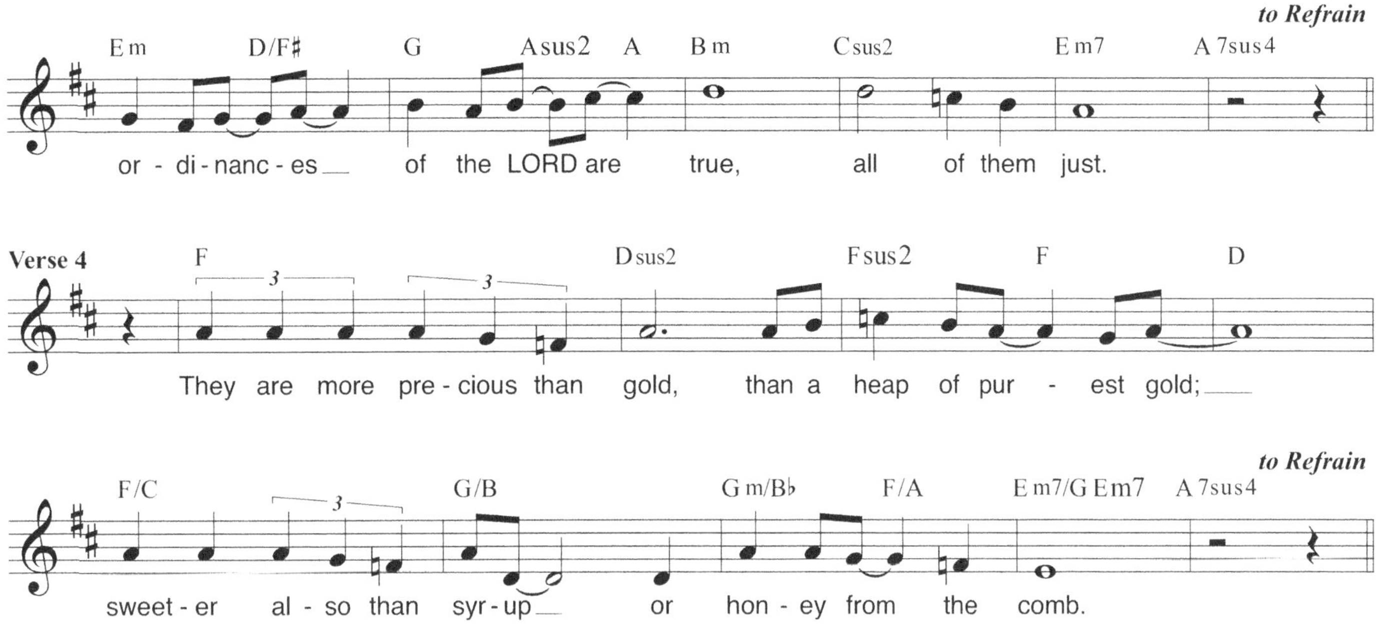
to Refrain
Em D/F♯ G Asus2 A Bm Csus2 Em7 A7sus4
or - di - nanc - es of the LORD are true, all of them just.
Verse 4
F Dsus2 Fsus2 F D
They are more pre - cious than gold, than a heap of pur - est gold;
to Refrain
F/C G/B Gm/B♭ F/A Em7/G Em7 A7sus4
sweet - er al - so than syr - up or hon - ey from the comb.

Option A, when Baptism is celebrated

Responsorial Psalm (following seventh reading)

Psalm 42:3, 5; 43:3, 4

(M.M. ♩ = c. 64)

REFRAIN
Capo 3: A/E C/G
A C
D/A F/C
Like a deer that longs for run - ning streams, my soul longs for you, my
Asus2 Csus2
D/A F/C
A C
God, my soul longs for you, my God.
Verse 1
D F
Asus2 Csus2
Em Gm
A - thirst is my soul for God, the liv - ing God. When shall I
D/F♯ F/A
G B♭
Asus2 Csus2
G/D B♭/F
A/E C/G
to Refrain
go and be - hold the face of God?
Verse 2
D F
Asus2 Csus2
Em Gm
D/F♯ F/A
G B♭
Asus2 Csus2
I went with the throng and led them in pro - ces - sion to the house of God, a - mid loud
Em Gm
D/F♯ F/A
G B♭
Asus2 Csus2
G/D B♭/F
A/E C/G
to Refrain
cries of joy and thanks - giv - ing, with the mul - ti - tude keep - ing fes - ti - val.

Verse 3
D
F
Asus2
Csus2
Send forth your light and your fi - del - i - ty; they shall lead me on and
Em Gm
D/F♯ F/A
G B♭
Asus2 Csus2
G/D B♭/F
A/E C/G
to Refrain
bring me to your ho - ly moun - tain, to your dwell - ing-place.
Verse 4
D
F
Then will I go in to the al - tar of God, the God of my glad - ness and
Asus2 Csus2
Em Gm
D/F♯ F/A
G B♭
Asus2 Csus2
G/D B♭/F
A/E C/G
to Refrain
joy; then will I give you thanks up - on the harp, O God, my God!

Responsorial Psalm (following seventh reading)
Or: Option B, when Baptism is not celebrated

(M.M. ♩ = c. 120) Isaiah 12:2-3, 4bcd, 5-6

REFRAIN

Capo 2: D E
C/D D/E D E C/D D/E
D/A E/B
D/F♯ E/G♯ Gsus2 Asus2
Asus4 Bsus4
You will draw wat-er joy-ful-ly from the springs of sal - va - tion.
Verse 1
Asus4 Bsus4
Csus2 Dsus2
Bm7 C♯m7
D/F♯ E/G♯
Gsus2 Asus2
God in - deed is my sav - ior; I am con - fi - dent and un - a -
Asus4 Bsus4
Em F♯m
Bm/D C♯m/E
Asus4 Bsus4
fraid. My strength and my cour - age is the LORD, and
D/F♯ E/G♯
Gsus2 Asus2
Asus4 Bsus4
D/F♯ E/G♯
Gsus2 Asus2
Asus4 Bsus4
he has been my sav - ior. With
C/E D/F♯
Bm/D C♯m/E
C D
Asus4 Bsus4
to Refrain
joy you will draw wa - ter at the foun - tain of sal - va-tion.
Verse 2
Asus4 Bsus4
D E
C/D D/E
D E
Give thanks to the LORD, ac - claim his name; a - mong the
D/F♯ E/G♯
Gsus2 Asus2
Asus4 Bsus4
Em F♯m
na - tions make known his deeds, pro - claim how ex -

Bm/D C♯m/E C D G/B A/C♯ Asus4 Bsus4
to Refrain
alt - ed is his name.
Verse 3
Asus4 Bsus4 D E C/D D/E
Sing praise to the LORD for his glo - rious a -
D E D/F♯ E/G♯ Gsus2 Asus2 Asus4 Bsus4
chieve - ment; let this be known through-out all the earth. Shout with ex - ul -
Em F♯m Bm/D C♯m/E G/B A/C♯ C D
ta - tion, O cit - y of Zi - on, for great in your midst is the
C D D E C/E D/F♯ G/B A/C♯ Asus4 Bsus4
to Refrain
Ho - ly One of Is - ra - el!

Or: Option C, when Baptism is not celebrated

Responsorial Psalm (following seventh reading)

Psalm 51:12-13, 14-15, 18-19

(M.M. ♩ = c. 77)

REFRAIN

G Bsus4 Bsus4/A Em7 F♯m7 D/F♯ Gmaj7
Cre - ate a clean heart, a clean heart in me, O God.

Verse 1 (M.M. ♩ = c. 69)

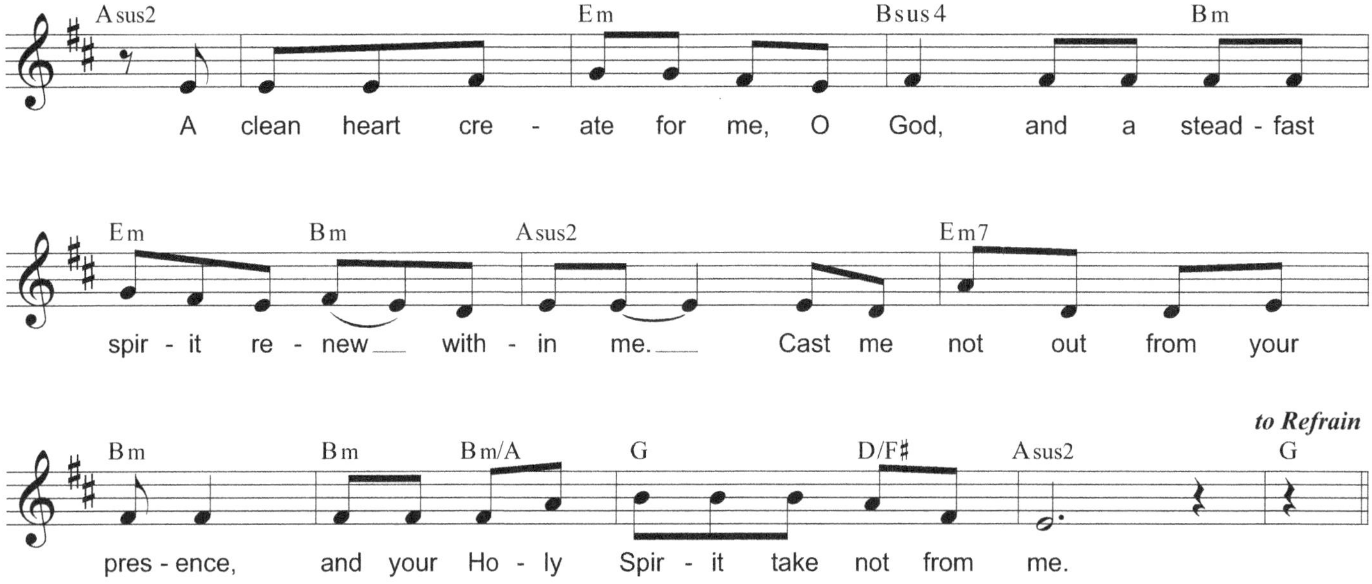
Asus2 Em Bsus4 Bm
A clean heart cre - ate for me, O God, and a stead - fast
Em Bm Asus2 Em7
spir - it re - new with - in me. Cast me not out from your
to Refrain
Bm Bm Bm/A G D/F♯ Asus2 G
pres - ence, and your Ho - ly Spir - it take not from me.

Verse 2 (M.M. ♩ = c. 69)

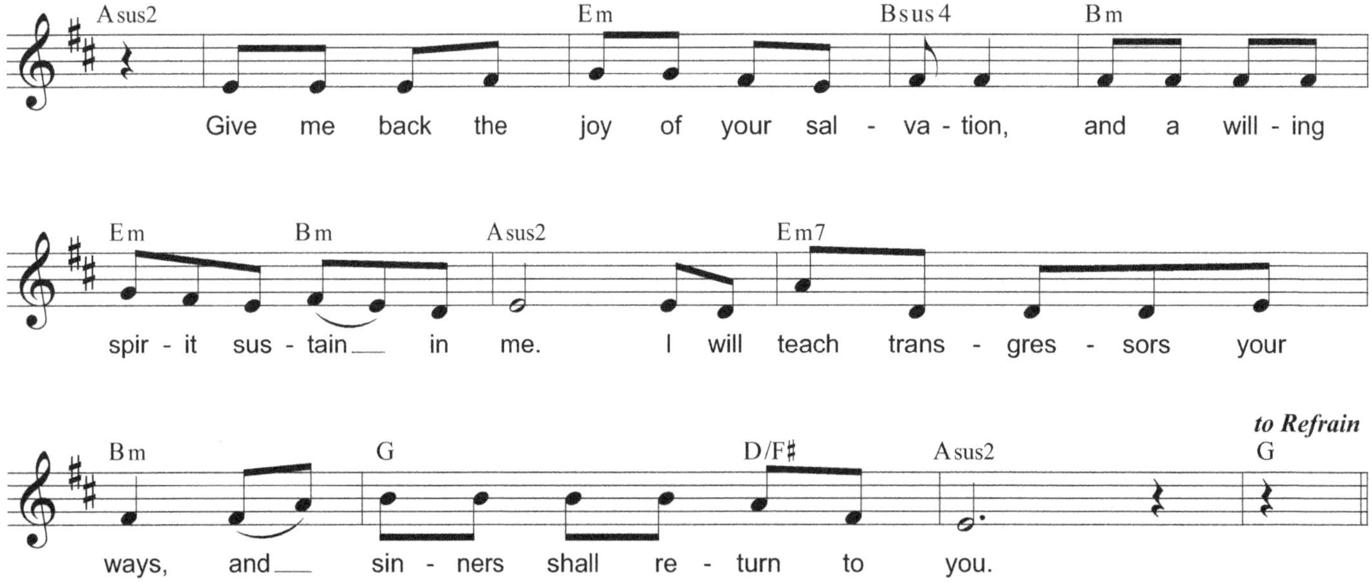
Asus2 Em Bsus4 Bm
Give me back the joy of your sal - va - tion, and a will - ing
Em Bm Asus2 Em7
spir - it sus - tain in me. I will teach trans - gres - sors your
to Refrain
Bm G D/F♯ Asus2 G
ways, and sin - ners shall re - turn to you.

Verse 3 (M.M. ♩ = c. 69)

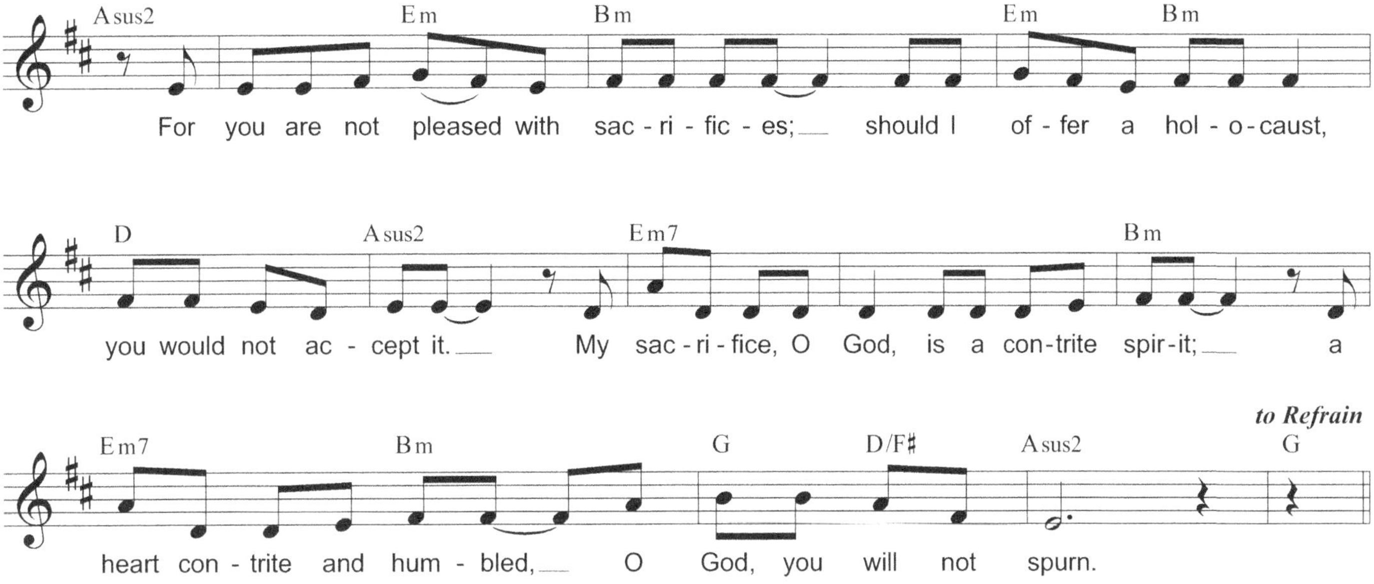
Asus2 Em Bm Em Bm
For you are not pleased with sac - ri - fic - es; should I of - fer a hol - o - caust,
D Asus2 Em7 Bm
you would not ac - cept it. My sac - ri - fice, O God, is a con - trite spir - it; a
to Refrain
Em7 Bm G D/F♯ Asus2 G
heart con - trite and hum - bled, O God, you will not spurn.

The Easter Vigil in the Holy Night, cont. (21)

Responsorial Psalm: Psalm 118:1-2, 16-17, 22-23

Acclamation: (Keyboard/SATB) NO. II

(M.M. ♩ = c. 154)

Capo 3: A C
G B♭
D/F♯ F/A
E G
E/D G/F
A/C♯ C/E
D F
D/F♯ F/A
Esus4 Gsus4
E G
Al - le - lu - ia, al - le - lu - ia, al - le - lu - ia.
Verse 1
E7 G7
A C
D/A F/C
E7/A G7/C
Give thanks to the LORD, for he is good, for his mer - cy en - dures for - ev - er.
Let the house of Is - ra - el say, "His mer - cy en - dures for - ev - er."
to Refrain
Verse 2
The right hand of the LORD has struck with pow'r; the right hand of the Lord is ex - alt - ed.
I shall not die, but live, and de - clare the works of the LORD.
to Refrain

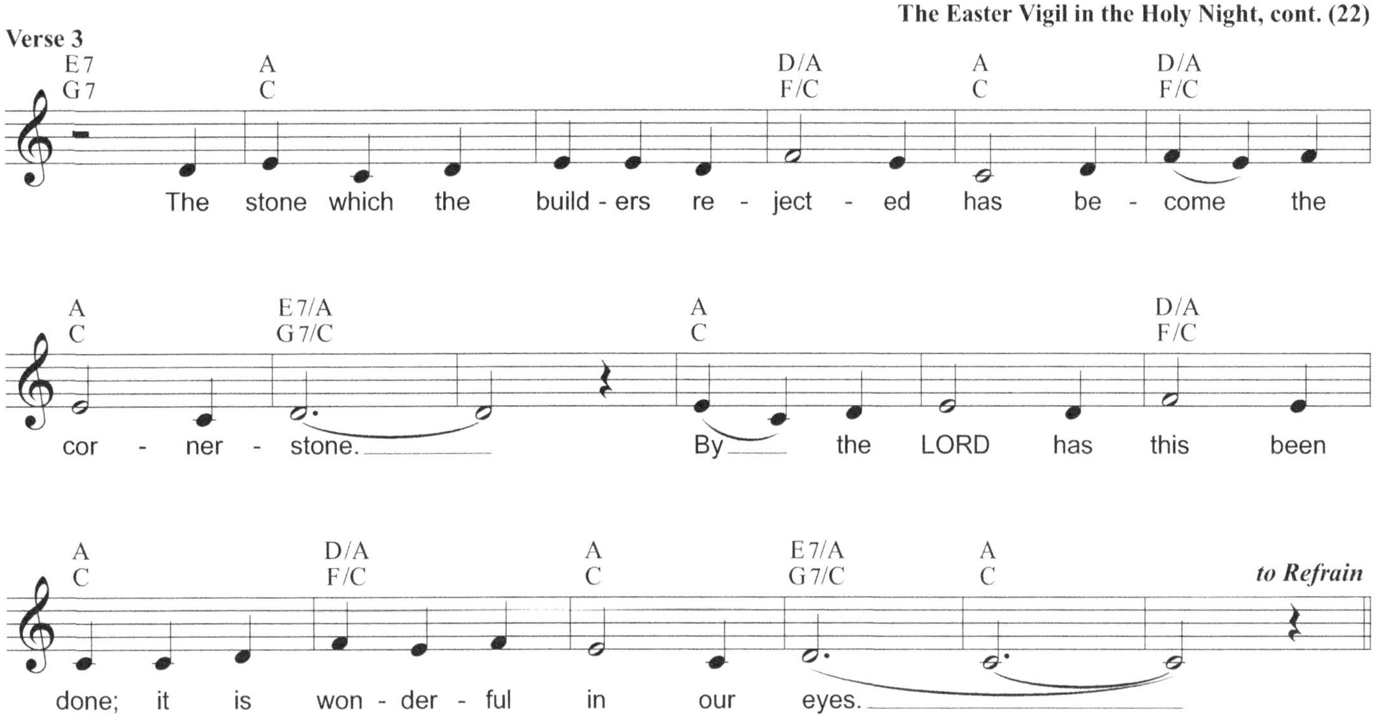
Verse 3
E7 G7
A C
D/A F/C
A C
D/A F/C
The stone which the build - ers re - ject - ed has be - come the
A C
E7/A G7/C
A C
D/A F/C
cor - ner - stone. By the LORD has this been
A C
D/A F/C
A C
E7/A G7/C
A C
to Refrain
done; it is won - der - ful in our eyes.

Easter Sunday of the Resurrection of the Lord: At the Mass during the Day

(M.M. ♩= c. 156)

REFRAIN [or: Alleluia]

April 4

Psalm 118:1-2, 16-17, 22-23

G/B C C/E C Dm7 C/F G C C/E C F C/E C Gsus4 G
This is the day the Lord has made; let us re-joice and be glad.
Verse 1
G7 C F/C C F/C
Give thanks to the LORD, for he is good, for his mer-cy en-
C G7/C C C F/C
dures for-ev-er. Let the house of Is-ra-el
C F/C C G7/C C
to Refrain
say, "His mer-cy en-dures for-ev-er."
Verse 2
G7 C F/C C F/C
"The right hand of the LORD has struck with pow'r; the right hand of the
G7/C C G7/C C C F/C
LORD is ex-alt-ed. I shall not die, but live,
C F/C C G7/C C
to Refrain
and de-clare the works of the LORD."

Verse 3

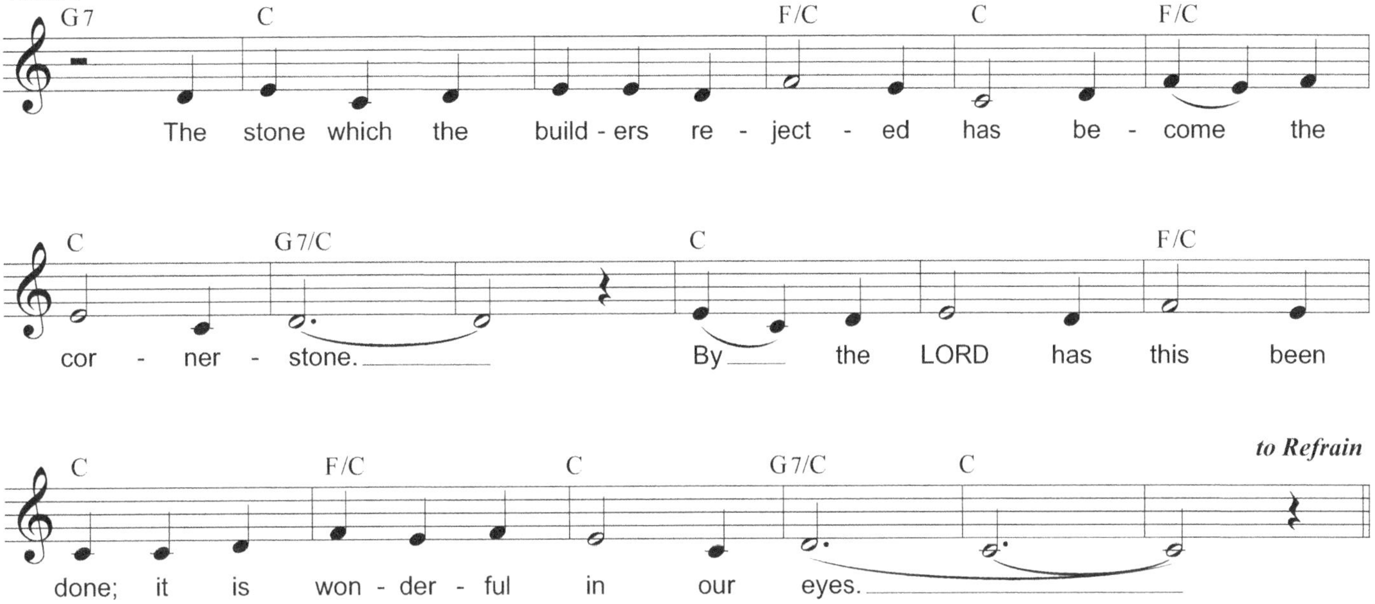
G7 C F/C C F/C
The stone which the build - ers re - ject - ed has be - come the
C G7/C C F/C
cor - ner - stone. By the LORD has this been
C F/C C G7/C C
to Refrain
done; it is won - der - ful in our eyes.

Gospel Acclamation: cf. 1 Corinthians 5:7b-8a

Acclamation: (Keyboard/SATB) NO. V

(M.M. ♪ = c. 150)
C Dm Am Dm F/A G/B G
Al - le - lu - ia, al - le - lu - ia. Al - le - lu - ia, al - le - lu - ia.

Verse: (Cantor)

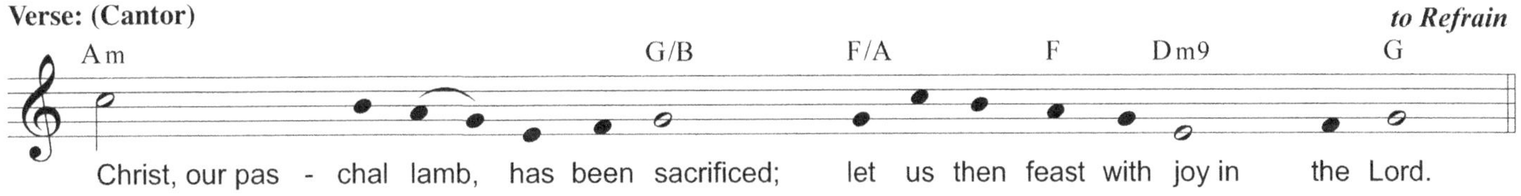
to Refrain
Am G/B F/A F Dm9 G
Christ, our pas - chal lamb, has been sacrificed; let us then feast with joy in the Lord.

Second Sunday of Easter (or Sunday of Divine Mercy)

April 11

(M.M. ♩ = c. 114)

Psalm 118:2-4, 13-15, 22-24

REFRAIN [or: Alleluia]

A/C♯ D D/F♯ D G D/F♯ D
Give thanks to the Lord for he is good, his
G/B A/C♯ A G/B G D
love is ev - er - last - ing.
Verse 1
D D D/F♯ G Bm F♯m/A D/F♯ D Em7 D/F♯
Let the house of Is - rael say, "His mer - cy en - dures for -
G D D/F♯ G Bm F♯m/A D/F♯ D
ev - er." Let the house of Aa - ron say, "His
Em7 D/F♯ Asus4 A D D/F♯ G Bm
mer - cy en - dures for - ev - er." Let those who
to Refrain
F♯m/A D/F♯ D Em7 G/B D G/D D
fear the LORD say, "His mer - cy en - dures for - ev - er."
Verse 2
D D/F♯ G Bm F♯m/A F♯m Gmaj7 G/B A/C♯
I was hard pressed and fall - ing, but the LORD helped me.

Through composed octavo Ed. 92525 available at www.ocp.org.

D D/F♯ G Bm A A/C♯ Bm A F♯m A/G
My strength and my cour - age is the LORD,
G D/F♯ D/A Em/G G/B A/C♯
and he has been my sav - ior.
D/A A Em D/F♯ Gmaj7 G/B A/C♯
The joy - ful shout of vic - to - ry in the
to Refrain
Em7 D/F♯ Gmaj7 G/B Asus4 D/A A
tents of the just.
Verse 3
D D/F♯ G Bm F♯m/A D/F♯ D D/A Gmaj7 G/B D A/C♯
The stone which the build - ers re - jec - ted has be - come the cor - ner - stone.
D D/F♯ G Bm A A/C♯ Bm A F♯m
By the LORD has this been done; [it is
A/G G D/F♯ D/A Em/G G/B A/C♯
won - der - ful,] it is won - der - ful in our eyes.
A D/A A Asus4 Em7 D/F♯ Gsus2 G/B A/C♯
This is the day the LORD has made
to Refrain
A D/F♯ Em7 D/F♯ Gmaj7 G/B A/C♯ D/A A
let us be glad and re - joice in it.

Gospel Acclamation: John 20:29

Acclamation: (Keyboard/SATB) NO. III

(M.M. ♩= c. 160)

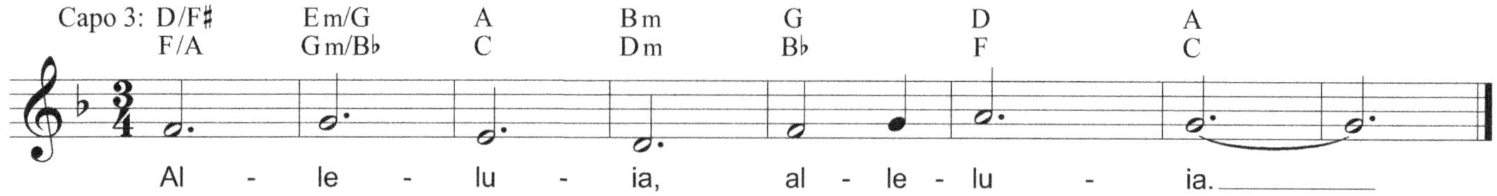
Capo 3: D/F♯ Em/G A Bm G D A
F/A Gm/B♭ C Dm B♭ F C
Al - le - lu - ia, al - le - lu - ia.

Verse: (Cantor)

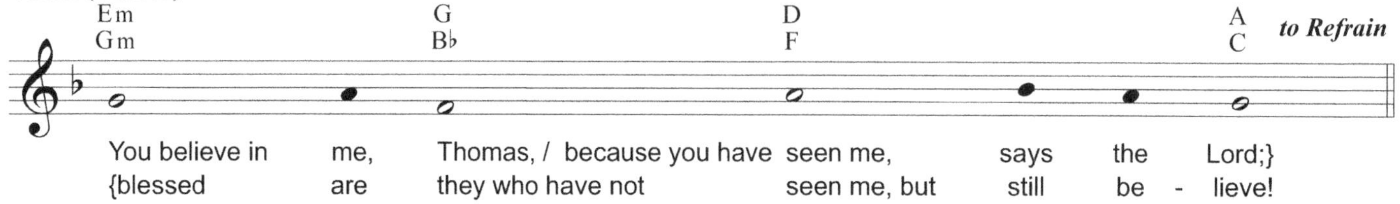
Em G D A
Gm B♭ F C
to Refrain
You believe in me, Thomas, / because you have seen me, says the Lord;}
{blessed are they who have not seen me, but still be - lieve!

Third Sunday of Easter

April 18

(M.M. 𝅗𝅥 = c. 63)
REFRAIN [or: Alleluia]
Psalm 4:2, 4, 7–8, 9
D D/C G/B D/A Gsus2 G/B D/A
Lord, let your face shine on us. (shine on us.) Lord, let your face shine on us.
(shine on us.)
Verse 1
D/A Am C/E Dsus2 Gsus2 C/E
When I call, an - swer me, O my just God, you who re -
D/F♯ F C/E D F/C G/B
lieve me when I am in dis - tress; have pit - y on
D/A Bm7 D/A G C/E D
me, and hear my prayer!
to Refrain
Verse 2
Am C/E Dsus2 Gsus2 C/E D/F♯ C/E F C/E
Know that the LORD does won-ders for his faith - ful one; the LORD will
D F/C G/B D/A G/B Am7 G C/E D
hear me when I call up - on him.
to Refrain
Verse 3
D/A Am C/E Dsus2 Gsus2 C/E D/F♯
O LORD, let the light of your coun - te - nance shine up - on us!

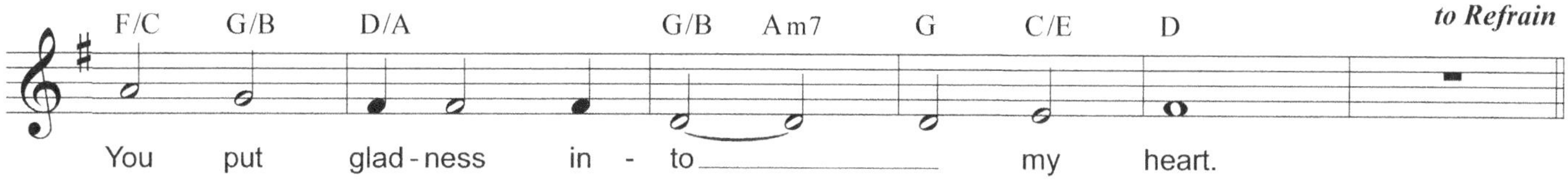
F/C G/B D/A G/B Am7 G C/E D
to Refrain
You put glad - ness in - to my heart.

Verse 4

D/A Am C/E Dsus2 Gsus2 C/E D/F♯ F C/E
As soon as I lie down, I fall peace-ful - ly a - sleep, for you a - lone, O

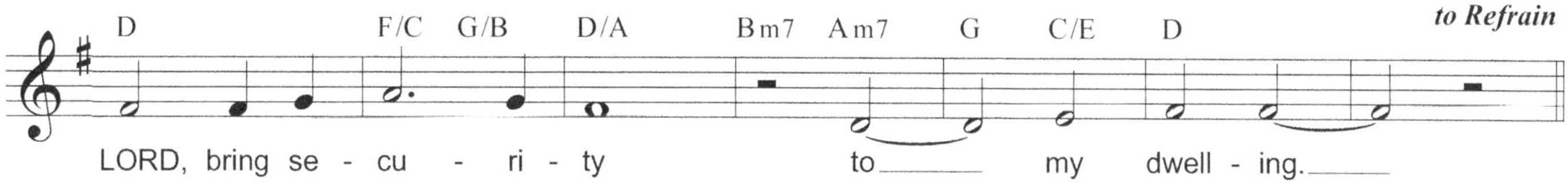
D F/C G/B D/A Bm7 Am7 G C/E D
to Refrain
LORD, bring se - cu - ri - ty to my dwell - ing.

Gospel Acclamation: Luke 24:32

Acclamation: (Keyboard/SATB) NO. III

(M.M. ♩ = c. 160)

Capo 3: D/F♯ Em/G A Bm G D A
F/A Gm/B♭ C Dm B♭ F C
Al - le - lu - ia, al - le - lu - ia.

Verse: (Cantor)

Em G D A
Gm B♭ F C
to Refrain
Lord Jesus, open the Scrip - tures to us;}
{make our hearts burn while you speak to us.

Fourth Sunday of Easter

April 25

(M.M. ♩ = c. 75)

Psalm 118:1, 8–9, 21–23, 26, 28, 29

REFRAIN [or: Alleluia]
Capo 3:
The stone re - jec - ted by the build - ers has be - come the cor - ner - stone.
Verse 1
Give thanks to the LORD, for he is good, for his mer - cy en - dures for -
ev - er. It is bet - ter to take ref - uge in the LORD than to trust in
man. It is bet - ter to take ref - uge in the LORD than to trust in princ - es.
to Refrain
Verse 2
I will give thanks to you, for you have an - swered me and have been my
sav - ior. The stone which the build - ers re - ject - ed has be - come the cor - ner - stone.
By the LORD has this been done; it is won - der - ful in our eyes.
to Refrain

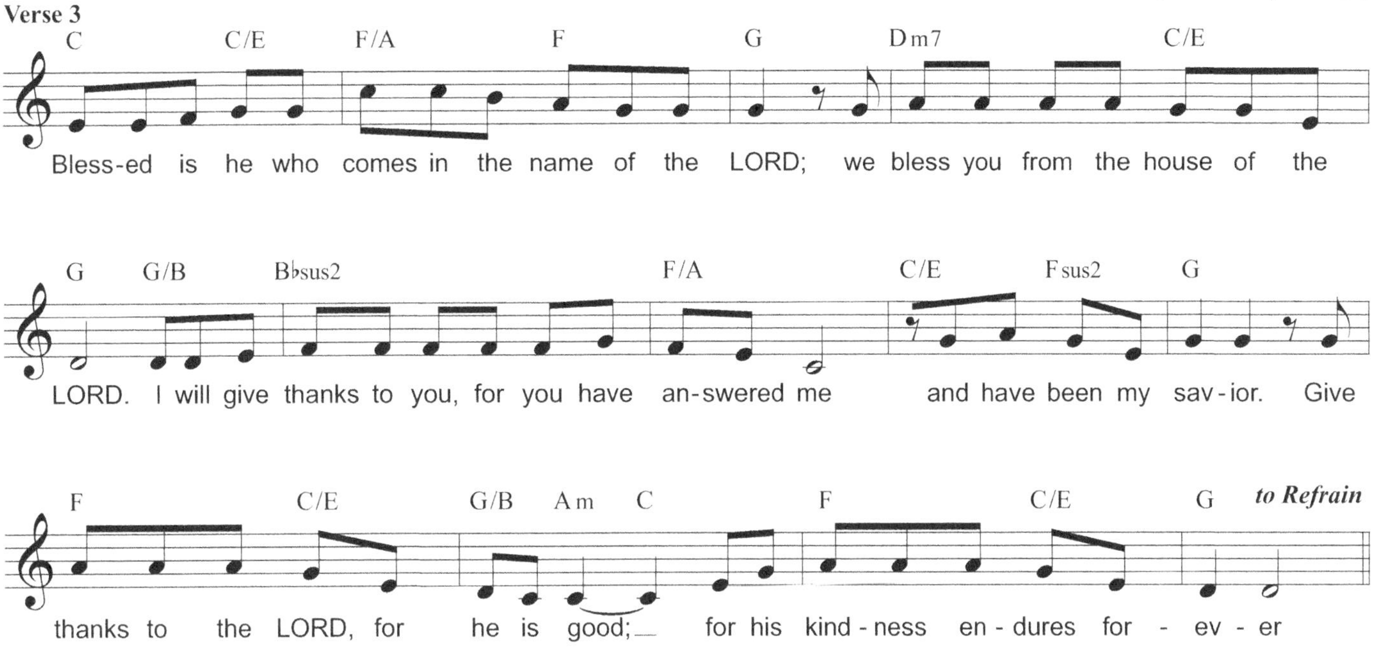
Verse 3
C C/E F/A F G Dm7 C/E
Bless-ed is he who comes in the name of the LORD; we bless you from the house of the
G G/B B♭sus2 F/A C/E Fsus2 G
LORD. I will give thanks to you, for you have an-swered me and have been my sav-ior. Give
F C/E G/B Am C F C/E G
to Refrain
thanks to the LORD, for he is good; for his kind-ness en-dures for-ev-er

Gospel Acclamation: John 10:14

Acclamation: (Keyboard/SATB) NO. IV

(M.M. ♩ = c. 116)
Capo 5: G Am F C Dm7
C Dm B♭ F Gm7
Al-le-lu-ia, al-le-lu-ia, al-le-
C/E Fmaj7 Gsus4 Gsus4
F/A B♭maj7 Csus4 Csus4
1.
2 and onward
lu-ia. ia.
Verse: (Cantor)
to Refrain
Asus4 Fadd2 C C/F G
Dsus4 B♭add2 F F/B♭ C
I am the good shepherd, says the Lord; / I know my sheep, / and mine know me.

Fifth Sunday of Easter

May 2

(M.M. ♩ = c. 68)

REFRAIN [or: Alleluia]

Psalm 22:26–27, 28, 30, 31–32

Gsus4 C C/E F Am G Dm7 C/F G
I will praise you, Lord, in the as - sem - bly of your peo - ple.
Verse 1 (M.M. ♩ = c. 62)
E E/G♯ Am C7/G Fsus4 F Fm
I will ful - fill my vows be - fore those who fear the LORD. The
C/G D7/G G7sus4 G E/G♯ Am C7/G
low - ly shall eat their fill; they who seek the LORD shall
Fsus4 F Fm/A♭ C/G D7/G G7sus4 G
praise him: "May your hearts live for - ev - er!"
to Refrain
Verse 2 (M.M. ♩ = c. 62)
E/G♯ Am C7/G F Fm C/G D7/G
All the ends of the earth shall re - mem - ber and turn to the
G7sus4 E/G♯ Am C7/G Fsus4 F F/A♭ C/G D7/G G7sus4
LORD; all the fam - 'lies of the na - tions shall bow down be - fore him.
to Refrain
Verse 3 (M.M. ♩ = c. 62)
E/G♯ Am C7/G Fsus4 F Fm C/G D7/G G7sus4 E/G♯
To him a - lone shall bow down all who sleep in the earth; be -

to Refrain
Am C7/G F Fm/A♭ C/G D7/G G7sus4
fore him shall bend all who go down in - to the dust.

Verse 4 (M.M. ♩ = c. 62)

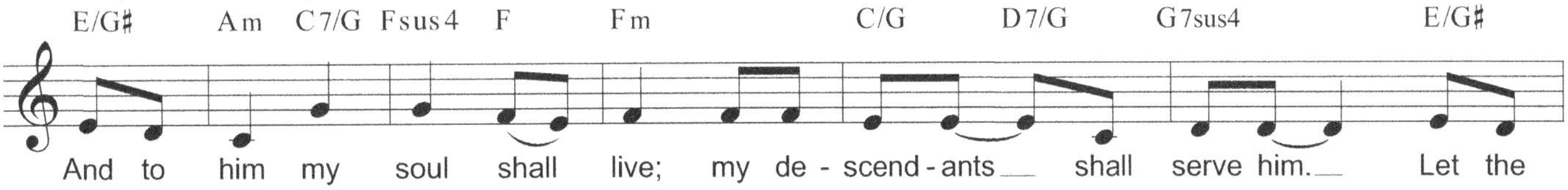
E/G♯ Am C7/G Fsus4 F Fm C/G D7/G G7sus4 E/G♯
And to him my soul shall live; my de - scend - ants shall serve him. Let the

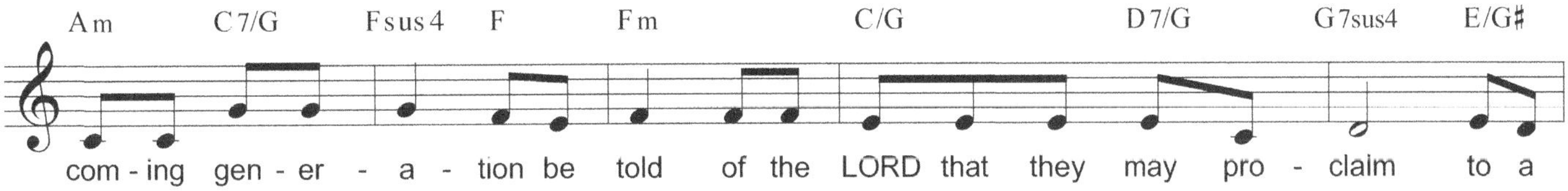
Am C7/G Fsus4 F Fm C/G D7/G G7sus4 E/G♯
com - ing gen - er - a - tion be told of the LORD that they may pro - claim to a

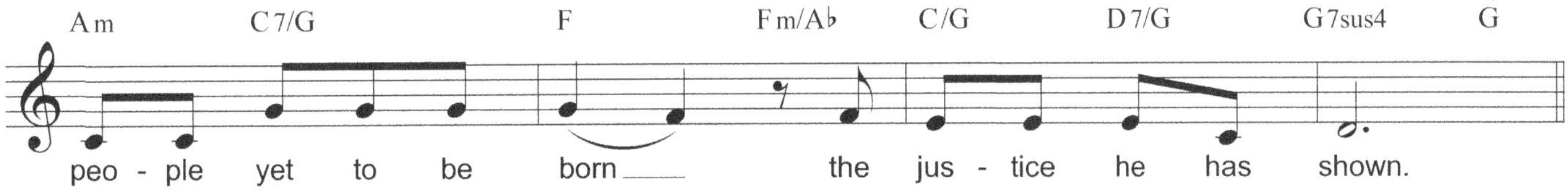
to Refrain
Am C7/G F Fm/A♭ C/G D7/G G7sus4 G
peo - ple yet to be born the jus - tice he has shown.

Gospel Acclamation: John 15:4a, 5b

Acclamation: (Keyboard/SATB) NO. IV

(M.M. ♩ = c. 116)

Capo 5: G C Am Dm F B♭ C F Dm7 Gm7
Al - le - lu - ia, al - le - lu - ia, al - le -

1. 2 and onward
C/E F/A Fmaj7 B♭maj7 Gsus4 Csus4 Gsus4 Csus4
lu - ia. ia.

Verse: (Cantor)

to Refrain
Asus4 Dsus4 Fadd2 B♭add2 C F C/F F/B♭ G C
Remain in me as I remain in you, says the Lord. / Who –
{ever re - mains in me will bear much fruit.

Sixth Sunday of Easter

May 9

(M.M. ♩ = c. 146)

REFRAIN [or: Alleluia]

Psalm 98:1, 2-3, 3-4

The Lord has re-vealed to the na-tions his
sav-ing pow'r, sav-ing pow'r, sav-ing pow'r.

Verse 1

Sing to the LORD a new song, for he has done won-drous deeds; his
right hand has won vic-t'ry for him, his ho-ly arm.
to Refrain

Verse 2

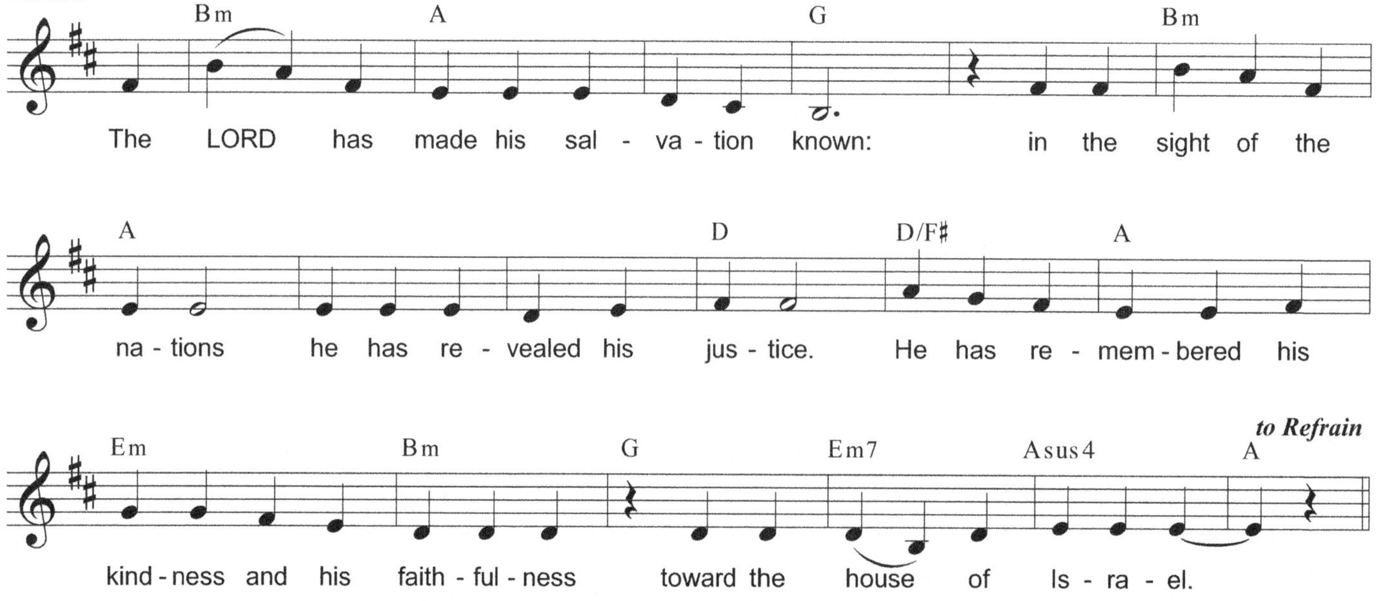
The LORD has made his sal-va-tion known: in the sight of the
na-tions he has re-vealed his jus-tice. He has re-mem-bered his
kind-ness and his faith-ful-ness toward the house of Is-ra-el.
to Refrain

Verse 3

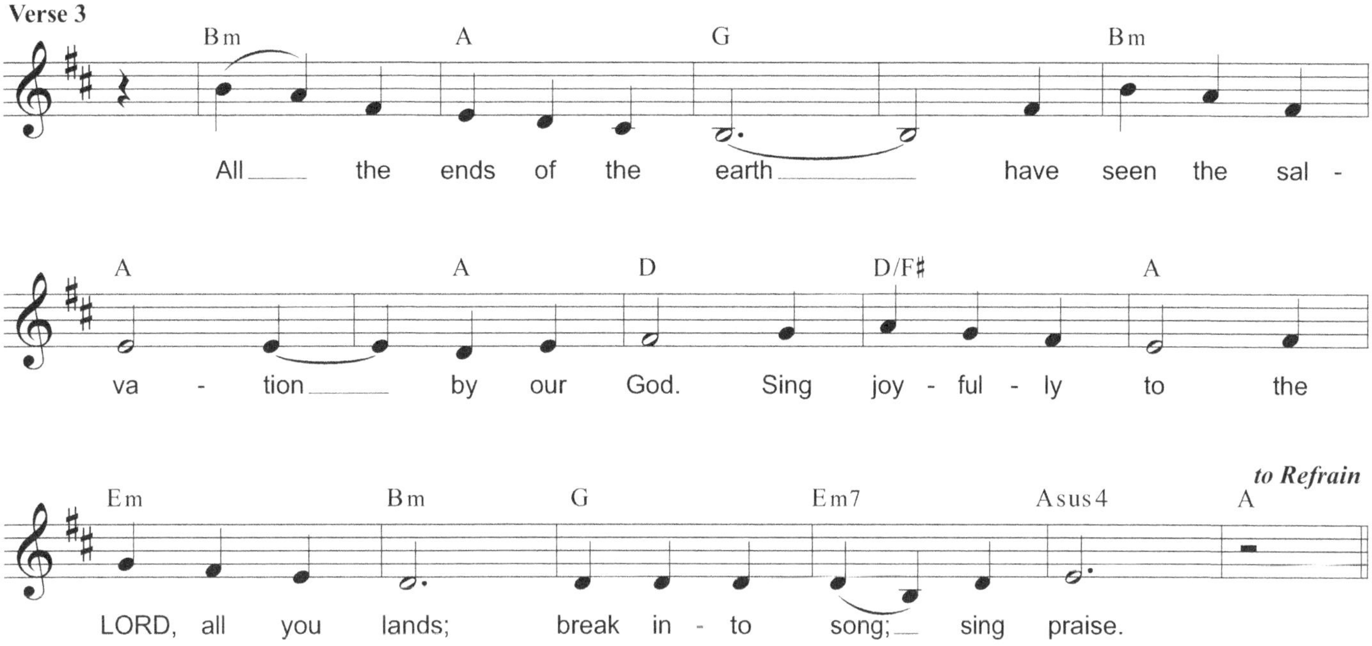
Bm A G Bm
All the ends of the earth have seen the sal -
A A D D/F♯ A
va - tion by our God. Sing joy - ful - ly to the
to Refrain
Em Bm G Em7 Asus4 A
LORD, all you lands; break in - to song; sing praise.

Gospel Acclamation: John 14:23

Acclamation: (Keyboard/SATB) NO. II

(M.M. ♩ = c. 130)

Capo 3: A G D/F♯ E E/D A/C♯ D D/F♯ Esus4 E
C B♭ F/A G G/F C/E F F/A Gsus4 G
Al - le - lu - ia, al - le - lu - ia, al - le - lu - ia.
Verse: (Cantor)
Esus2 Gsus2 D/F♯
Gsus2 B♭sus2 F/A
Whoever loves me will keep my word, says the Lord, / and my
A/C♯ Dsus2 E
C/E Fsus2 G
to Refrain
Father will love him / and we will come to him.

The Ascension of the Lord

May 13

The Ascension of the Lord may be celebrated on May 13 or transferred to May 16, depending upon the practice of each province.

(M.M. ♪ = c. 138)

REFRAIN [or: Alleluia]

Psalm 47:2-3, 6-7, 8-9

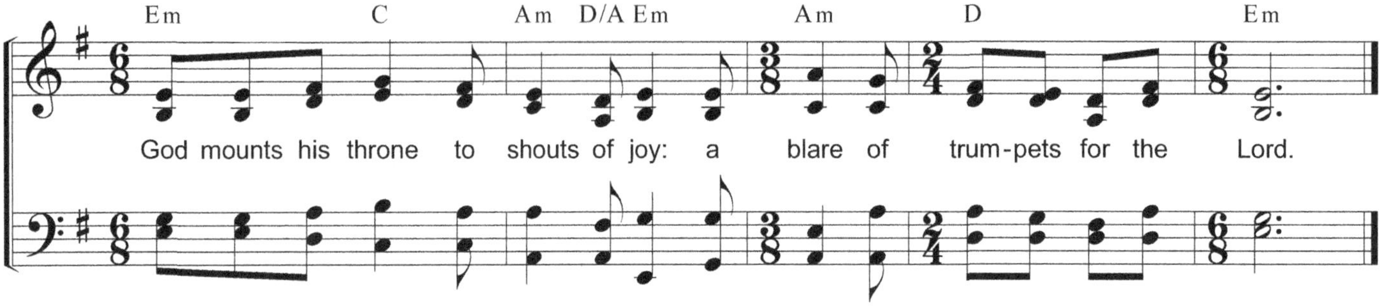
Em C Am D/A Em Am D Em
God mounts his throne to shouts of joy: a blare of trum-pets for the Lord.

Verse 1

Em D/F♯ G G/B D Am
All you peo - ples, clap your hands, shout to God with cries of
Em Cmaj7 D A/E
glad - ness. For the LORD, the Most High, the awe - some, is the great
Cmaj7 D G C F♯dm7 B
king o - ver all the earth.
to Refrain

Verse 2

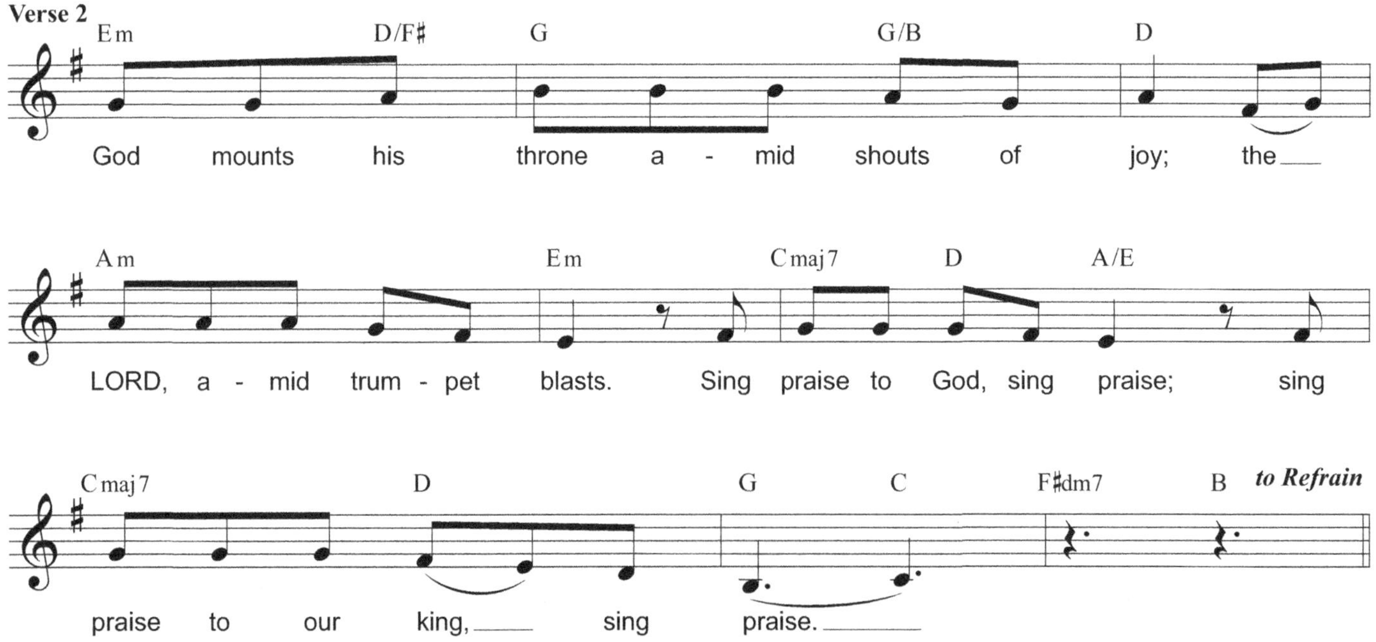
Em D/F♯ G G/B D
God mounts his throne a - mid shouts of joy; the
Am Em Cmaj7 D A/E
LORD, a - mid trum - pet blasts. Sing praise to God, sing praise; sing
Cmaj7 D G C F♯dm7 B
praise to our king, sing praise.
to Refrain

Verse 3

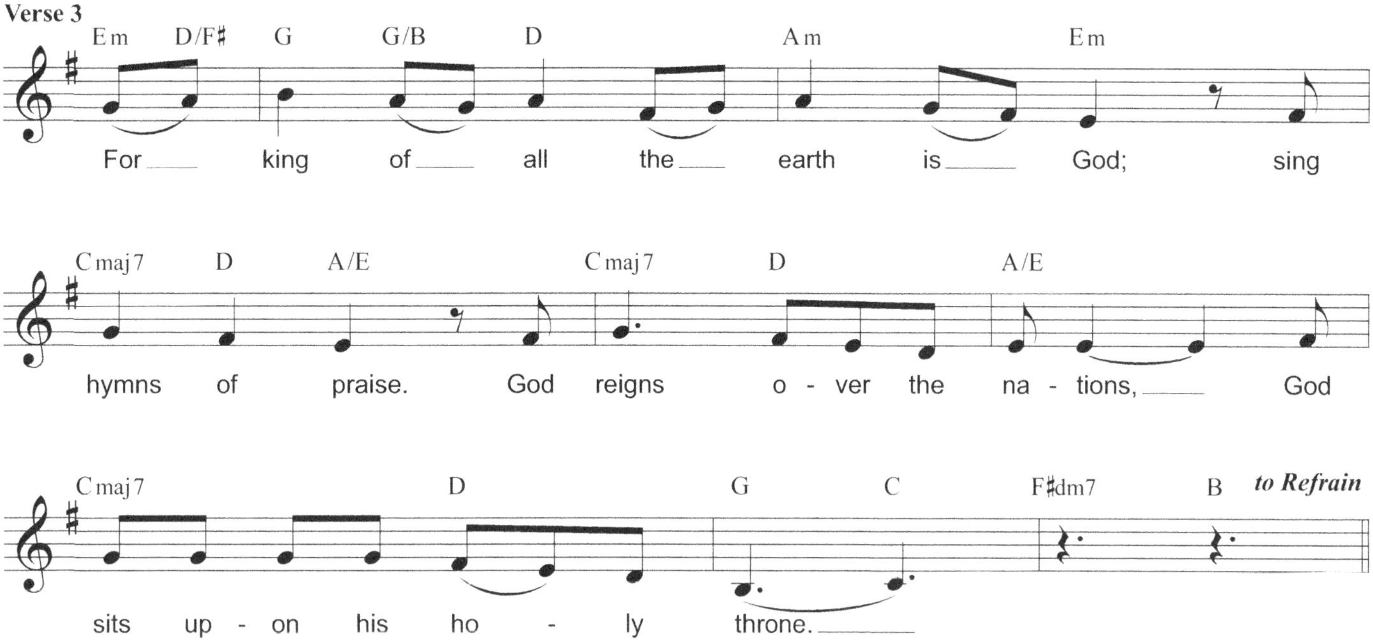
Em D/F♯ G G/B D Am Em
For king of all the earth is God; sing
Cmaj7 D A/E Cmaj7 D A/E
hymns of praise. God reigns o - ver the na - tions, God
Cmaj7 D G C F♯dm7 B
to Refrain
sits up - on his ho - ly throne.

Gospel Acclamation: Matthew 28:19a, 20b

Acclamation: (Keyboard/SATB) NO. III

(M.M. ♩ = c. 160)

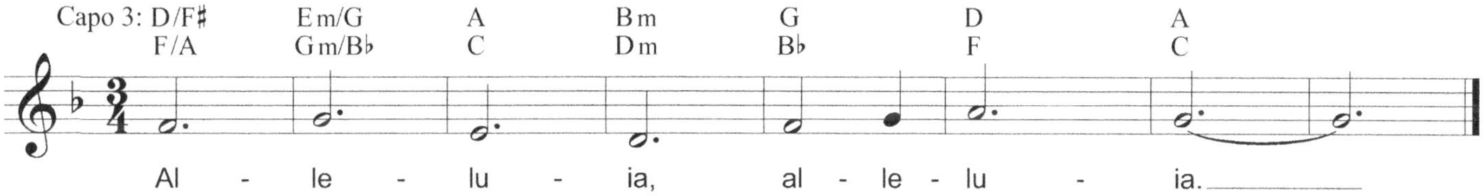
Capo 3: D/F♯ Em/G A Bm G D A
F/A Gm/B♭ C Dm B♭ F C
Al - le - lu - ia, al - le - lu - ia.

Verse: (Cantor)

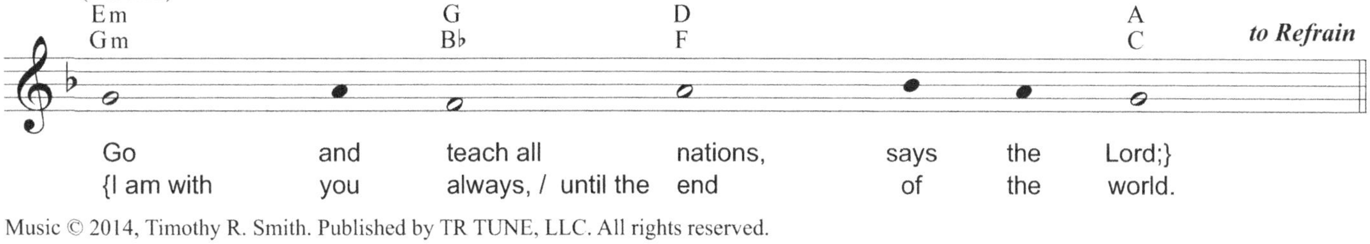
Em G D A
Gm B♭ F C
to Refrain
Go and teach all nations, says the Lord;}
{I am with you always, / until the end of the world.

Seventh Sunday of Easter

May 16

(M.M. ♩ = c. 68)

REFRAIN [or: Alleluia]

Psalm 103:1–2, 11–12, 19–20

Capo 1: D Eb G/B Ab/C G Ab D/A Eb/Bb D/G Eb/Ab A Bb
The Lord has set his throne in heav - en, in heav - en.
Verse 1
G7sus4 Bb7sus4 C Eb G/B Bb/D A C Am7/G Cm7/Bb
Bless the LORD, O my soul; and all my
Fsus2 Absus2 C/E Eb/G Dm7 Fm7 G Bb Am Cm Em/G Gm/Bb
be - ing, bless his ho - ly name. Bless the LORD, O my
F Ab C/E Eb/G Dm Fm C/E Eb/G Fsus2 Absus2 G Bb
soul, and for - get not all his ben - e - fits.
to Refrain
Verse 2
G7sus4 Bb7sus4 C Eb G/B Bb/D Am Cm Am7/G Cm7/Bb
For as the heav - ens are high a - bove the earth, so sur -
Fsus2 Absus2 C/E Eb/G Dm7 Fm7 G Bb Am Cm Em/G Gm/Bb
pass-ing is his kind - ness toward those who fear him. As far as the east is from the
F Ab C/E Eb/G Dm Fm C/E Eb/G F Ab G Bb
west, so far has he put our trans - gres - sions from us.
to Refrain

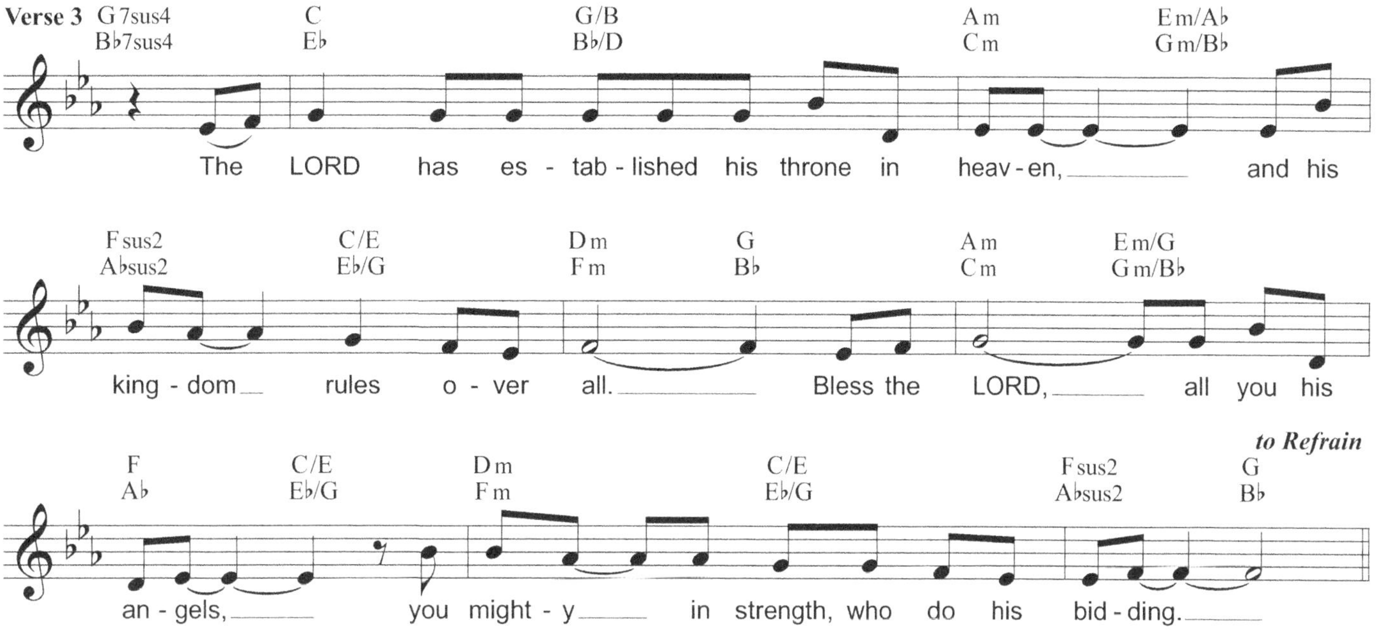
Verse 3
G7sus4 C G/B Am Em/A♭
B♭7sus4 E♭ B♭/D Cm Gm/B♭
The LORD has es - tab - lished his throne in heav - en, and his
Fsus2 C/E Dm G Am Em/G
A♭sus2 E♭/G Fm B♭ Cm Gm/B♭
king - dom rules o - ver all. Bless the LORD, all you his
to Refrain
F C/E Dm C/E Fsus2 G
A♭ E♭/G Fm E♭/G A♭sus2 B♭
an - gels, you might - y in strength, who do his bid - ding.

Gospel Acclamation: cf. John 14:18

Acclamation: (Keyboard/SATB) NO. IV

(M.M. ♩ = c. 116)
Capo 5: G Am F C Dm7
C Dm B♭ F Gm7
Al - le - lu - ia, al - le - lu - ia, al - le -
1.
2 and onward
C/E Fmaj7 Gsus4 Gsus4
F/A B♭maj7 Csus4 Csus4
lu - ia. ia.
Verse: (Cantor)
Asus4 Fadd2 C C/F G
Dsus4 B♭add2 F F/B♭ C
to Refrain
I will not leave you orphans, / says the Lord. / I will come back to you, / and your}
{hearts will re - joice.

Pentecost Sunday: At the Vigil Mass

(Extended Form)

May 22

(M.M. ♪ = c. 128)

Psalm 33:10-11, 12-13, 14-15

REFRAIN
Alternate ending
Capo 2:
Bless-ed the peo-ple the Lord has chos-en, the Lord has chos-en to be his own.
Optional Interlude before Verse 3 & after final Refrain
Verse 1
The LORD brings to nought the plans of na-tions; he foils the de-signs of peo-ples. But the plan of the LORD stands for-ev-er; the de-sign of his heart, through all gen-er-a-tions.
to Refrain
Verse 2
Bless-ed the na-tion whose God is the LORD, the peo-ple he has cho-sen for his own in-her-it-ance. From heav-en the LORD looks

www.timothyrsmith.com

to Refrain
D/A E/B G/B A/C♯ A/C♯ B/D♯ D E A 7/D B 7/E D E G/D A/E
down; he sees all man - kind.
Verse 3
D E G/D A/E D E
From his fixed throne he be - holds all who dwell on the
A 7/D B 7/E D E F♯m G♯m G/B A/C♯
earth, He who fash - ioned the heart of
to Refrain
D/A E/B G/B A/C♯ A/C♯ B/D♯ D E A 7/D B 7/E D E G/D A/E
each, he who knows all their works.

Option 1:

Responsorial Psalm (following second reading)

(M.M. ♩ = c. 74)

Daniel 3:52, 53, 54, 55, 56

REFRAIN

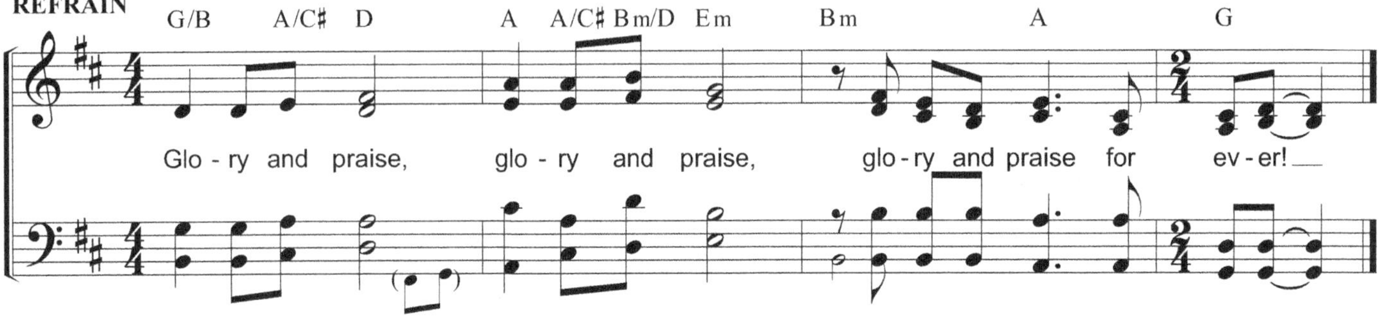
G/B A/C# D A A/C# Bm/D Em Bm A G
Glo - ry and praise, glo - ry and praise, glo - ry and praise for ev - er!

Verse 1

G Bm D G D Em A/C#
"Bless-ed are you, O Lord, the God of our fa-thers, praise-wor - thy and ex -

D A F#m7 G Bm D
alt - ed a - bove all for - ev - er; and bless - ed is your ho - ly and

G D/A Em A/C# D A F#m7 G
to Refrain
glo - rious name, praise-wor - thy and ex - alt - ed a - bove all for all ag - es."

Verse 2

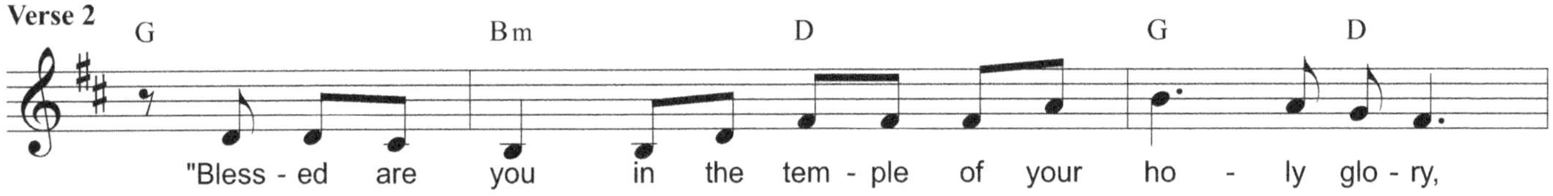
G Bm D G D
"Bless - ed are you in the tem - ple of your ho - ly glo - ry,

Em A/C# D A F#m7 G
to Refrain
praise - wor - thy and glo - rious a - bove all for - ev - er."

Verse 3

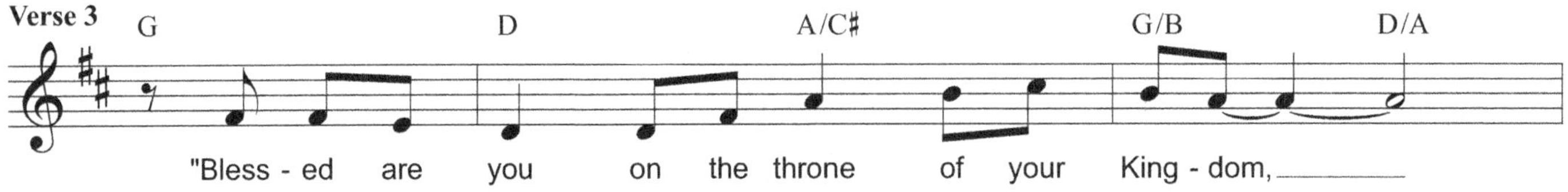
G D A/C# G/B D/A
"Bless - ed are you on the throne of your King - dom,

Em A/C♯ D A F♯m7 G
to Refrain
praise - wor - thy and ex - alt - ed a - bove all for - ev - er."
Verse 4
G D A/C♯ G/B A A/G
"Bless-ed are you who look in - to the depths from your throne up-on the
Bm Em A/C♯ D A F♯m7 G
to Refrain
cher-u-bim, praise-wor - thy and ex - alt - ed a - bove all for - ev - er."
Verse 5
G D A/C♯ G/B D/A
"Bless - ed are you in the fir - ma - ment of heav - en
Em A/C♯ D F♯m7 G
to Refrain
praise - wor - thy and glo - ri - ous for - ev - er."

Responsorial Psalm (following second reading)

(M.M. ♩ = c. 124)

Psalm 19:8, 9, 10, 11

REFRAIN
A/C♯ D D/F♯ Gsus2 D/F♯ G Dmaj7/F♯
Lord, you have the words, Lord, you have the words,
Em7 D/F♯ Gsus2 D/A A Bm Asus2
you have the words of ev - er - last - ing life.
(Keyboard)
Verse 1
D/C G/B G Dmaj7/F♯
The law of the LORD is per - fect, re - fresh - ing the soul; the de-
D/C G/B Em7 D/F♯ G A7sus4
cree of the LORD is trust - wor - thy, giv - ing wis - dom to the sim - ple.
to Refrain
Verse 2
D/C G/B G Dmaj7/F♯
The pre - cepts of the LORD are right, re - joic - ing the heart; the com-
D/C Bm7 Em7 D/F♯ Em7/G A7sus4
mand of the LORD is clear, en - light - en - ing the eye.
to Refrain
Verse 3
D/C G/B G Dmaj7/F♯
The fear of the LORD is pure, en - dur - ing for - ev - er; the

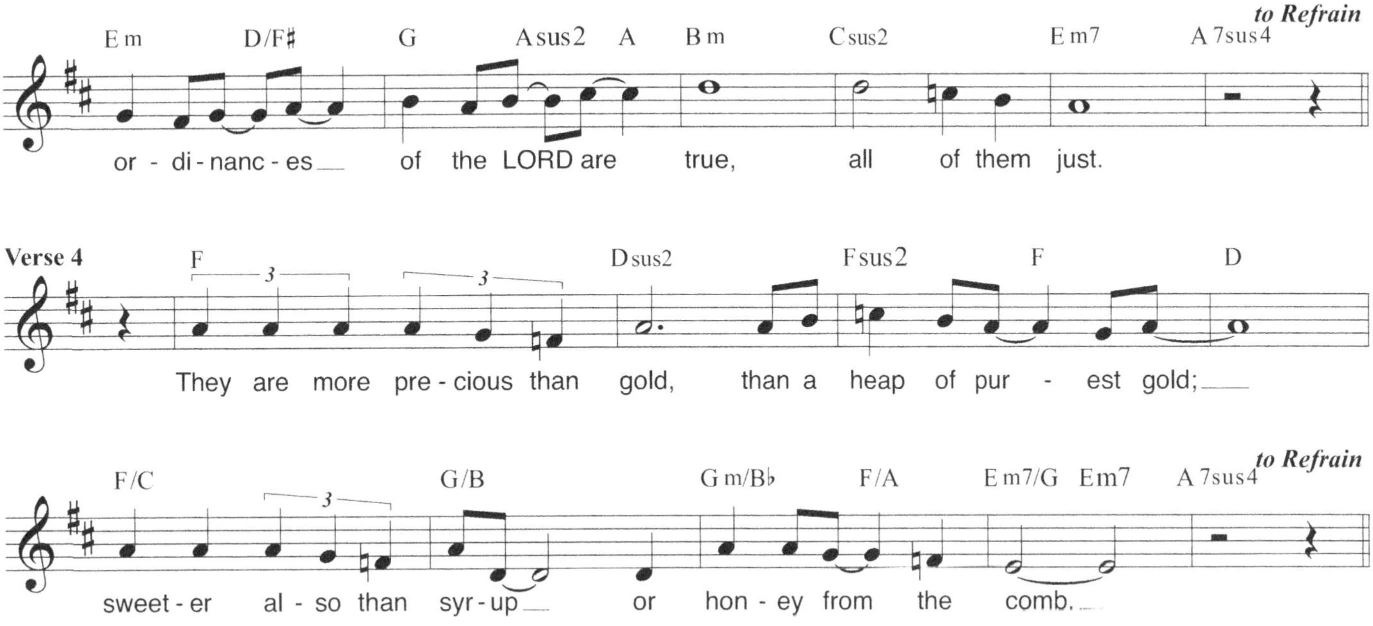
to Refrain
Em D/F♯ G Asus2 A Bm Csus2 Em7 A7sus4
or - di - nanc - es of the LORD are true, all of them just.
Verse 4
F Dsus2 Fsus2 F D
They are more pre - cious than gold, than a heap of pur - est gold;
to Refrain
F/C G/B Gm/B♭ F/A Em7/G Em7 A7sus4
sweet - er al - so than syr - up or hon - ey from the comb.

Responsorial Psalm (following third reading)

(M.M. ♩= c. 136)

Psalm 107:2-3, 4-5, 6-7, 8-9

REFRAIN [or: Alleluia]

Bm D Em Em/G
Give thanks to the Lord; his love is ev - er -
Bm A/C♯ A Bm
last - ing, his love is ev - er - last - ing.
Verse 1
Bm A/B Bm Em Em/G Bm
Let the re - deemed of the LORD say, those whom he has re - deemed
Em Em/G Bm D A/C♯ G
from the hand of the foe And gath - ered from the lands,
G Em Asus2 Em A
from the east and the west, from the north and the south.
to Refrain
Verse 2
A/B Bm Em Em/G Bm
They went a - stray in the de - sert wil - der - ness; the

D A/C♯ G Em Asus2
way to an in - hab - it - ed cit - y they did not find. Hun - gry and
to Refrain
D A/C♯ G Em A
thirst - y, their life was wast - ing a - way with - in them.
Verse 3
Bm A/B Bm
They cried to the LORD in their dis - tress;
Em Em/G Bm F♯m/A
from their straits he res - cued them. And he led them by a di -
to Refrain
F♯m G Em G A
rect way to reach an in - hab - it - ed cit - y.
Verse 4
Bm A/B Bm Em Em/G
Let them give thanks to the LORD for his mer - cy and his won - drous
Bm Em Em/G Bm
deeds to the chil - dren of men, Be - cause he sat - is - fied the
to Refrain
F♯m/A G Em Em G A
long - ing soul and filled the hun - gry soul with good things.

Responsorial Psalm (following fourth reading)

(M.M. ♩ = c. 116)

REFRAIN [or: Alleluia]

Psalm 104:1-2, 24 & 35, 27-28, 29-30

D C/D D Bm7 C D
Lord, send out your Spir - it, and re-new the face of the earth.
Verse 1
D C/D G/D
Bless the LORD, O my soul! O LORD, my God, you are great in -
D Bm7 C
deed! You are clothed with maj - es - ty and
G C/E Gsus2 Gsus 4 G
glo - ry, robed in light as with a cloak.
to Refrain
Verse 2
D C/D G/D D
How man - i - fold are your works, O LORD! In
Bm7 C G C/G G
wis - dom you have wrought them all— the earth is full of your crea - tures. Bless the
C/E Gsus2
LORD, O my soul! Al - le - lu - ia.
to Refrain

Verse 3
D C/D G/D
Crea-tures all look to you to give them food in due
D Bm7 C C/G
time. When you give it to them, they gath-er it; when you o - pen your
G C/E Gsus2 Gsus4 G
to Refrain
hand, they are filled with good things.
Verse 4
D C/D G/D
If you take a - way their breath, they per-ish and re - turn to their
D Bm7 C C/G
dust. When you send forth your spir - it, they are cre -
Gsus2 C/E Gsus2 Gsus4 G
to Refrain
3
at - ed, and you re - new the face of the earth.

Gospel Acclamation:

Acclamation: (Keyboard/SATB) NO. V

(M.M. ♪ = c. 150)

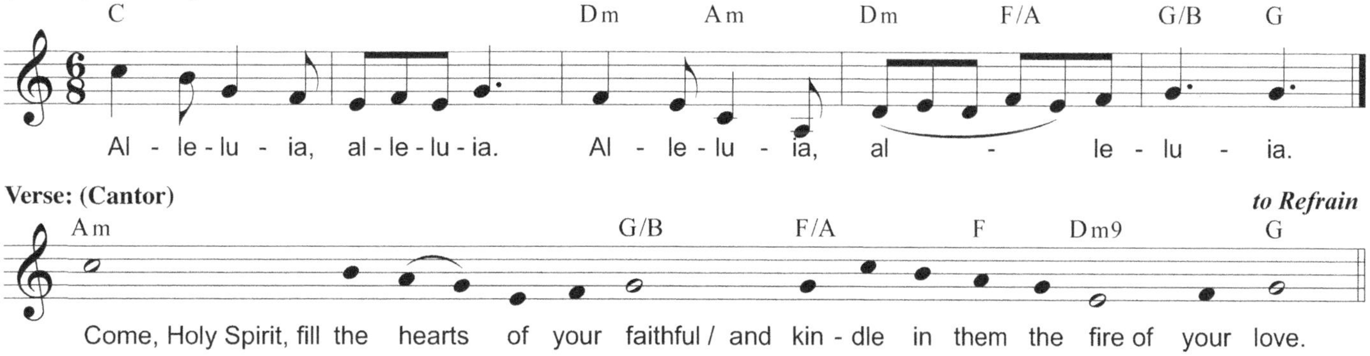
C Dm Am Dm F/A G/B G
Al - le-lu - ia, al-le-lu-ia. Al - le-lu - ia, al - le - lu - ia.
Verse: (Cantor)
to Refrain
Am G/B F/A F Dm9 G
Come, Holy Spirit, fill the hearts of your faithful / and kin - dle in them the fire of your love.

Pentecost Sunday: At the Mass during the Day

May 23

(M.M. ♩ = c. 116)

Psalm 104:1, 24, 29-30, 31, 34

REFRAIN [or: Alleluia]

D C/D D Bm7 C D
Lord, send out your Spir - it, and re-new the face of the earth.
Verse 1
D C/D G/D D
Bless the LORD, O my soul! O LORD, my God, you are great in - deed!
Bm7 C C/G Gsus2
How man - i - fold are your works, O LORD. The
C/E Gsus2 Gsus4 G
earth is full of your crea - tures.
to Refrain
Verse 2
D C/D G/D
If you take a - way their breath, they per - ish and re - turn to their
D Bm7 C C/G
dust. When you send forth your spir - it, they are cre -
Gsus2 C/E Gsus2 Gsus4 G
at - ed, and you re - new the face of the earth.
to Refrain

Verse 3

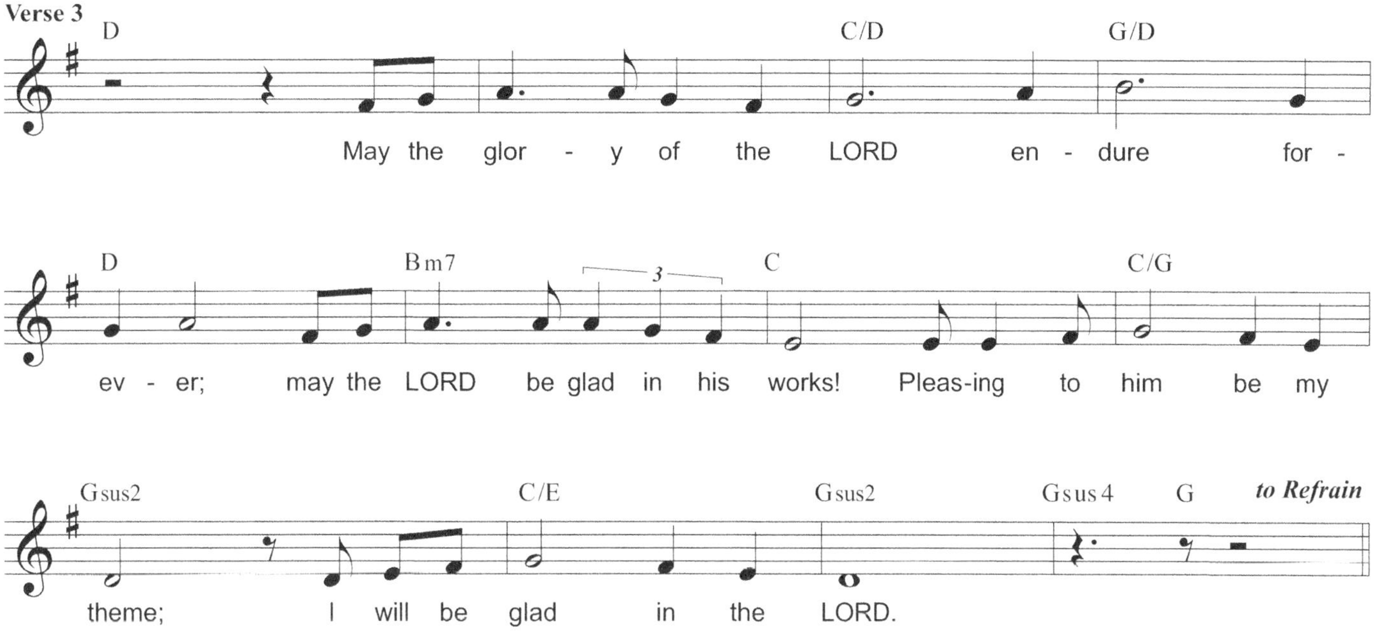
D
C/D
G/D
May the glor - y of the LORD en - dure for -
D
Bm7
C
C/G
3
ev - er; may the LORD be glad in his works! Pleas-ing to him be my
Gsus2
C/E
Gsus2
Gsus4
G
to Refrain
theme; I will be glad in the LORD.

Gospel Acclamation:

Acclamation: (Keyboard/SATB) NO. V

(M.M. ♪ = c. 150)

C
Dm
Am
Dm
F/A
G/B
G
Al - le - lu - ia, al - le - lu - ia. Al - le - lu - ia, al - le - lu - ia.

Verse: (Cantor)

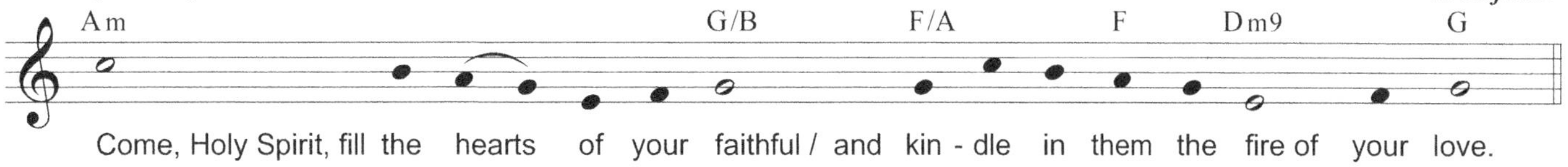
to Refrain
Am
G/B
F/A
F
Dm9
G
Come, Holy Spirit, fill the hearts of your faithful / and kin - dle in them the fire of your love.

The Most Holy Trinity

May 30

Psalm 33:4–5, 6, 9, 18–19, 20, 22

(M.M. ♪ = c. 124)
REFRAIN
Alternate ending
Capo 2: D G/D D A/D G/D D G/D Em7/D G/D A/D D
E A/E E B/E A/E E A/E F♯m7/E A/E B/E E
Bless-ed the peo-ple the Lord has chos-en, the Lord has chos-en to be his own.
Optional Interlude before Verse 3 & after final Refrain
D Em7/D D A/D D
E F♯m7/E E B/E E
Verse 1
D G/D D A7/D D
E A/E E B7/E E
Up-right is the word of the LORD, and all his works are trust-wor-thy.
to Refrain
F♯m G/B D/A G/B D A7/D D G/D
G♯m A/C♯ E/B A/C♯ E B7/E E A/E
He loves jus-tice and right; of the kind-ness of the LORD the earth is full.
Verse 2
D G/D D
E A/E E
By the word of the LORD the heav-ens were made; by the
A7/D D F♯m G/B
B7/E E G♯m A/C♯
breath of his mouth all their host. For he spoke, and it was
to Refrain
D/A G/B D A7/D D G/D
E/B A/C♯ E B7/E E A/E
made; he com-mand-ed, and it stood forth.

Verse 3
D
E
G/D
A/E
See, the eyes of the LORD are up - on those who fear him,
A 7/D
B 7/E
F♯m
G♯m
G/B
A/C♯
up - on those who hope for his kind - ness, to de - liv - er them from
to Refrain
D/A
E/B
death and pre - serve them in spite of fam - ine.
Verse 4
Our soul waits for the LORD, who is our help and our shield. May your
to Refrain
kind - ness, O LORD, be up - on us who have put our hope in you.

Gospel Acclamation: cf. Revelation 1:8

Acclamation: (Keyboard/SATB) NO. I

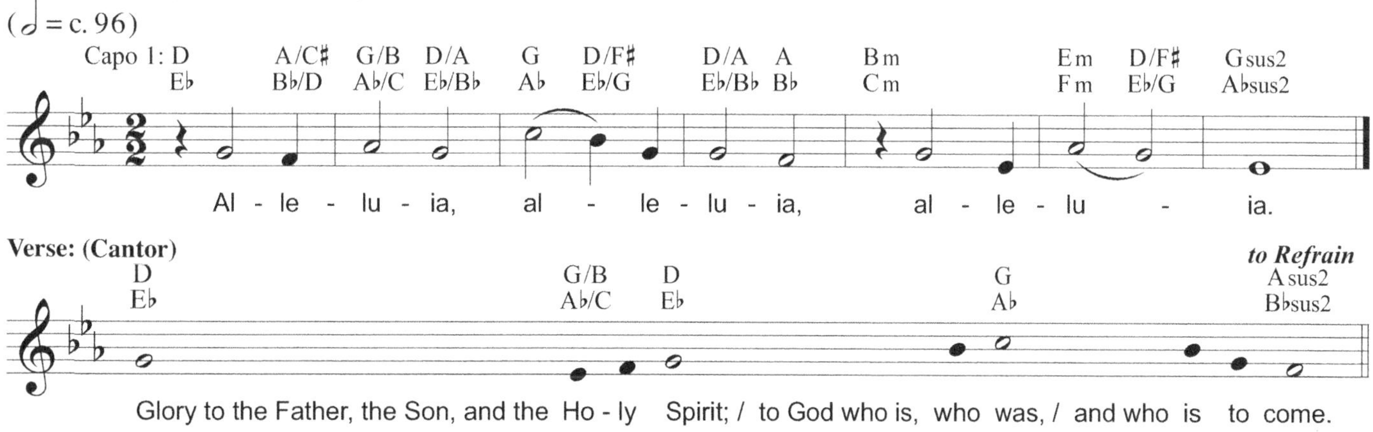
(𝅗𝅥 = c. 96)
Capo 1: D
E♭
A/C♯
B♭/D
G/B
A♭/C
D/A
E♭/B♭
G
A♭
D/F♯
E♭/G
A
B♭
B m
C m
E m
F m
G sus2
A♭sus2
Al - le - lu - ia, al - le - lu - ia, al - le - lu - ia.
Verse: (Cantor)
to Refrain
A sus2
B♭sus2
Glory to the Father, the Son, and the Ho - ly Spirit; / to God who is, who was, / and who is to come.

The Most Holy Body and Blood of Christ

(Corpus Christi)

(M.M. 𝅗𝅥 = c. 65)

June 6

REFRAIN [or: Alleluia]

Psalm 116:12-13,15-16, 17-18

Capo 3: D F
Bm7 Dm7
D/C F/E♭
C E♭
I will take the cup of sal - va - tion, and
Gsus2 B♭sus2
Gm B♭m
Gm7 B♭m7
C E♭
D F
call on the name of the Lord.
Verse 1
Em Gm
Bm/D Dm/F
G/B B♭/D
A C
G B♭
How shall I make a re - turn to the LORD for all the
D F
Asus4 Csus4
A C
Em Gm
Bm/D Dm/F
good he has done for me? The cup of sal - va - tion
G/B B♭/D
A C
G B♭
D F
Asus4 Csus4
A C
to Refrain
I will take up, and I will call up - on the name of the LORD.
Verse 2
Em Gm
G/B B♭/D
A C
G B♭
Pre - cious in the eyes of the LORD is the

D F
Asus4 Csus4
A C
Em Gm
Bm/D Dm/F
death of his faith - ful ones.
I am your ser - vant, the
G/B B♭/D
A C
G B♭
D F
Asus4 Csus4
A C
to Refrain
son of your hand-maid; you have loosed my bonds.
Verse 3
A C
Em Gm
Bm/D Dm/F
G/B B♭/D
A C
To you will I of - fer sac - ri - fice of thanks - giv - ing,
G B♭
D F
Asus4 Csus4
A C
Em Gm
and I will call up - on the name of the LORD. My vows to the
Bm/D Dm/F
G/B B♭/D
A C
G B♭
D F
Asus4 Csus4
A C
to Refrain
LORD I will pay in the pres-ence of all his peo - ple.

Gospel Acclamation: John 6:51

Acclamation: (Keyboard/SATB) NO. II

(M.M. ♩ = c. 130)

Capo 3: A C
G B♭
D/F♯ F/A
E G
A/C♯ C/E
D F
D/F♯ F/A
Esus4 Gsus4
E G
Al - le - lu - ia, al - le - lu - ia, al - le - lu - ia.

Verse: (Cantor)

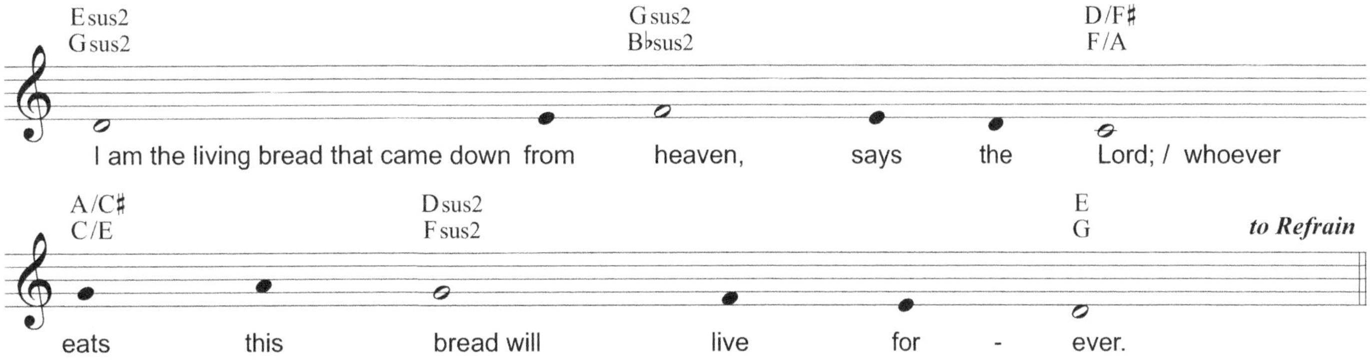
Esus2 Gsus2
Gsus2 B♭sus2
D/F♯ F/A
I am the living bread that came down from heaven, says the Lord; / whoever
A/C♯ C/E
Dsus2 Fsus2
E G
to Refrain
eats this bread will live for - ever.

11th Sunday in Ordinary Time

June 13

(M.M. ♩ = c. 72)
REFRAIN
Psalm 92:2–3, 13–14, 15–16
D D7 Em7/D Edm7/D D
Lord, it is good to give thanks, give thanks to you.
NOTE: Refrain Vocals SAB in Treble Clef
D D7 Em7/D Edm7/D D
Lord, it is good to give thanks, give thanks to you.
Verse 1
D G/D D C/F G/C D/G Bm7
It is good to give thanks to the LORD, to sing praise to your name, Most
C D G/D D C
High, to pro-claim your kind - ness at dawn and your
B♭ Em7 A7sus4 D/A A7sus4
to Refrain
faith - ful - ness through - out the night.
Verse 2
D G/D D
The just one shall flour - ish like the palm tree, like a
C/F G/C Dsus4 Bm7 C D G/D
ce - dar of Leb - a - non shall he grow. They that are plant - ed in the

to Refrain
D C B♭ Em7 A7sus4 D/A A7sus4
house of the LORD shall flour - ish in the courts of our God.

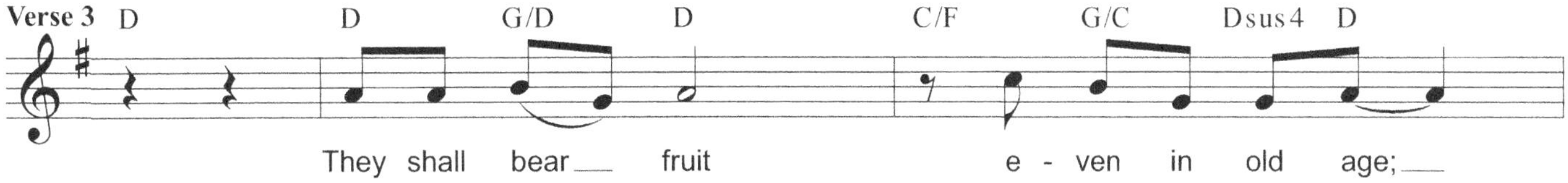
Verse 3
D D G/D D C/F G/C Dsus4 D
They shall bear fruit e - ven in old age;

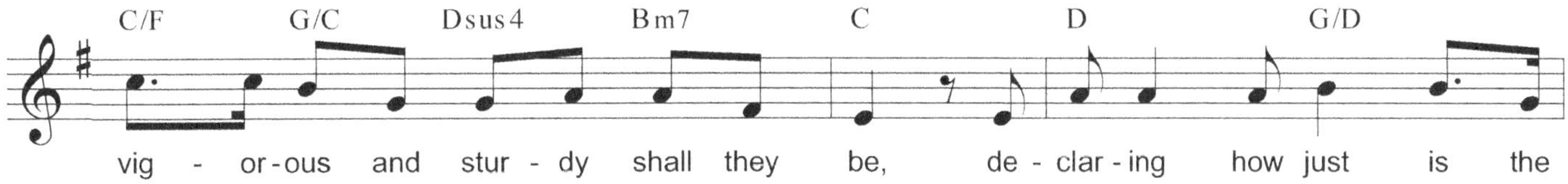
C/F G/C Dsus4 Bm7 C D G/D
vig - or-ous and stur - dy shall they be, de - clar - ing how just is the

to Refrain
D Bm7 C B♭ Em7 A7sus4 D/A A7sus4
LORD, my rock, in whom there is no wrong.

Gospel Acclamation:

Acclamation: (Keyboard/SATB) NO. IV

(M.M. ♩ = c. 116)

Capo 5: G Am F C Dm7
C Dm B♭ F Gm7
Al - le - lu - ia, al - le - lu - ia, al - le -

1.
2 and onward
C/E Fmaj7 Gsus4 Gsus4
F/A B♭maj7 Csus4 Csus4
lu - ia. ia.

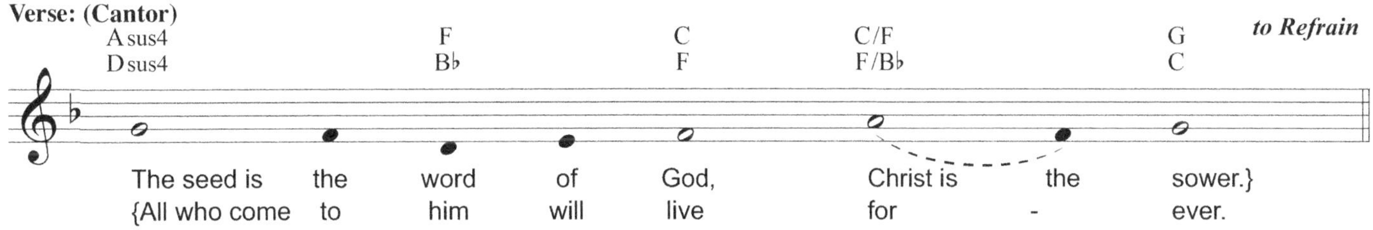
Verse: (Cantor)
to Refrain
Asus4 F C C/F G
Dsus4 B♭ F F/B♭ C
The seed is the word of God, Christ is the sower.}
{All who come to him will live for - ever.

12th Sunday in Ordinary Time

June 20

(M.M. ♩ = c. 132)

Psalm 107:23-24, 25-26, 28-29, 30-31

REFRAIN [or: Alleluia]
Bm D Em Em/G
Give thanks to the Lord; his love is ev - er -
Bm A/C♯ A Bm
last - ing, his love is ev - er - last - ing.
Verse 1
Bm A/B Bm Em Em/G Bm
They who sailed the sea in ships, trad-ing on the deep wa - ters,
D A/C♯ G G Em A
these saw the works of the LORD and his won-ders in the a - byss.
to Refrain
Verse 2
Bm A/B Bm Em Em/G
His com - mand raised up a storm wind which tossed its waves on
Bm D A/C♯ G Em Asus2
high. They mount - ed up to heav - en; they sank to the depths;
D A/C♯ G Em7 A Em A
their hearts melt - ed a - way in their plight.
to Refrain

Verse 3

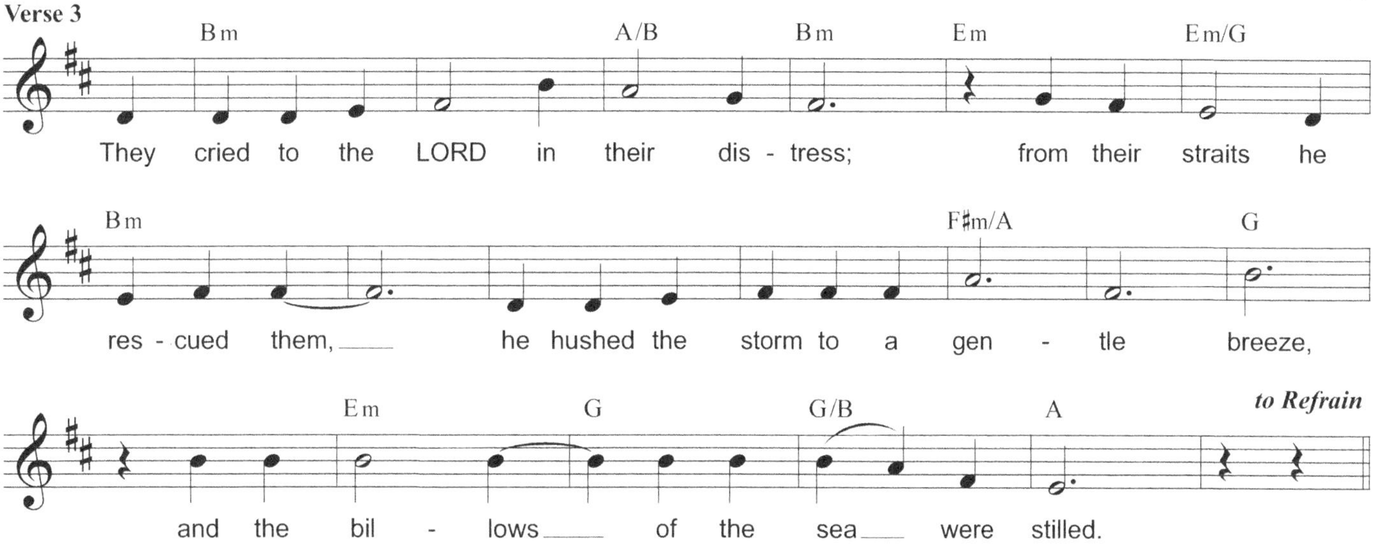
Bm A/B Bm Em Em/G
They cried to the LORD in their dis - tress; from their straits he
Bm F♯m/A G
res - cued them, he hushed the storm to a gen - tle breeze,
Em G G/B A
to Refrain
and the bil - lows of the sea were stilled.

Verse 4

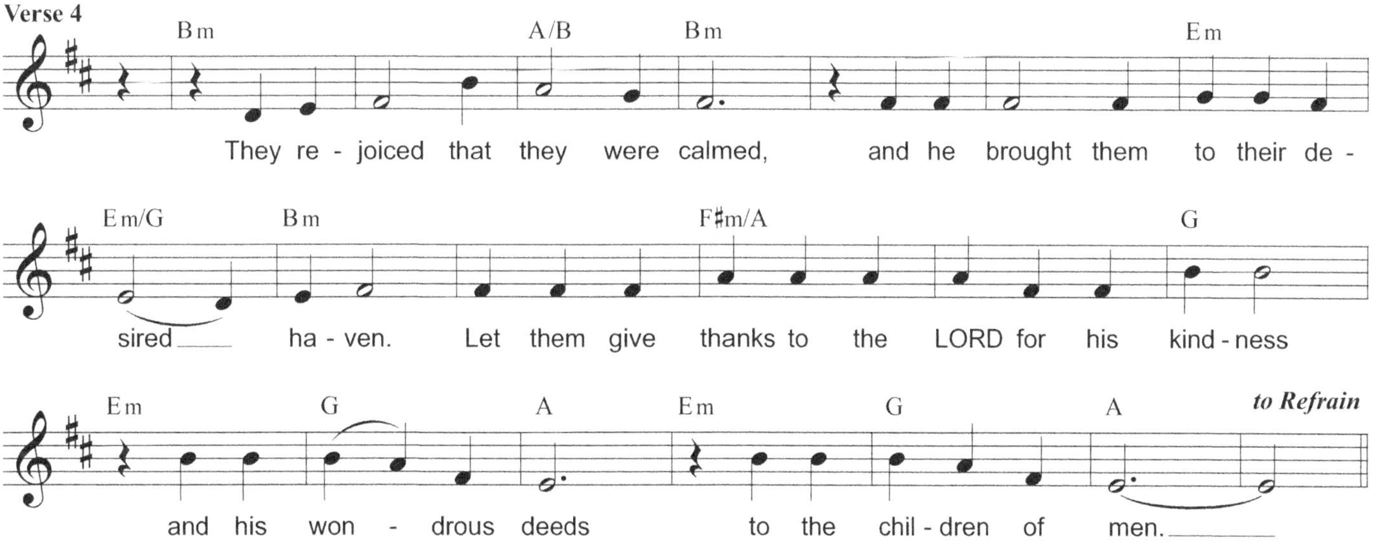
Bm A/B Bm Em
They re - joiced that they were calmed, and he brought them to their de -
Em/G Bm F♯m/A G
sired ha - ven. Let them give thanks to the LORD for his kind - ness
Em G A Em G A
to Refrain
and his won - drous deeds to the chil - dren of men.

Gospel Acclamation: Luke 7:16

Acclamation: (Keyboard/SATB) NO. IV

(M.M. ♩= c. 116)
Capo 5: G Am F C Dm7
C Dm B♭ F Gm7
Al - le - lu - ia, al - le - lu - ia, al - le -
C/E Fmaj7
F/A B♭maj7
1.
Gsus4
Csus4
2 and onward
Gsus4
Csus4
lu - ia. ia.

Verse: (Cantor)

Asus4 F C C/F G
Dsus4 B♭ F F/B♭ C
to Refrain
A great proph - et has risen in our midst.}
{God has visited his people.

13th Sunday in Ordinary Time

June 27

Psalm 30:2, 4, 5-6, 11-12, 13

(M.M. ♩ = c. 118)
REFRAIN
Bm Gmaj7 A F♯m7 G
I will praise you, Lord, for you have res - cued me.
Verse 1
D/A G D/A G/B A/C♯ Em D/F♯
I will ex - tol you, O LORD, for you drew me clear and did not let my en-e-mies re -
Asus2 G D/F♯ Em G/B
joice o - ver me. O LORD, you brought me up from the neth - er world; you pre -
D/A G/B Em7 D/F♯ G Asus2
served me from a - mong those go - ing down in-to the pit.
to Refrain
Verse 2
D/A G D/A G/B A/C♯ Em D/F♯
Sing praise to the LORD, you his faith - ful ones, and give thanks to his
Asus2 G D/F♯ Em Gsus2
ho - ly name. For his an - ger lasts but a mo-ment; a life - time, his good will. At
D/A G/B Em7 D/F♯ G Asus2
night - fall, weep - ing en - ters in, but with the dawn, re - joic - ing.
to Refrain

Verse 3
D/A G D/A G/B A/C♯ D/F♯ A
Hear, O LORD, and have pit - y [have pit - y] on me; O LORD, be my
G D/F♯ Em
help - er. You changed my mourn-ing in - to danc-ing; O LORD, my
G/B D/A G/B Em7 D/F♯ G Asus2
God, for - ev - er will I give you thanks.
to Refrain

Gospel Acclamation: cf. 2 Timothy 1:10

Acclamation: (Keyboard/SATB) NO. IV

(M.M. = c. 116)
Capo 5: G Am F C Dm7
C Dm B♭ F Gm7
Al - le - lu - ia, al - le - lu - ia, al - le -
C/E Fmaj7
F/A B♭maj7
1. Gsus4 Csus4
2 and onward Gsus4 Csus4
lu - ia. ia.
Verse: (Cantor)
Asus4 F C C/F G
Dsus4 B♭ F F/B♭ C
Our Sav - ior Je - sus Christ de - stroyed death}
{and brought life to light through the Gospel.
to Refrain

14th Sunday in Ordinary Time

July 4

(M.M. ♩ = c. 124)

Psalm 123:1–2, 2, 3–4

REFRAIN
A7sus4 D Dmaj7 G/D Gmaj7/D Em7/D
Our eyes are fixed on the Lord, plead - ing for his mer - cy,
G/D Em7/D D Dmaj7 G/D D
plead - ing for his mer - cy,
Verse 1
D A7/D G/D D
To you I lift up my eyes who are en -
Dmaj7 Em7/D Dmaj7/F♯ G/B D/A
throned in heav - en — As the eyes of ser - vants
Am/C Em7/B Em7/G A7sus4 A7
are on the hands of their mas - ters.
to Refrain
Verse 2
A7/D G/D D Dmaj7
As the eyes of a maid are on the hands of her
Em7/D A7/D G/D D Dmaj7
mis - tress, so are our eyes on the LORD, our God,

to Refrain
D/A Am/C Em7/B Em7/G A7sus4 A7
till he have pit - y on us.
Verse 3
D A7/D G/D D Em7/D
Have pit - y on us, O LORD, have pit - y on us, for
A7/D G/D D Em7/D
we are more than sat - ed with con - tempt; our
Dmaj7/F♯ G/B D/A G/B
souls are more than sat - ed with the mock - er - y of the
to Refrain
A/C♯ Asus4 Am/C Em7/B Em7/G A7sus4 A7
ar - ro - gant, with the con - tempt of the proud.

Gospel Acclamation: cf. Luke 4:18

Acclamation: (Keyboard/SATB) NO. IV

(M.M. ♩ = c. 116)

Capo 5: G C Am Dm F B♭ C F Dm7 Gm7
Al - le - lu - ia, al - le - lu - ia, al - le -
1.
2 and onward
C/E F/A Fmaj7 B♭maj7 Gsus4 Csus4 Gsus4 Csus4
lu - ia. ia.
Verse: (Cantor)
to Refrain
Asus4 Dsus4 Fadd2 B♭add2 C F C/F F/B♭ G C
The Spirit of the LORD is up - on me / for he sent me to bring glad tidings to the poor.

15th Sunday in Ordinary Time

July 11

(M.M. ♩ = c. 90)

Psalm 85:9, 10, 11-12, 13-14

REFRAIN
Em G D C
Lord, let us see your kind - ness, and grant us your sal - va - tion.
Verse 1 (M.M. ♩ = c. 76)
G D Am Dsus4
I will hear what God pro - claims; the LORD— for he pro - claims
Em Csus2 D
peace. Near in - deed is his sal - va - tion to
G/B G/D G C/E Am/C D
to Refrain
those who fear him, glo - ry dwell - ing in our land.
Verse 2 (M.M. ♩ = c. 76)
G D Am D Em Csus2
Kind - ness and truth shall meet; jus - tice and peace shall kiss. Truth shall spring out of the
D G/B G/D C/E Am/C D
to Refrain
earth, and jus - tice shall look down from heav - en.
Verse 3 (M.M. ♩ = c. 76)
G D Am
The LORD him - self will give his ben - e - fits; our land shall yield its

Em
Csus2
D
in - crease. Jus - tice shall walk be - fore him, and pre -

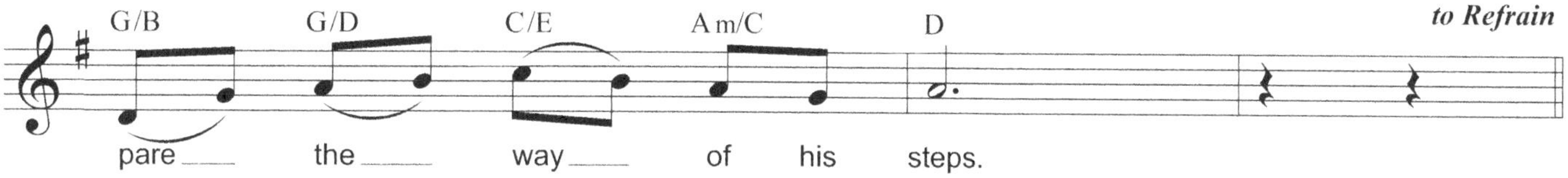
G/B
G/D
C/E
Am/C
D
to Refrain
pare the way of his steps.

Gospel Acclamation: Ephesians 1:17-18

Acclamation: (Keyboard/SATB) NO. II

(M.M. ♩ = c. 130)

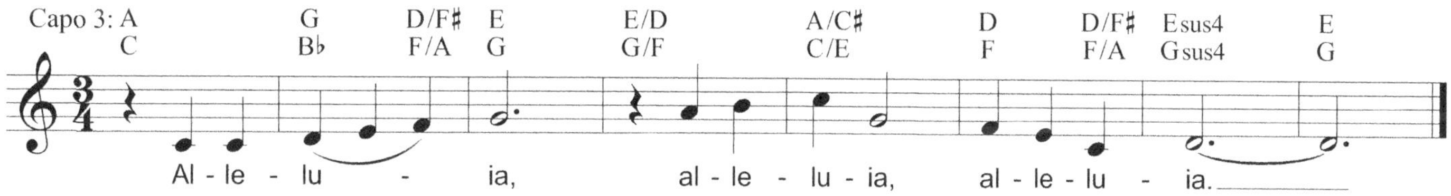
Capo 3: A
C
G
B♭
D/F♯
F/A
E
G
E/D
G/F
A/C♯
C/E
D
F
D/F♯
F/A
Esus4
Gsus4
E
G
Al - le - lu - ia, al - le - lu - ia, al - le - lu - ia.

Verse: (Cantor)

to Refrain
Esus2
Gsus2
Gsus2
B♭sus2
D/F♯
F/A
A/C♯
C/E
Dsus2
Fsus2
E
G
May the Father of our Lord Je - sus Christ en - lighten the eyes of our hearts,}
{that we may know what is the hope that be - longs to our call.

16th Sunday in Ordinary Time

July 18

Psalm 23:1-3a, 3b-4, 5, 6

(M.M. ♩ = c. 114)
REFRAIN
Capo 3:
The Lord is my shep-herd; there is noth-ing I shall want.
Verse 1
The LORD is my shep-herd; I shall not want. In ver-dant pas-tures he gives me re-pose; be-side rest-ful wa-ters he leads me; he re-fresh-es my soul.
to Refrain
Verse 2
He guides me in right paths for his name's sake. E-ven though I walk in the dark val-ley I fear no e-vil; for you are at my side with your rod and your staff that give me cour-age.
to Refrain
Verse 3
You spread the ta-ble be-fore me in the sight of my

Am Cm F A♭ G B♭ A/E C/G
foes; you a - noint my head with oil;
C/G E♭/B♭ F A♭ Gsus4 B♭sus4 G B♭
to Refrain
my cup o - ver - flows.
Verse 4
F A♭ G/F B♭/A♭ Em Gm Am Cm
On-ly good-ness and kind - ness fol-low me all the days of my life; and I shall
to Refrain
F A♭ G B♭ A/E C/G C/G E♭/B♭ F A♭ Gsus4 B♭sus4 G B♭
dwell in the house of the LORD for years to come.

Gospel Acclamation: John 10:27

Acclamation: (Keyboard/SATB) NO. IV

(M.M. ♩ = c. 116)

Capo 5: G C Am Dm F B♭ C F Dm7 Gm7
Al - le - lu - ia, al - le - lu - ia, al - le -
C/E F/A Fmaj7 B♭maj7
1. Gsus4 Csus4
2 and onward Gsus4 Csus4
lu - ia. ia.

Verse: (Cantor)

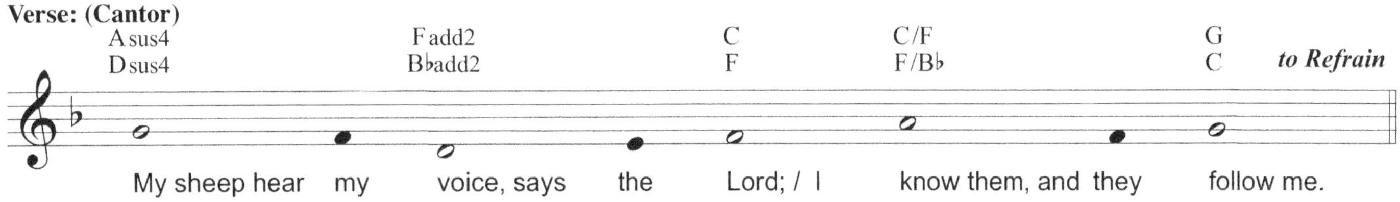
Asus4 Dsus4 Fadd2 B♭add2 C F C/F F/B♭ G C
to Refrain
My sheep hear my voice, says the Lord; / I know them, and they follow me.

17th Sunday in Ordinary Time

July 25

Psalm 145:10–11, 15–16, 17–18

(M.M. ♩ = c. 84)
REFRAIN
Gsus2 F♯m Gmaj7 F♯m/A G/B D/A Gsus2
The hand of the Lord feeds us; he an-swers all our needs.
(Keyboard)
Verse 1
Gsus2 Dmaj7 Gmaj7 F♯m/A G/B
Let all your works give you thanks, O LORD, and let your faith - ful ones
Asus2 Gsus2 Bm9 Em9
bless you. Let them dis - course of the glo - ry of your
A/C♯ G/B A A/G
king - dom and speak of your might.
to Refrain
Verse 2
Gsus2 Dmaj7 Gmaj7 F♯m/A G/B
The eyes of all look hope-ful - ly to you, and you give them their food in due
Asus2 Gsus2 Bm9 Em9 A/C♯
sea - son; you o - pen your hand and sat - is - fy the de -
G/B A A/G
sire of ev - 'ry liv - ing thing.
to Refrain

Verse 3

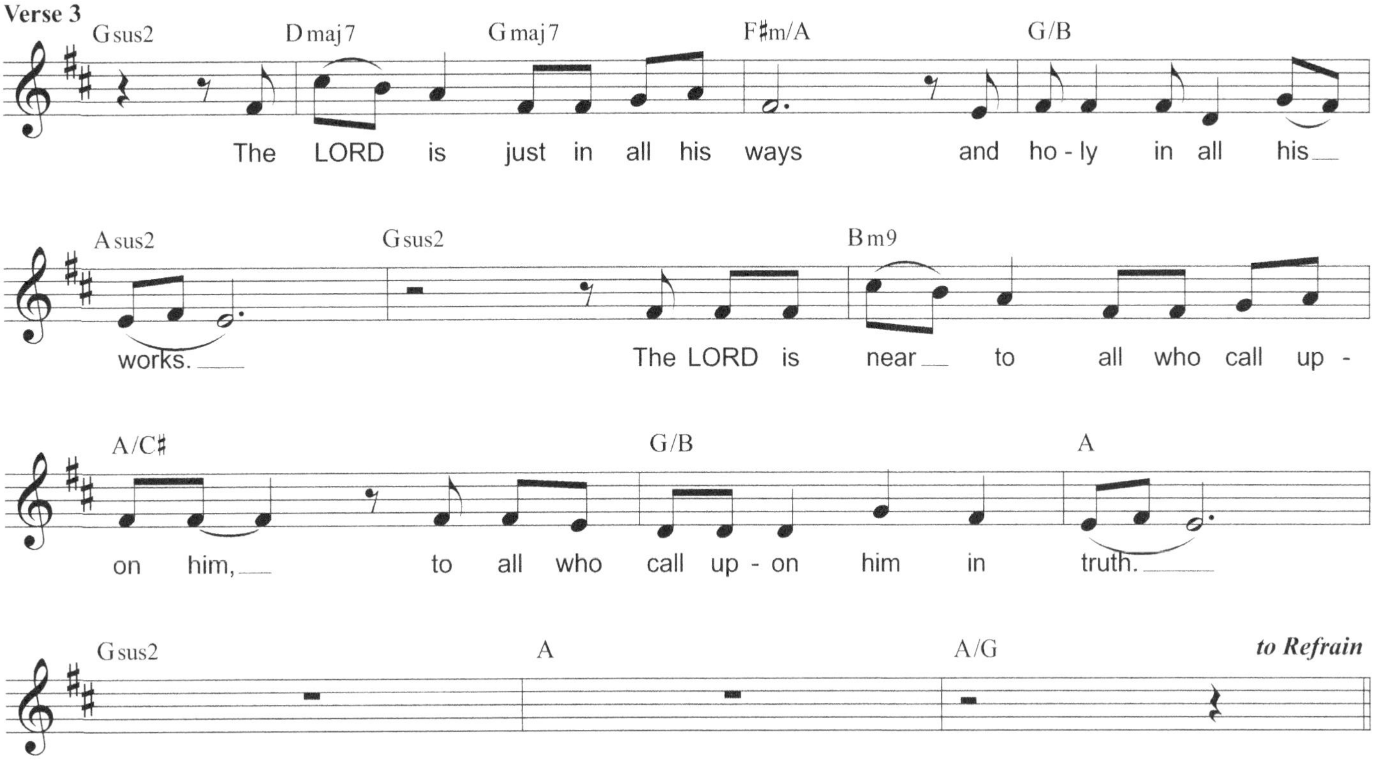
Gsus2 Dmaj7 Gmaj7 F♯m/A G/B
The LORD is just in all his ways and ho - ly in all his
Asus2 Gsus2 Bm9
works. The LORD is near to all who call up -
A/C♯ G/B A
on him, to all who call up - on him in truth.
Gsus2 A A/G
to Refrain

Gospel Acclamation: Luke 7:16

Acclamation: (Keyboard/SATB) NO. III

(M.M. ♩ = c. 160)

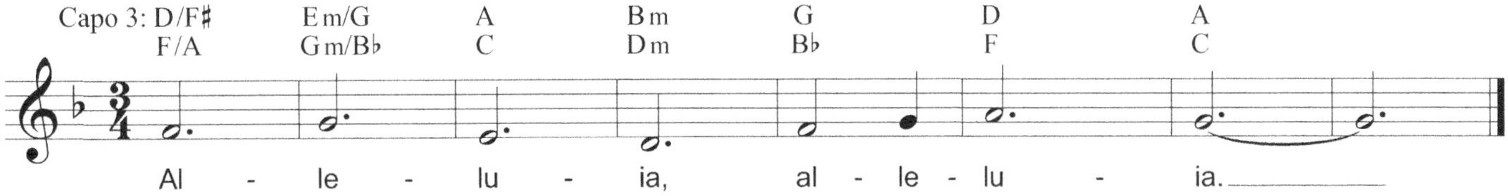
Capo 3: D/F♯ Em/G A Bm G D A
F/A Gm/B♭ C Dm B♭ F C
Al - le - lu - ia, al - le - lu - ia.

Verse: (Cantor)

Em G D A
Gm B♭ F C
to Refrain
A great prophet has risen in our midst. God has visited his people.

18th Sunday in Ordinary Time

August 1

(M.M. ♩ = c. 64)

Psalm 78:3-4, 23-24, 25, 54

REFRAIN

Am G/B Dm/F E
The Lord gave them bread from heav - en.

Verse 1

Am Em/G F C/G
What we have heard and know, and what our fa-thers have de-clared to us, we will de-

Am Em/G F C/G B♭sus2 Fm/A♭
clare to the gen-er-a-tion to come, the glo-rious deeds of the

C/G Dm7 F/A G
to Refrain
LORD and his strength and the won-ders that he wrought.

Verse 2

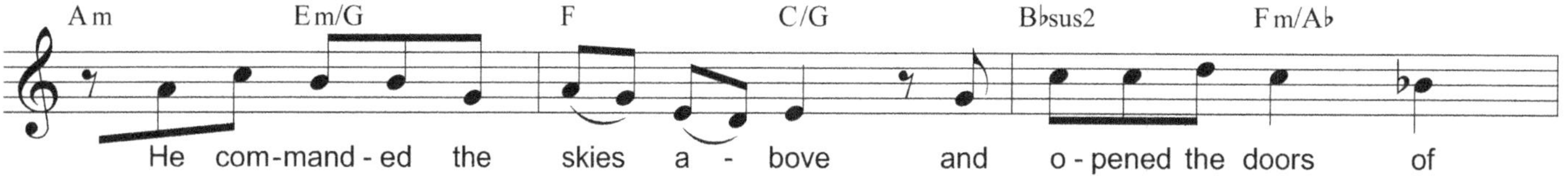
Am Em/G F C/G B♭sus2 Fm/A♭
He com-mand-ed the skies a-bove and o-pened the doors of

C/G Dm7 F/A C/G Dm7 F/A G
to Refrain
heav-en; he rained man-na up-on them for food and gave them heav-en-ly bread.

Verse 3

Am
Em/G
F
C/G
Man ate the bread of an - gels, food he sent them in a - bun - dance. And he

B♭sus2
Fm/A♭
C/G
Dm7
F/A
G
to Refrain
brought them to his ho - ly land, to the moun-tains his right hand had won.

Gospel Acclamation: Matthew 4:4b

Acclamation: (Keyboard/SATB) NO. IV

(M.M. ♩ = c. 116)

Capo 5: G
C
Am
Dm
F
B♭
C
F
Dm7
Gm7
Al - le - lu - ia, al - le - lu - ia, al - le -

1.
2 and onward
C/E
F/A
Fmaj7
B♭maj7
Gsus4
Csus4
Gsus4
Csus4
lu - ia. ia.

Verse: (Cantor)

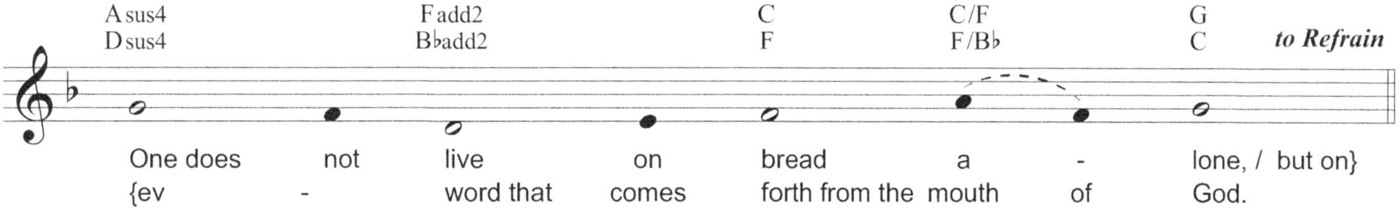
Asus4
Dsus4
Fadd2
B♭add2
C
F
C/F
F/B♭
G
C
to Refrain
One does not live on bread a - lone, / but on}
{ev - word that comes forth from the mouth of God.

19th Sunday in Ordinary Time

August 8

Psalm 34:2-3, 4-5, 6-7, 8-9

(M.M. ♩ = c. 100)
REFRAIN
Capo 1: Dmaj7 G/D D F♯m Gsus2
Ebmaj7 Ab/Eb Eb Gm Absus2
Taste and see the good - ness of the Lord.
(Keyboard)
Dmaj7 G/D D D/F♯ Em Gsus2
Ebmaj7 Ab/Eb Eb Eb/G Fm Absus2
Taste and see the good - ness of the Lord.
Verse 1 (M.M. ♩ = c. 79)
D/A A7sus4 D/A A7sus4 D/A
Eb/Bb Bb7sus4 Eb/Bb Bb7sus4 Eb/Bb
I will bless the LORD at all times; his praise shall be ev - er in my mouth.
Gsus2 F♯m Bm Em7 D/F♯ D/G
Absus2 Gm Cm Fm7 Eb/G Eb/Ab
to Refrain
Let my soul glo - ry in the LORD; the low - ly will hear me and be glad.
Verse 2 (M.M. ♩ = c. 79)
D/A A7sus4 D/A A7sus4 D/A
Eb/Bb Bb7sus4 Eb/Bb Bb7sus4 Eb/Bb
Glo - ri - fy the LORD with me, let us to - geth - er ex - tol his name. I
Gsus2 F♯m Bm Em7 D/F♯ D/G
Absus2 Gm Cm Fm7 Eb/G Eb/Ab
to Refrain
sought the LORD, and he an - swered me__ and de - liv - ered me from all my fears.

Verse 3 (M.M. ♩ = c. 79)

D/A Eb/Bb A7sus4 Bb7sus4 D/A Eb/Bb A7sus4 Bb7sus4
Look to him that you may be ra-diant with joy, and your fac-es may not blush with
D/A Eb/Bb Gsus2 Absus2 F#m Gm Bm Cm
shame. When the af-flic-ted man called out, the LORD heard, and from
Em7 Fm7 D/F# Eb/G D/G Eb/Ab
all his dis-tress he saved him.
to Refrain
Verse 4 (M.M. ♩ = c. 79)
D/A Eb/Bb A7sus4 Bb7sus4
The an-gel of the LORD en-
D/A Eb/Bb A7sus4 Bb7sus4 D/A Eb/Bb Gsus2 Absus2
camps a-round those who fear him and de-liv-ers them. Taste and see how
F#m Gm Bm Cm Em7 Fm7 D/F# Eb/G D/G Eb/Ab
good the LORD is; bless-ed the man who takes ref-uge in him.
to Refrain

Gospel Acclamation: John 6:51

Acclamation: (Keyboard/SATB) NO. II

(M.M. ♩ = c. 130)

Capo 3: A C G Bb D/F# F/A E G A/C# C/E D F D/F# F/A Esus4 Gsus4 E G
Al-le-lu-ia, al-le-lu-ia, al-le-lu-ia.
Verse: (Cantor)
Esus2 Gsus2 Gsus2 Bbsus2 D/F# F/A
I am the living bread that came down from heaven, says the Lord; / whoever
A/C# C/E Dsus2 Fsus2 E G
eats this bread will live for-ever.
to Refrain

The Assumption of the Blessed Virgin Mary:

At the Vigil Mass

August 14

Psalm 132:6-7, 9-10, 13-14

(M.M. ♩= c. 128)

REFRAIN
Em D G Am/C D G D Em Am7 D
Lord, go up to the place of your rest, you and the ark of your hol - i - ness.
Verse 1
D Em C G
Be - hold, we heard of it in Eph - rat - hah; we found it in the
D Am Em/G D/F♯
fields of Jaar. Let us en - ter his dwell - ing,
D/A C/E Am7 D
let us wor - ship at his foot - stool.
to Refrain
Verse 2
D Em C G
May your priests be clothed with jus - tice; let your faith - ful ones shout mer - ri - ly for
D Am Em/G D/F♯
joy. For the sake of Da - vid your ser - vant,
D/A C/E Am7 D
re - ject not the plea of your a - noint - ed.
to Refrain

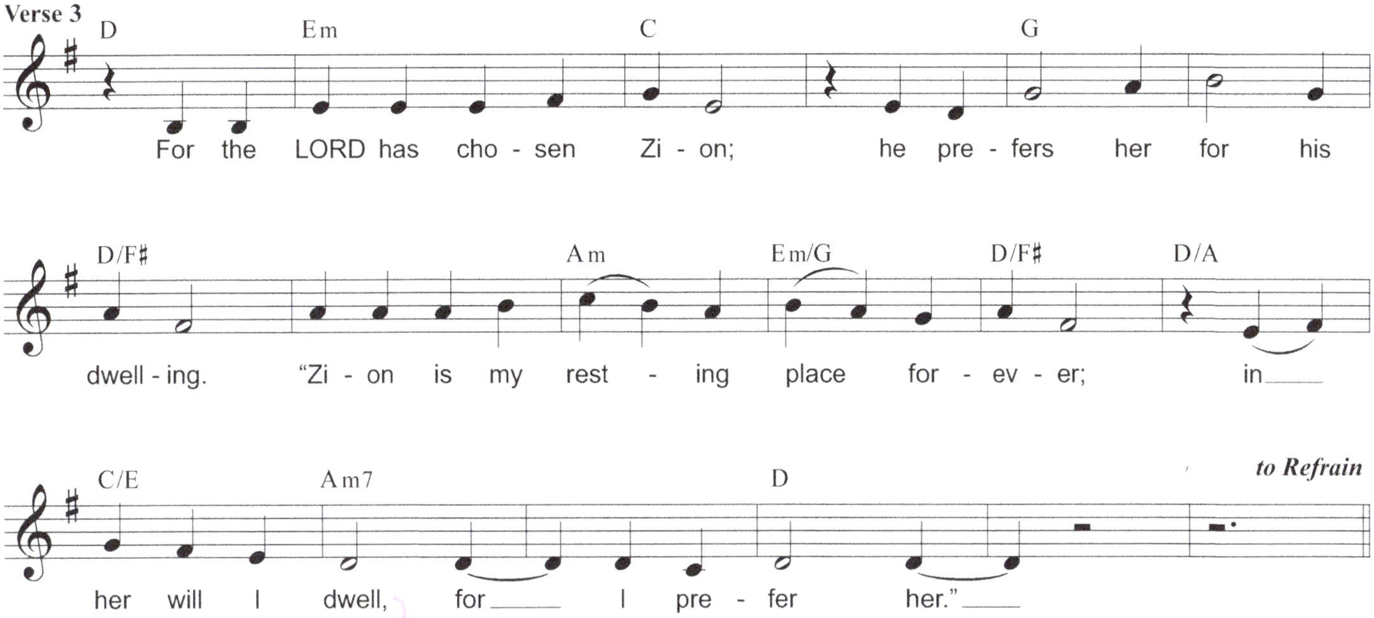
Verse 3
D Em C G
For the LORD has cho - sen Zi - on; he pre - fers her for his
D/F♯ Am Em/G D/F♯ D/A
dwell - ing. "Zi - on is my rest - ing place for - ev - er; in
C/E Am7 D
her will I dwell, for I pre - fer her."
to Refrain

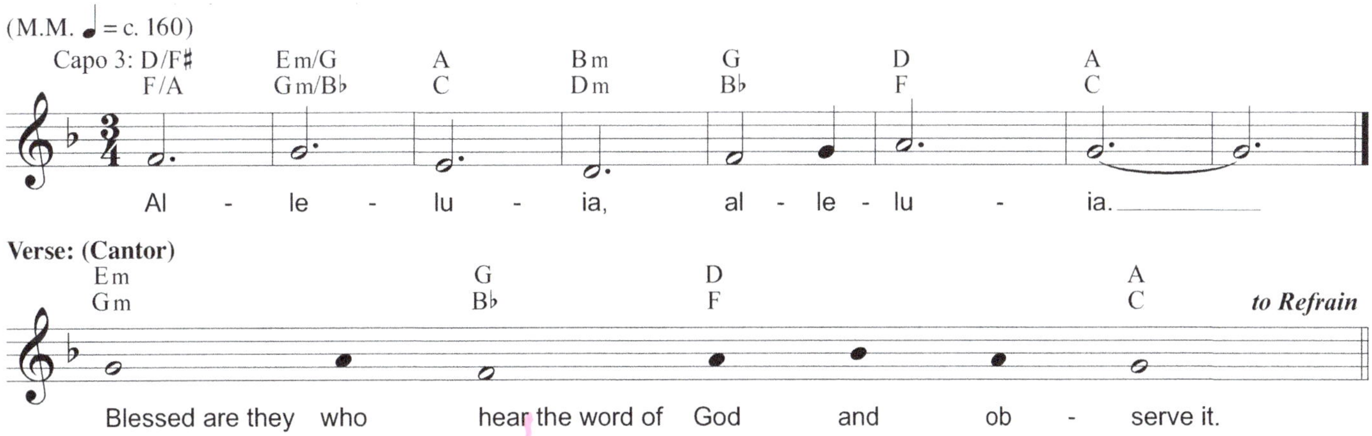
(M.M. ♩ = c. 160)
Capo 3: D/F♯ Em/G A Bm G D A
F/A Gm/B♭ C Dm B♭ F C
Al - le - lu - ia, al - le - lu - ia.
Verse: (Cantor)
Em G D A
Gm B♭ F C
Blessed are they who hear the word of God and ob - serve it.
to Refrain

The Assumption of the Blessed Virgin Mary:
At the Mass during the Day

August 15

(M.M. ♩ = c. 68)

Psalm 45:10, 11, 12, 16

REFRAIN

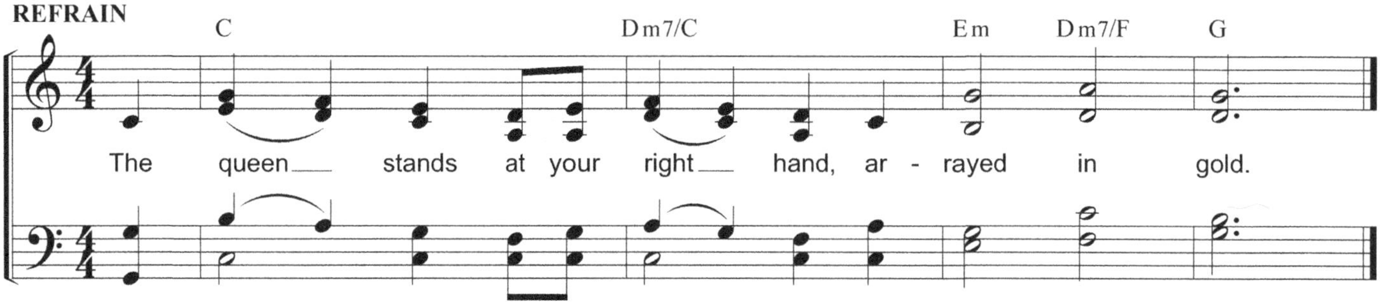
C Dm7/C Em Dm7/F G
The queen stands at your right hand, ar - rayed in gold.

Verse 1

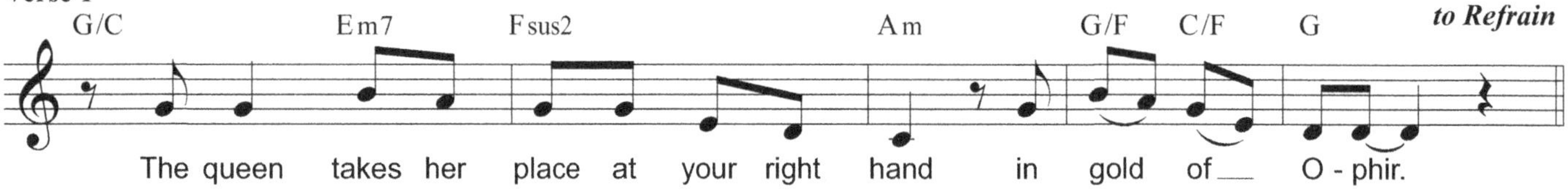
G/C Em7 Fsus2 Am G/F C/F G
to Refrain
The queen takes her place at your right hand in gold of O - phir.

Verse 2

G/C Em7 Fsus2 Am G/F C/F G
to Refrain
Hear, O daugh-ter, and see; turn your ear, for-get your peo-ple and your fa-ther's house.

Verse 3

G/C Em7 C/F Am G/F C/F G
to Refrain
So shall the king de - sire your beau-ty; for he is your lord.

Verse 4

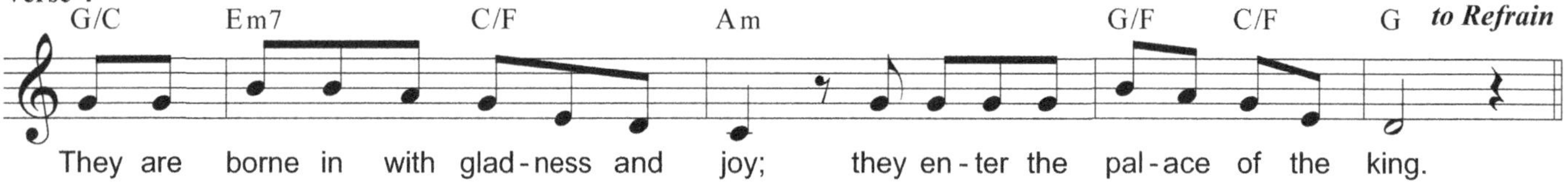
G/C Em7 C/F Am G/F C/F G
to Refrain
They are borne in with glad-ness and joy; they en-ter the pal-ace of the king.

Gospel Acclamation:

Acclamation: (Keyboard/SATB) NO. III

(M.M. ♩ = c. 160)

Capo 3: D/F♯ Em/G A Bm G D A
F/A Gm/B♭ C Dm B♭ F C
Al - le - lu - ia, al - le - lu - ia.

Verse: (Cantor)

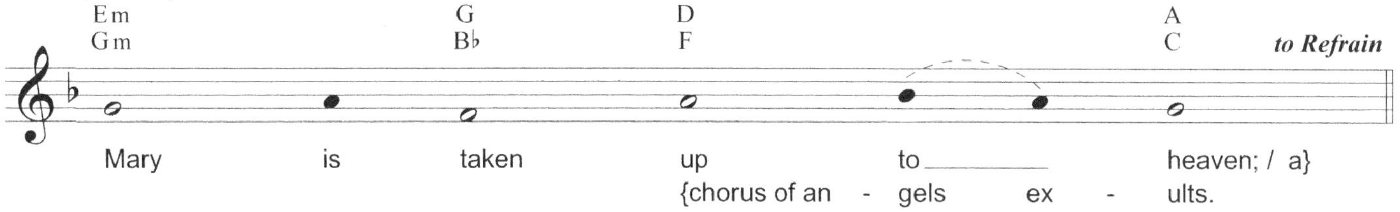
Em G D A
Gm B♭ F C
to Refrain
Mary is taken up to heaven; / a}
{chorus of an - gels ex - ults.

21st Sunday in Ordinary Time

August 22

Psalm 34:2–3, 16–17, 18–19, 20–21

(M.M. ♩ = c. 100)
REFRAIN
Capo 1: Dmaj7 G/D D F♯m Gsus2
E♭maj7 A♭/E♭ E♭ Gm A♭sus2
Taste and see the good - ness of the Lord.
(Keyboard)
Dmaj7 G/D D D/F♯ Em Gsus2
E♭maj7 A♭/E♭ E♭ E♭/G Fm A♭sus2
Taste and see the good - ness of the Lord.
Verse 1 (M.M. ♩ = c. 79)
D/A A7sus4 D/A A7sus4
E♭/B♭ B♭7sus4 E♭/B♭ B♭7sus4
I will bless the LORD at all times; his praise shall be ev - er in my
D/A Gsus2 F♯m Bm
E♭/B♭ A♭sus2 Gm Cm
mouth. Let my soul glo - ry in the LORD; the
Em7 D/F♯ D/G
Fm7 E♭/G E♭/A♭
low - ly will hear me and be glad.
to Refrain
Verse 2 (M.M. ♩ = c. 79)
D/A
E♭/B♭
The LORD has
A7sus4 D/A A7sus4 D/A
B♭7sus4 E♭/B♭ B♭7sus4 E♭/B♭
eyes for the just, and ears for their cry. The LORD con -

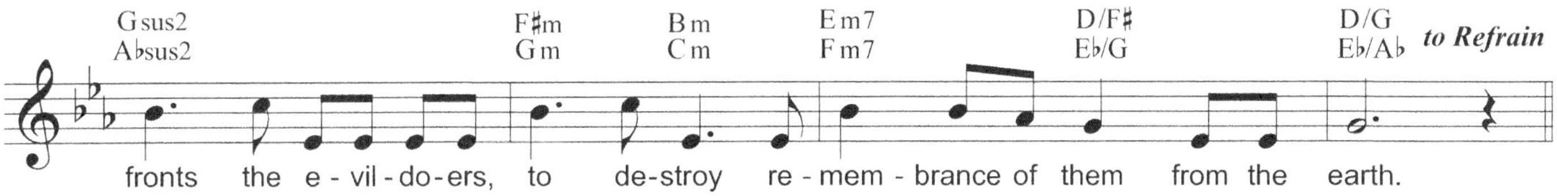
Gsus2 Absus2
F♯m Gm
Bm Cm
Em7 Fm7
D/F♯ E♭/G
D/G E♭/A♭
to Refrain
fronts the e-vil-do-ers, to de-stroy re-mem-brance of them from the earth.

Verse 3 (M.M. ♩ = c. 79)

D/A E♭/B♭
A7sus4 B♭7sus4
D/A E♭/B♭
When the just cry out, the LORD hears them, and from

A7sus4 B♭7sus4
D/A E♭/B♭
Gsus2 A♭sus2
F♯m Gm
all their dis-tress he res-cues them. The LORD is close to the bro-ken-

to Refrain
Verse 4 (M.M. ♩ = c. 79)
Bm Cm
Em7 Fm7
D/F♯ E♭/G
D/G E♭/A♭
D/A E♭/B♭
A7sus4 B♭7sus4
heart-ed; and those who are crushed in spir-it he saves.
Man-y are the trou-bles of the

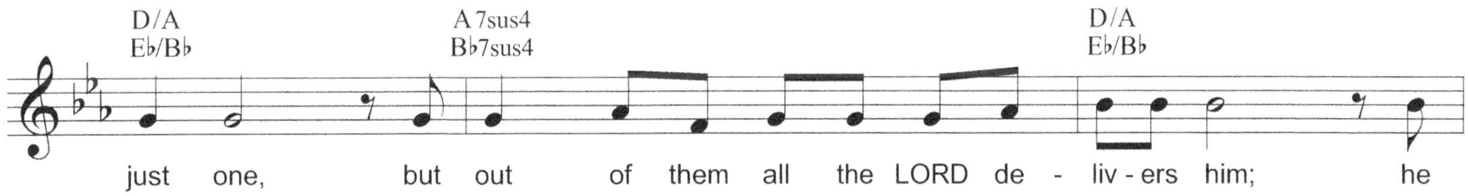
D/A E♭/B♭
A7sus4 B♭7sus4
D/A E♭/B♭
just one, but out of them all the LORD de-liv-ers him; he

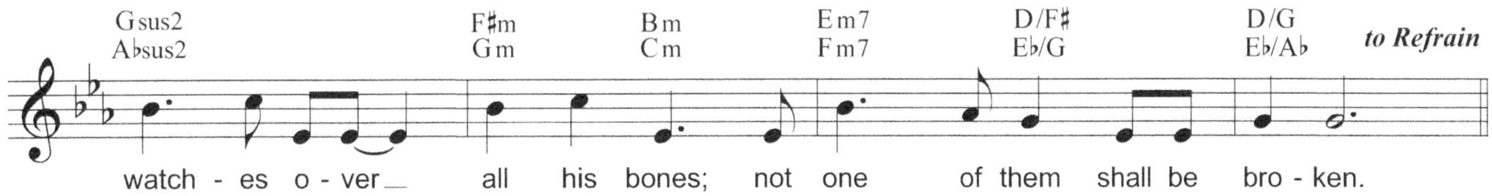
Gsus2 A♭sus2
F♯m Gm
Bm Cm
Em7 Fm7
D/F♯ E♭/G
D/G E♭/A♭
to Refrain
watch-es o-ver all his bones; not one of them shall be bro-ken.

Gospel Acclamation: John 6:63c, 68c

Acclamation: (Keyboard/SATB) NO. III

(M.M. ♩ = c. 160)

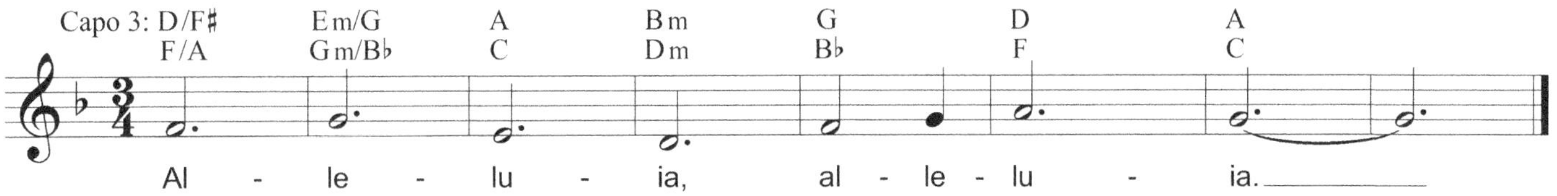
Capo 3: D/F♯ F/A
Em/G Gm/B♭
A C
Bm Dm
G B♭
D F
A C
Al-le-lu-ia, al-le-lu-ia.

Verse: (Cantor)

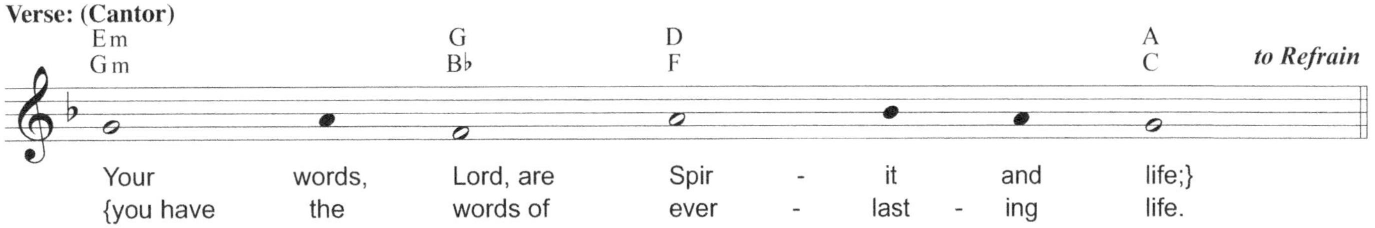
Em Gm
G B♭
D F
A C
to Refrain
Your words, Lord, are Spir-it and life;}
{you have the words of ever-last-ing life.

22nd Sunday in Ordinary Time

August 29

Psalm 15:2–3, 3–4, 4–5

(M.M. ♩ = c. 122)
REFRAIN
Capo 3:
Am Cm G/A B♭/C Fsus2 A♭sus2 Em7 Gm7 Fsus2 A♭sus2
The one who does jus-tice will live in the pres-ence of the Lord.
Verse 1
Fsus2 A♭sus2 C E♭ C/F E♭/A♭ G B♭
Who - ev - er walks blame-less - ly and does jus - tice; who thinks the
Em Gm F A♭ C/G E♭/B♭ Gsus2 B♭sus2 Am Cm
to Refrain
truth in his heart and slan - ders not with his tongue.
Verse 2
Fsus2 A♭sus2 C E♭
Who harms not his fel - low man, nor takes up a re -
C/F E♭/A♭ G B♭ Em Gm
proach a - gainst his neigh - bor; by whom the rep - ro - bate is de -
F A♭ C/G E♭/B♭ Gsus2 B♭sus2 Am Cm
to Refrain
spised, while he hon - ors those who fear the LORD.
Verse 3
Fsus2 A♭sus2 C E♭
Who lends not his mon - ey at u - su - ry and ac -

C/F
E♭/A♭
G
B♭
cepts no bribe a - gainst the in - no - cent. Who - ev - er does these things shall

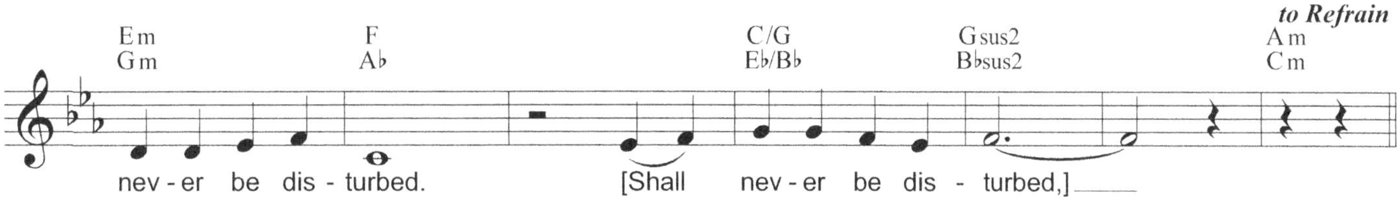
to Refrain
Em
Gm
F
A♭
C/G
E♭/B♭
Gsus2
B♭sus2
Am
Cm
nev - er be dis - turbed. [Shall nev - er be dis - turbed,]

Gospel Acclamation: James 1:18

Acclamation: (Keyboard/SATB) NO. I

(𝅗𝅥 = c. 96)

Capo 1: D A/C♯ G/B D/A G D/F♯ D/A A Bm Em D/F♯ Gsus2
E♭ B♭/D A♭/C E♭/B♭ A♭ E♭/G E♭/B♭ B♭ Cm Fm E♭/G A♭sus2
Al - le - lu - ia, al - le - lu - ia, al - le - lu - ia.

Verse: (Cantor)

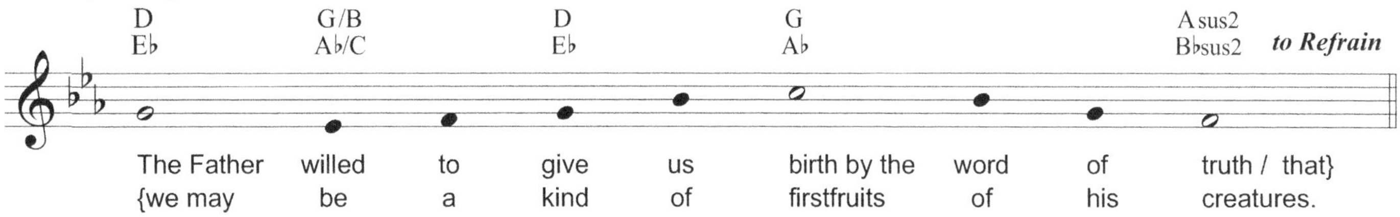
D G/B D G Asus2
E♭ A♭/C E♭ A♭ B♭sus2
to Refrain
The Father willed to give us birth by the word of truth / that}
{we may be a kind of firstfruits of his creatures.

23rd Sunday in Ordinary Time

September 5

(M.M. ♩ = c. 120)

Psalm 146:6-7, 8-9, 9-10

REFRAIN [or: Alleluia]
Capo 3: C F/C C C Em Dm/F G7 C
Eb Ab/Eb Eb Eb Gm Fm/Ab Bb7 Eb
Praise the Lord, my soul! Praise the Lord, my soul!
Verse 1
C Em Fsus2
Eb Gm Absus2
The God of Jac - ob keeps faith for - ev - er, se-cures
Dm7 Gsus4 G Am Em7/G
Fm7 Bbsus4 Bb Cm Gm7/Bb
jus - tice for the op - pressed, gives food to the hun -
F C/E Dm7 Fsus2 Gsus4 G
Ab Eb/G Fm7 Absus2 Bbsus4 Bb
- gry. The LORD sets cap - tives free.
to Refrain
Verse 2
C Em Fsus2
Eb Gm Absus2
The LORD gives sight to the blind; the LORD
Dm7 Gsus4 G Am Em7/G
Fm7 Bbsus4 Bb Cm Gm7/Bb
rais - es up those who were bowed down. The LORD loves the just;
F C/E Dm7 Fsus2 Gsus4 G
Ab Eb/G Fm7 Absus2 Bbsus4 Bb
the LORD pro - tects stran - gers.
to Refrain

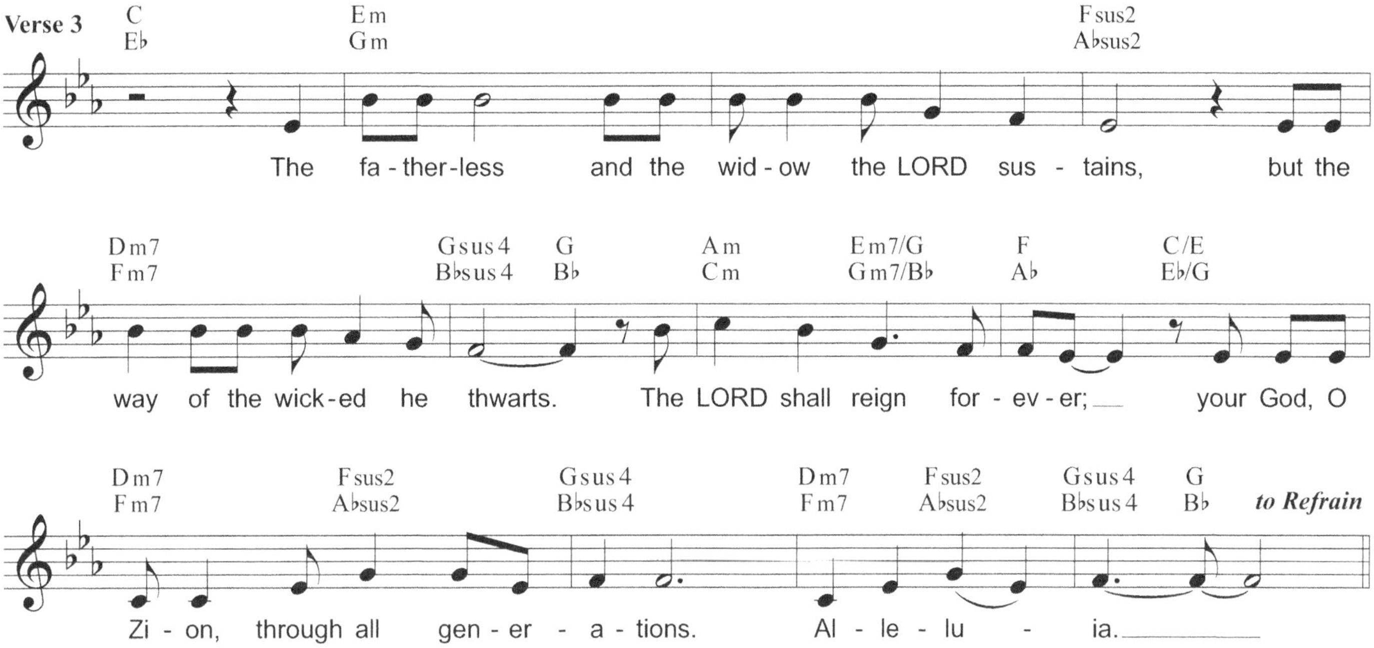
Verse 3
C Em Fsus2
E♭ Gm A♭sus2
The fa - ther - less and the wid - ow the LORD sus - tains, but the
Dm7 Gsus4 G Am Em7/G F C/E
Fm7 B♭sus4 B♭ Cm Gm7/B♭ A♭ E♭/G
way of the wick - ed he thwarts. The LORD shall reign for - ev - er; your God, O
Dm7 Fsus2 Gsus4 Dm7 Fsus2 Gsus4 G
Fm7 A♭sus2 B♭sus4 Fm7 A♭sus2 B♭sus4 B♭
to Refrain
Zi - on, through all gen - er - a - tions. Al - le - lu - ia.

Gospel Acclamation: cf. Matthew 4:23

Acclamation: (Keyboard/SATB) NO. I

(𝅗𝅥 = c. 96)
Capo 1: D A/C♯ G/B D/A G D/F♯ D/A A Bm Em D/F♯ Gsus2
E♭ B♭/D A♭/C E♭/B♭ A♭ E♭/G E♭/B♭ B♭ Cm Fm E♭/G A♭sus2
Al - le - lu - ia, al - le - lu - ia, al - le - lu - ia.

Verse: (Cantor)

to Refrain
D G/B D G Asus2
E♭ A♭/C E♭ A♭ B♭sus2
Jesus proclaimed the Gospel of the kingdom and cured every dis - ease a - mong the people.

24th Sunday in Ordinary Time

September 12

Psalm 116:1–2, 3–4, 5–6, 8–9

(M.M. ♩ = c. 72)
REFRAIN [or: Alleluia]
A Em7 Em/G A F Em G/B A
I will walk be-fore the Lord, in the land of the liv - ing.
Verse 1
Asus2 Em7 G/B A C/G Bm7
I love the LORD be-cause he has heard my voice [my voice] in sup-pli - ca-tion, be-
A C/G Fmaj7 Esus4
to Refrain
cause he has in - clined his ear to me the day I called.
Verse 2
Asus2 Em7 G/B A C/G
The cords of death en-com-passed me; the snares of the neth-er-world seized up -
Bm7 Csus2 G/B Gm6/B♭
poco rit.
on me; I fell in - to dis - tress and sor - row,__ and I
A C/G Fmaj7 Esus4
a tempo
to Refrain
called up - on the name of the LORD, “O LORD, save my life!”
Verse 3
Asus2 Em7 G/B A C/G Bm7
Gra-cious is the LORD and__ just; yes, our God is__ mer-ci - ful. The

C G/B Gm/B♭ A C/G Fmaj7 Esus4
poco rit.
a tempo
to Refrain
LORD keeps the lit - tle ones; I was brought low, and he saved me.
Verse 4
Asus2 Em7 G/B A C/G
For he has freed my soul from death, my eyes from
Bm7 Csus2 G/B Gm6/B♭
poco rit.
tears, my feet from stum - bling. I shall
A a tempo C/G Fmaj7 Esus4
to Refrain
walk be - fore the LORD in the land of the liv - ing.

Gospel Acclamation: Galatians 6:14

Acclamation: (Keyboard/SATB) NO. II

(M.M. ♩ = c. 130)

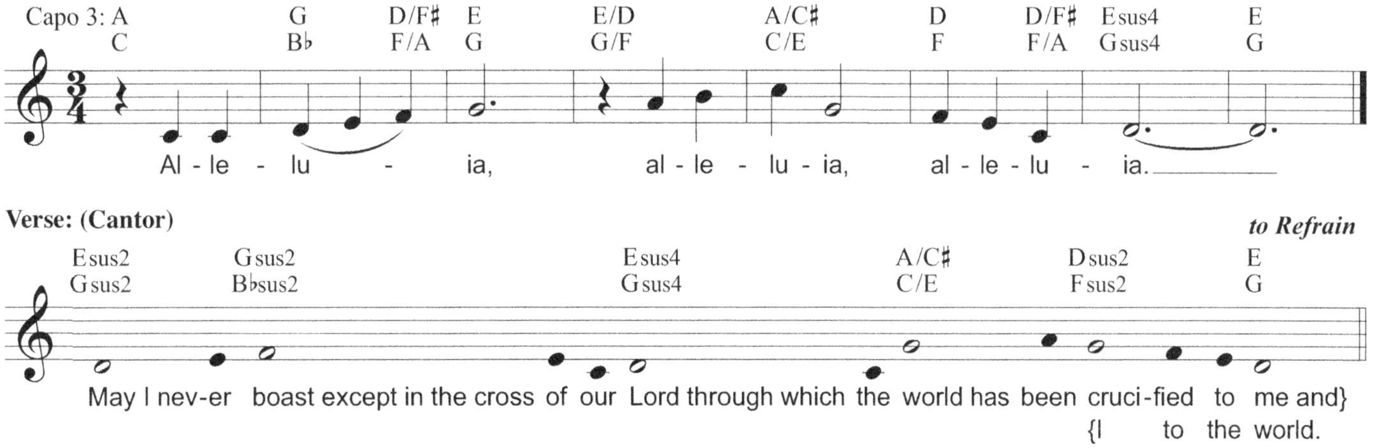
Capo 3: A G D/F♯ E E/D A/C♯ D D/F♯ Esus4 E
C B♭ F/A G G/F C/E F F/A Gsus4 G
Al - le - lu - ia, al - le - lu - ia, al - le - lu - ia.
Verse: (Cantor)
to Refrain
Esus2 Gsus2 Esus4 A/C♯ Dsus2 E
Gsus2 B♭sus2 Gsus4 C/E Fsus2 G
May I nev-er boast except in the cross of our Lord through which the world has been cruci-fied to me and}
{I to the world.

25th Sunday in Ordinary Time

September 19

(M.M. 𝅗𝅥 = c. 63)

Psalm 54:3–4, 5, 6 & 8

REFRAIN
Capo 3: C C Em Dm/F G
E♭ E♭ Gm Fm/A♭ B♭
The Lord up - holds my life.
Verse 1
Dm Am/C G/B F
Fm Cm/E♭ B♭/D A♭
O God, by your name save me, and by your might de -
C C/E Gsus2 G F/A C
E♭ E♭/G B♭sus2 B♭ A♭/C E♭
fend my cause. O God, hear my
to Refrain
Gsus2 G F/A C C/E Gsus2 G
B♭sus2 B♭ A♭/C E♭ E♭/G B♭sus2 B♭
prayer; heark-en to the words of my mouth.
Verse 2
Dm Am/C G/B
Fm Cm/E♭ B♭/D
For the haugh - ty men have ris - en up a - gainst me,
F C C/E Gsus2
A♭ E♭ E♭/G B♭sus2
the ruth - less seek my life;
to Refrain
G F/A C Gsus2 G
B♭ A♭/C E♭ B♭sus2 B♭
they set not God be - fore their eyes.

Verse 3
Dm Fm
Am/C Cm/E♭
G/B B♭/D
Be - hold, God is my help - er; the
F A♭
C E♭
Gsus2 B♭sus2
G B♭
Lord sus - tains my life.
F/A A♭/C
C E♭
G/B B♭/D
Free - ly will I of - fer you sac - ri - fice; I will
F A♭
C E♭
C/E E♭/G
Gsus2 B♭sus2
G B♭
praise your name, O LORD,
to Refrain
F/A A♭/C
C E♭
C/E E♭/G
Gsus2 B♭sus2
G B♭
for its good - ness.

Gospel Acclamation: cf. 2 Thessalonians 2:14

Acclamation: (Keyboard/SATB) NO. IV

(M.M. ♩ = c. 116)

Capo 5: G C
Am Dm
F B♭
C F
Dm7 Gm7
Al - le - lu - ia, al - le - lu - ia, al - le -
C/E F/A
Fmaj7 B♭maj7
1.
Gsus4 Csus4
2 and onward
Gsus4 Csus4
lu - ia. ia.

Verse: (Cantor)

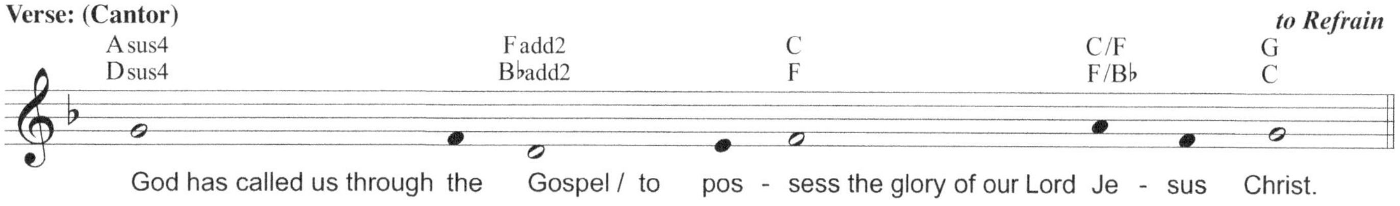
to Refrain
Asus4 Dsus4
Fadd2 B♭add2
C F
C/F F/B♭
G C
God has called us through the Gospel / to pos - sess the glory of our Lord Je - sus Christ.

26th Sunday in Ordinary Time

September 26

(M.M. 𝅗𝅥 = c. 74)

Psalm 19:8, 10, 12-13, 14

REFRAIN
D A/C♯ G/B C Em7 D/F♯ G D/A
The precepts of the Lord give joy to the heart, joy to the heart.
Verse 1
D/A Bm F♯m/A G Gsus2
The law of the LORD is per - fect, re - fresh - ing the
D/A D Em9 Bm/D
soul; the de - cree of the LORD is trust - wor - thy, giv - ing
Cmaj7 D/G D/A Dsus4 D
wis - dom to the sim - ple.
to Refrain
Verse 2
D/A Bm F♯m/A G Gsus2
The fear of the LORD is pure, en - dur - ing for -
D/A D Em9 Bm7/D
ev - er; the or - di - nanc - es of the LORD are true,
Cmaj7 D/G D/A Dsus4 D
all of them just.
to Refrain
Verse 3
D/A Bm F♯m/A G
Though your ser - vant is care - ful of them, ver - y dil - i - gent in

D/A D Em9 Bm7/D
keep - ing them, yet who can de - tect fail - ings?
Cmaj7 D/G D/A D
to Refrain
Cleanse me from my un - known faults!
Verse 4
D/A Bm F♯m/A G
From wan - ton sin es - pe - cial - ly, re - strain your
D/A G D/A
ser - vant; let it not rule o - ver me.
Em9 Bm7/D Cmaj7
Then shall I be blame - less and in - no - cent of
D/G D/A D
to Refrain
se - ri - ous sin.

Gospel Acclamation: cf. John 17:17b, 17a

Acclamation: (Keyboard/SATB) NO. I

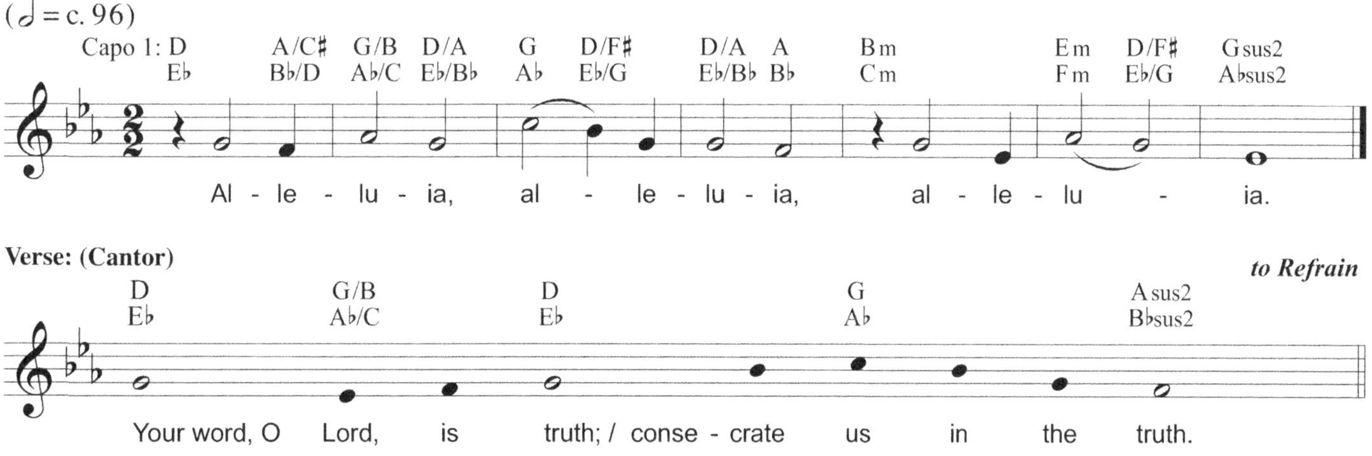
(𝅗𝅥 = c. 96)
Capo 1: D A/C♯ G/B D/A G D/F♯ D/A A Bm Em D/F♯ Gsus2
E♭ B♭/D A♭/C E♭/B♭ A♭ E♭/G E♭/B♭ B♭ Cm Fm E♭/G A♭sus2
Al - le - lu - ia, al - le - lu - ia, al - le - lu - ia.
Verse: (Cantor)
to Refrain
D G/B D G Asus2
E♭ A♭/C E♭ A♭ B♭sus2
Your word, O Lord, is truth; / conse - crate us in the truth.

27th Sunday in Ordinary Time

October 3

(M.M. ♩ = c. 74)

REFRAIN

Psalm 128:1-2, 3, 4-5, 6

Capo 1: D
Eb
A 7/D
Bb7/Eb
D
Eb
C/E
Db/F
C
Db
G/B
Ab/C
May the Lord bless us all the days of our
G
Ab
Em
Fm
Em/G
Fm/Ab
G/B
Ab/C
Asus4
Bbsus4
A
Bb
lives, all the days of our lives.
Verse 1 (M.M. ♩ = c. 68)
D
Eb
G
Ab
D/F♯
Eb/G
G
Ab
Asus2
Bbsus2
Asus4
Bbsus4
Bless-ed are you who fear the LORD, who walk in his ways! For you shall
D
Eb
G
Ab
Bm
Cm
Em9
Fm9
Gmaj7
Abmaj7
Asus2
Bbsus2
to Refrain
eat the fruit of your hand-i-work; bless-ed shall you be, and fa-vored.
Verse 2 (M.M. ♩ = c. 68)
D
Eb
G
Ab
D/F♯
Eb/G
G
Ab
Your wife shall be like a fruit-ful vine in the re-cess-es of your
Asus2
Bbsus2
D
Eb
G
Ab
Bm
Cm
Em9
Fm9
G
Ab
Asus2
Bbsus2
to Refrain
home; your chil-dren like ol-ive plants a-round your ta-ble.

Verse 3 (M.M. ♩ = c. 68)

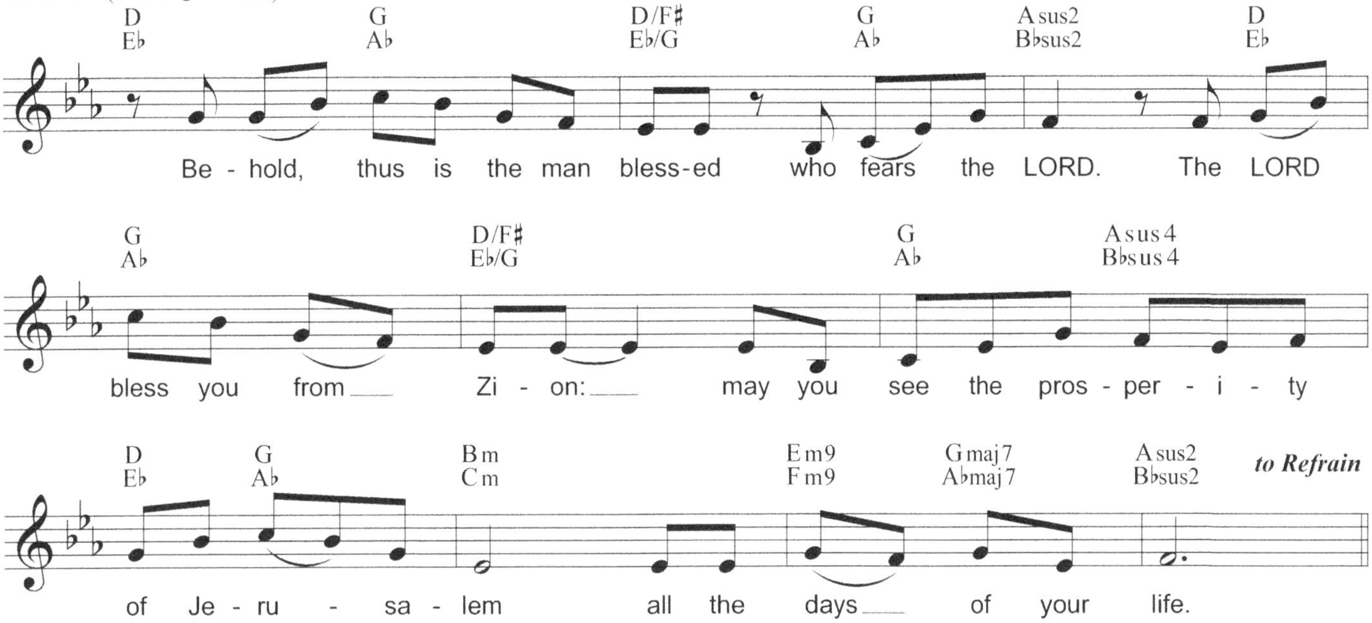
D Eb | G Ab | D/F♯ Eb/G | G Ab | Asus2 Bbsus2 | D Eb
Be - hold, thus is the man bless-ed who fears the LORD. The LORD
G Ab | D/F♯ Eb/G | G Ab | Asus4 Bbsus4
bless you from Zi - on: may you see the pros - per - i - ty
D Eb | G Ab | Bm Cm | Em9 Fm9 | Gmaj7 Abmaj7 | Asus2 Bbsus2
to Refrain
of Je - ru - sa - lem all the days of your life.

Verse 4 (M.M. ♩ = c. 68)

D/A Eb/Bb | D Eb | G Ab | Bm Cm | Em9 Fm9 | Gmaj7 Abmaj7 | Asus2 Bbsus2
to Refrain
May you see your child - ren's chil - dren. Peace be up - on Is - ra - el!

Gospel Acclamation: 1 John 4:12

Acclamation: (Keyboard/SATB) NO. I

(𝅗𝅥 = c. 96)

Capo 1: D Eb | A/C♯ Bb/D | G/B Ab/C | D/A Eb/Bb | G Ab | D/F♯ Eb/G | D/A Eb/Bb | A Bb | Bm Cm | Em Fm | D/F♯ Eb/G | Gsus2 Absus2
Al - le - lu - ia, al - le - lu - ia, al - le - lu - ia.

Verse: (Cantor) *to Refrain*

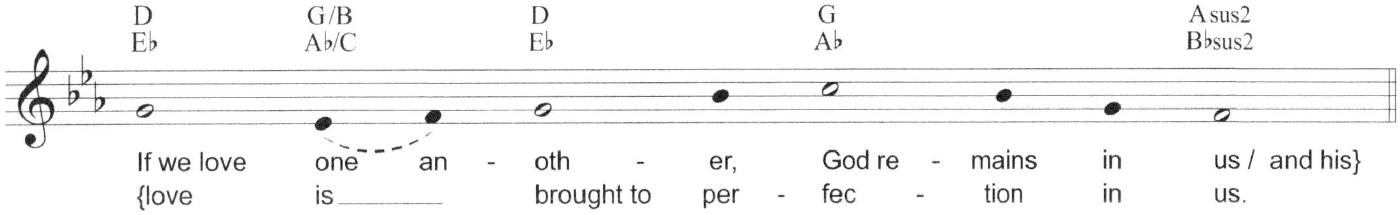
D Eb | G/B Ab/C | D Eb | G Ab | Asus2 Bbsus2
If we love one an - oth - er, God re - mains in us / and his}
{love is brought to per - fec - tion in us.

28th Sunday in Ordinary Time

October 10

Psalm 90:12–13, 14–15, 16–17

(M.M. ♩ = c. 100)

REFRAIN

Am Am/C C/E D Bm7 C Am9 C D
Fill us with your love, O Lord, and we will sing for joy!

Verse 1

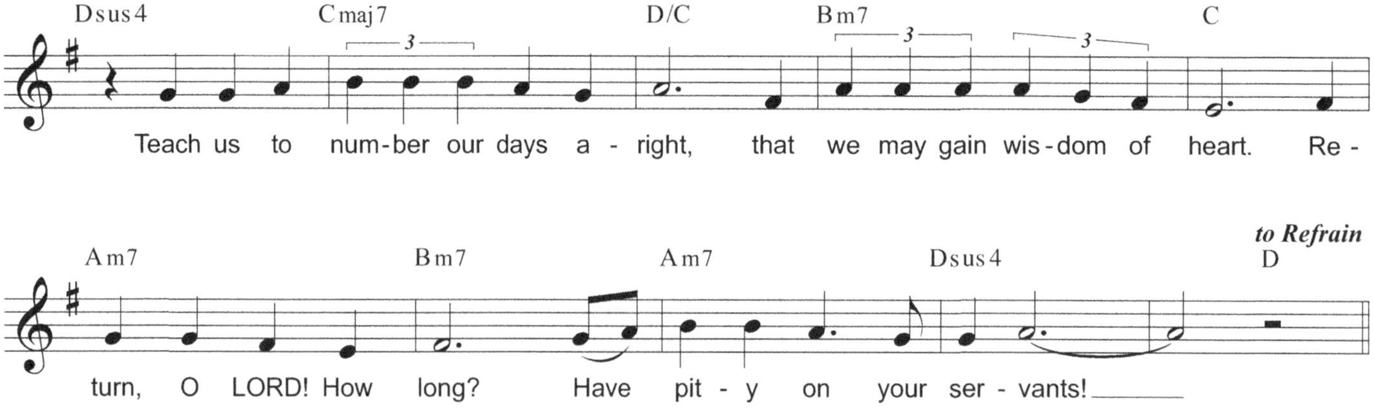
Dsus4 Cmaj7 D/C Bm7 C
Teach us to num-ber our days a - right, that we may gain wis-dom of heart. Re -
Am7 Bm7 Am7 Dsus4 D
turn, O LORD! How long? Have pit - y on your ser - vants!
to Refrain

Verse 2

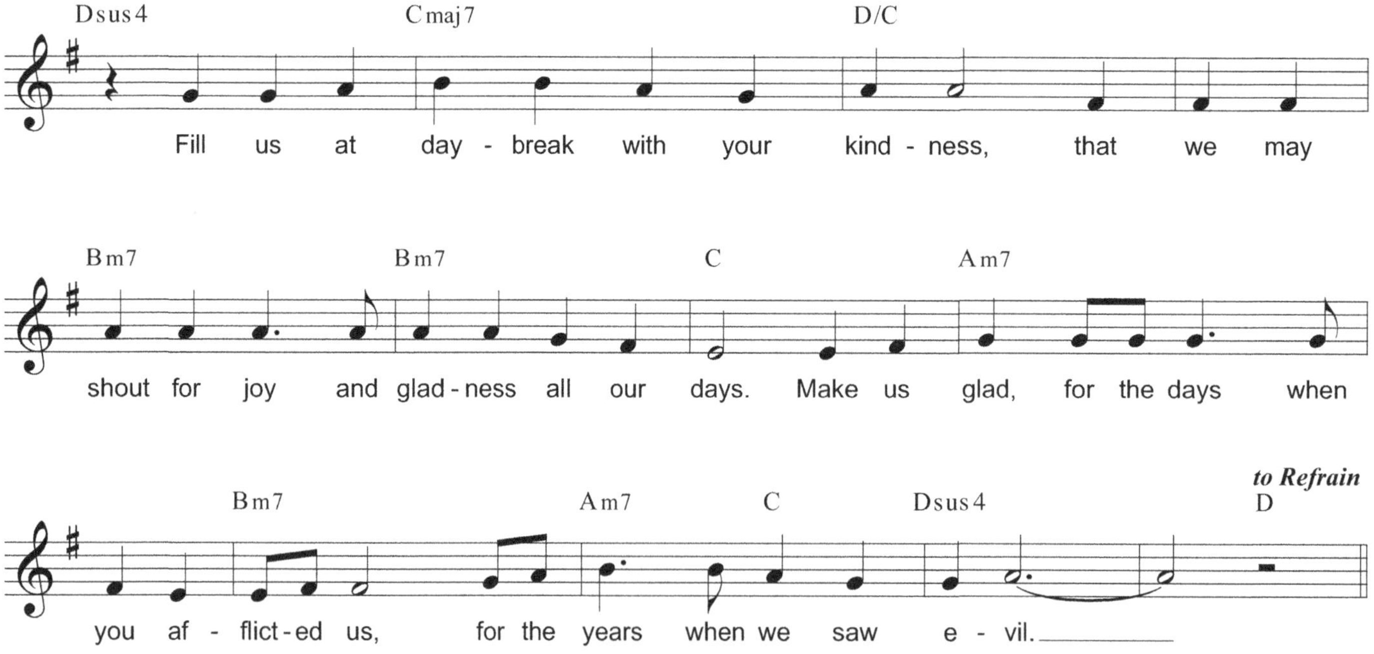
Dsus4 Cmaj7 D/C
Fill us at day - break with your kind - ness, that we may
Bm7 Bm7 C Am7
shout for joy and glad - ness all our days. Make us glad, for the days when
Bm7 Am7 C Dsus4 D
you af - flict - ed us, for the years when we saw e - vil.
to Refrain

Verse 3

Dsus4 Cmaj7 Dsus4/C Bm7 C
Let your work be seen by your ser - vants and your glo - ry by their chil - dren; and
Am7 D/A Am7
may the gra - cious care of the LORD our God be ours; pros - per the work of our
Bm7 G/B Am7 Dsus4 D
to Refrain
hands for us! Pros - per the work of our hands!

Gospel Acclamation: Matthew 5:3

Acclamation: (Keyboard/SATB) NO. III

(M.M. ♩ = c. 160)

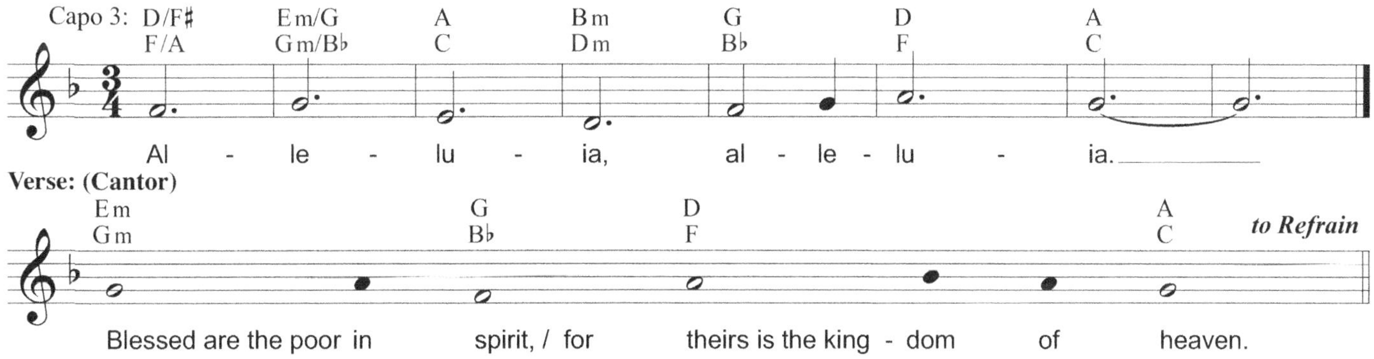
Capo 3: D/F♯ Em/G A Bm G D A
F/A Gm/B♭ C Dm B♭ F C
Al - le - lu - ia, al - le - lu - ia.
Verse: (Cantor)
Em G D A
Gm B♭ F C
to Refrain
Blessed are the poor in spirit, / for theirs is the king - dom of heaven.

29th Sunday in Ordinary Time

October 17

(M.M. ♪ = c. 136)

REFRAIN

Psalm 33:4–5, 18–19, 20, 22

Capo 2: D
E
C
D
Lord, let your mer - cy be on ___ as we
Bm G/B G Em9 Asus4 A
C♯m A/C♯ A F♯m9 Bsus4 B
place our trust in you. ___
Verse 1
D G/D D A7/D D
E A/E E B7/E E
Up - right ___ is the word of the LORD, and all his works are trust-wor - thy. ___
to Refrain
F♯m G/B D/A G/B D A7/D D G/D
G♯m A/C♯ E/B A/C♯ E B7/E E A/E
He loves jus - tice and right; of the kind - ness of the LORD the earth is full. ___
Verse 2
D G/D D
E A/E E
See, the eyes of the LORD are up - on those who fear him,
A7/D D F♯m G/B
B7/E E G♯m A/C♯
up - on those who hope for his kind - ness, to de - liv - er them from

to Refrain
D/A E/B G/B A/C♯ D E A7/D B7/E D E G/D A/E
death and pre - serve them in spite of fam - ine.

Verse 3

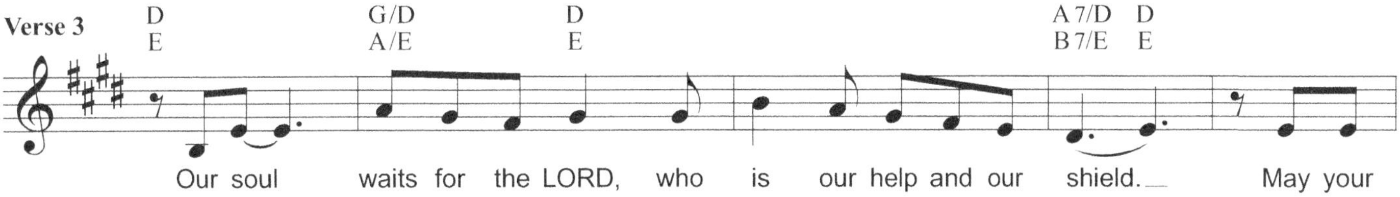
D E G/D A/E D E A7/D B7/E D E
Our soul waits for the LORD, who is our help and our shield. May your

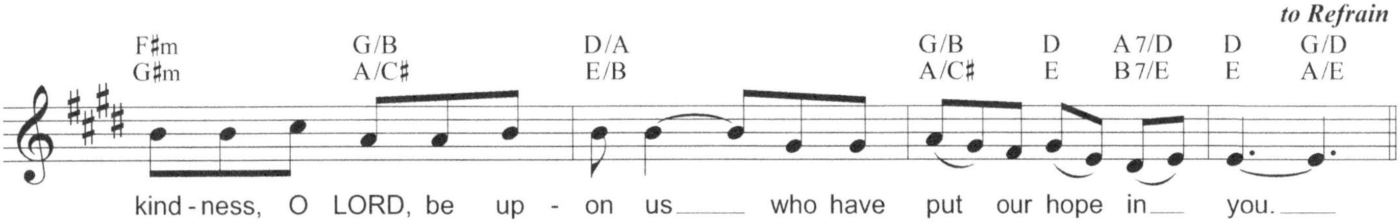
to Refrain
F♯m G♯m G/B A/C♯ D/A E/B G/B A/C♯ D E A7/D B7/E D E G/D A/E
kind-ness, O LORD, be up - on us who have put our hope in you.

Gospel Acclamation: Mark 10:45

Acclamation: (Keyboard/SATB) NO. V

(M.M. ♪ = c. 150)

C Dm Am Dm F/A G/B G
Al - le - lu - ia, al - le - lu - ia. Al - le - lu - ia, al - le - lu - ia.

Verse: (Cantor)

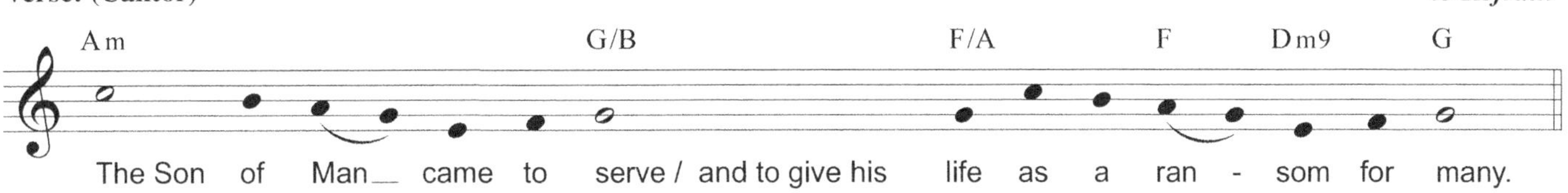
to Refrain
Am G/B F/A F Dm9 G
The Son of Man came to serve / and to give his life as a ran - som for many.

30th Sunday in Ordinary Time

October 24

Psalm 126:1–2, 2–3, 4–5, 6

(M.M. ♩ = c. 104)
REFRAIN
C G/C C G/C C G/C C A/C♯ C/E
The Lord has done great things for us;
F G F♯m Am F♯m/E Am/G Fsus2 Gsus2 C
we are filled with joy, we are filled with joy.
Verse 1
C F/A G/B Em F Em F G
When the LORD brought back the cap - tives of Zi - on,
F/A Dm7 Em Fmaj7 Cmaj7/E
we were like men dream - ing. Then our mouth was filled with laugh-
B♭maj7/D B♭ Dm7 Gsus4 G
- ter, and our tongue with re - joic - ing.
to Refrain
Verse 2
C F/A G/B Em F Em F G F/A Dm7 Em
Then they said a - mong the na - tions, "The LORD has done great things

Am Am7/G Fmaj7 Cmaj7/E
for them." The LORD has done great things for
Bbmaj7/D Bb Dm7 Gsus4 G
to Refrain
us; we are glad in - deed.
Verse 3
C F/A G/B Em F G
Re - store our for - tunes, O LORD, like the
F/A Dm Em Am Am7/G Fmaj7 Cmaj7/E
tor - rents in the south - ern des - ert. Those that sow in tears
Bbmaj7/D Bb Dm7 Gsus4 G
to Refrain
shall reap re - joic - ing.
Verse 4
F/A G/B Em F G
Al - though they go forth weep - ing,
F/A F Em Fmaj7 Cmaj7/E
car - ry - ing the seed to be sown, they shall come back re - joic -
Bbmaj7/D Bb Dm7 Gsus4 G
to Refrain
- ing, car - ry - ing their sheaves.

Gospel Acclamation: cf. 2 Timothy 1:10

Acclamation: (Keyboard/SATB) NO. IV

(M.M. ♩ = c. 116)

Capo 5: G C
Am Dm
F B♭
C F
Dm7 Gm7
Al - le - lu - ia, al - le - lu - ia, al - le -

C/E F/A
Fmaj7 B♭maj7
1.
Gsus4 Csus4
2 and onward
Gsus4 Csus4
lu - ia. ia.

Verse: (Cantor) ***to Refrain***

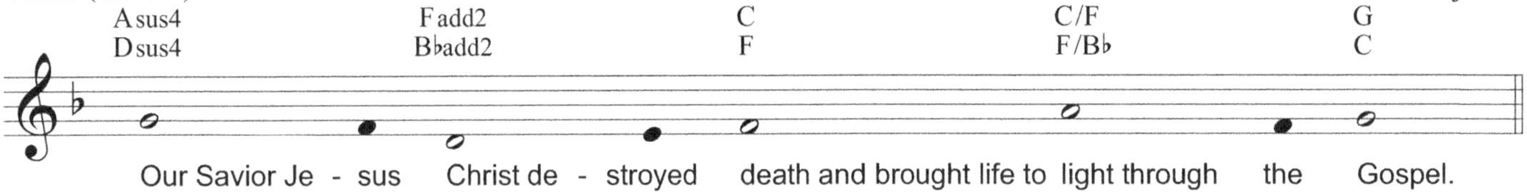
Asus4 Dsus4
Fadd2 B♭add2
C F
C/F F/B♭
G C
Our Savior Je - sus Christ de - stroyed death and brought life to light through the Gospel.

31st Sunday in Ordinary Time

October 31

(M.M. 𝅗𝅥 = c. 68)

REFRAIN

Psalm 18:2-3, 3-4, 47, 51

Bm A/B Bm7 E/B D
I love you, Lord, my strength. I
G A D D/F♯ A E Esus4 E
love you, Lord, my strength.
(Keyboard)
Verse 1
B7sus4 E D/E A/E E
I love you, O LORD, my strength, O LORD, my
to Refrain
G A D D/F♯ A Esus4 E Esus4 E
rock, my for - tress, my de - liv - er - er.
Verse 2
B7sus4 E D/E Asus2 E
My God, my rock of ref - uge, my shield, the
G A D D/F♯ A A/C♯ E
horn of my sal - va - tion, my strong - hold!
E D/E Asus2/E E G A
Praised be the LORD, I ex - claim, and I am

Through composed version in *Blessed Assurance* songbook Ed. 10747 available at www.ocp.org.

to Refrain
D D/F♯ A Esus4 E Esus4 E
safe from my en - e - mies.
Verse 3
E D/E A/E E
The LORD lives! And bless-ed be my rock! Ex -
G A D D/F♯ A E Esus4
tolled be God my sav - ior, you who
E D/E A/E E
gave great vic - t'ries to your king and showed
to Refrain
G A D D/F♯ A Esus4 E Esus4 E
kind - ness to your a - noint - ed.

Gospel Acclamation: John 14:23

Acclamation: (Keyboard/SATB) NO. II

(M.M. ♩ = c. 130)

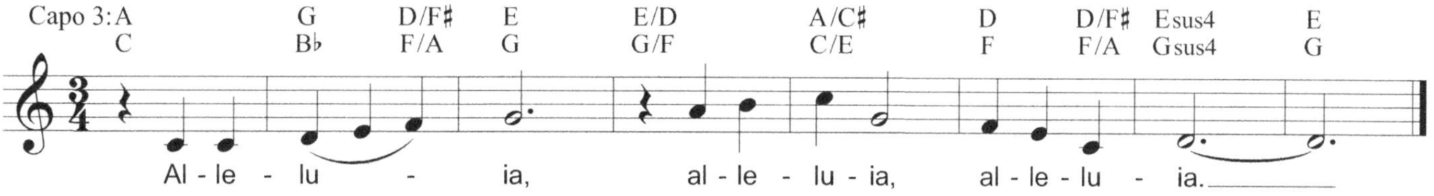
Capo 3: A G D/F♯ E E/D A/C♯ D D/F♯ Esus4 E
C B♭ F/A G G/F C/E F F/A Gsus4 G
Al - le - lu - ia, al - le - lu - ia, al - le - lu - ia.

Verse: (Cantor)

Esus2 Gsus2 D/F♯
Gsus2 B♭sus2 F/A
Whoever loves me will keep my word, says the Lord, / and my
A/C♯ Dsus2 E
C/E Fsus2 G
to Refrain
Father will love him / and we will come to him.

All Saints

November 1

Psalm 24:1bc-2, 3-4ab, 5-6

(M.M. ♩ = c. 94)
REFRAIN
G C/G G G/B Csus2
Lord, this is the peo - ple that longs to see your face.
Bm Cmaj7/E G/F F Em/G Am7 Dsus4 D G
Lord, this is the peo - ple that longs to see your face.
Verse 1
C D/C G/B Am
The LORD's are the earth and its full - ness; the world and those who
G C G/B B♭/F
dwell in it. For he found - ed it up - on the seas and es -
Fsus2 C Am7 Dsus4 D
tab - lished it up - on the riv - ers.
to Refrain
Verse 2
C D/C G/B Am
Who can as - cend the moun - tain of the LORD? or who may stand in his

G C G/B B♭/F F C
ho - ly place? One whose hands are sin - less, whose heart is clean, who de -
to Refrain Verse 3
Am7 Dsus4 D C D/C
sires not what is vain. He shall re - ceive a bless - ing from the
G/B Am G C G/B
LORD, a re - ward from God his sav - ior. Such is the race that seeks him, that
B♭/F F C Am7 Dsus4 D
to Refrain
seeks the face of the God of Ja - cob.

Gospel Acclamation: Matthew 11:28

Acclamation: (Keyboard/SATB) NO. I

(M.M. 𝅗𝅥 = c. 96)

Capo 1: D A/C♯ G/B D/A G D/F♯ D/A A Bm Em D/F♯ Gsus2
E♭ B♭/D A♭/C E♭/B♭ A♭ E♭/G E♭/B♭ B♭ Cm Fm E♭/G A♭sus2
Al - le - lu - ia, al - le - lu - ia, al - le - lu - ia.
Verse: (Cantor)
to Refrain
D G/B D G Asus2
E♭ A♭/C E♭ A♭ B♭sus2
Come to me, all you who labor and are burdened, / and I will give you rest, says the Lord.

32nd Sunday in Ordinary Time

November 7

(M.M. ♩ = c. 120)

REFRAIN [or: Alleluia]

Psalm 146:7, 8-9, 9-10

Capo 3:
C F/C C C Em Dm/F G7 C
E♭ A♭/E♭ E♭ E♭ Gm Fm/A♭ B♭7 E♭
Praise the Lord, my soul! Praise the Lord, my soul!
Verse 1
C Em Fsus2
E♭ Gm A♭sus2
The LORD keeps faith for-ev-er, se-cures
Dm7 Gsus4 G Am Em7/G
Fm7 B♭sus4 B♭ Cm Gm7/B♭
jus-tice for the op-pressed, gives food to the hun-
F C/E Dm7 Fsus2 Gsus4 G
A♭ E♭/G Fm7 A♭sus2 B♭sus4 B♭
-gry. The LORD sets cap-tives free.
to Refrain
Verse 2
C Em Fsus2
E♭ Gm A♭sus2
The LORD gives sight to the blind; the LORD rais-es
Dm7 Gsus4 G Am Em7/G
Fm7 B♭sus4 B♭ Cm Gm7/B♭
up those who were bowed down. The LORD loves the just;
F C/E Dm7 Fsus2 Gsus4 G
A♭ E♭/G Fm7 A♭sus2 B♭sus4 B♭
the LORD pro-tects stran-gers.
to Refrain

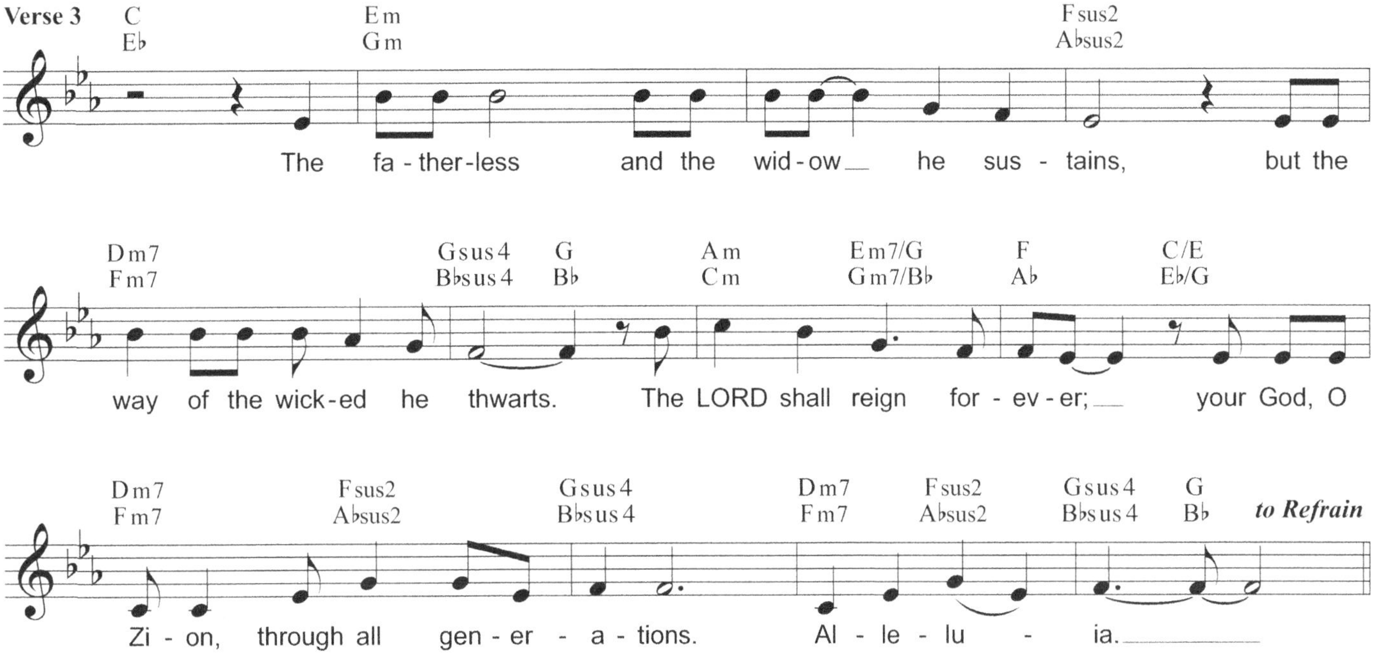
Verse 3
C Em Fsus2
E♭ Gm A♭sus2
The fa - ther-less and the wid - ow he sus - tains, but the
Dm7 Gsus4 G Am Em7/G F C/E
Fm7 B♭sus4 B♭ Cm Gm7/B♭ A♭ E♭/G
way of the wick-ed he thwarts. The LORD shall reign for - ev - er; your God, O
Dm7 Fsus2 Gsus4 Dm7 Fsus2 Gsus4 G
Fm7 A♭sus2 B♭sus4 Fm7 A♭sus2 B♭sus4 B♭
to Refrain
Zi - on, through all gen - er - a - tions. Al - le - lu - ia.

Gospel Acclamation: Matthew 5:3

Acclamation: (Keyboard/SATB) NO. III

(M.M. ♩= c. 160)
Capo 3: D/F♯ Em/G A Bm G D A
F/A Gm/B♭ C Dm B♭ F C
Al - le - lu - ia, al - le - lu - ia.
Verse: (Cantor)
Em G D A
Gm B♭ F C
to Refrain
Blessed are the poor in spirit, / for theirs is the king - dom of heaven.

33rd Sunday in Ordinary Time

November 14

(M.M. ♩ = c. 106)
REFRAIN
Capo 1: Bm7 F♯m7 G Bm7 F♯m7
Cm7 Gm7 A♭ Cm7 Gm7
You are my in - her - i - tance, you are my in - her -
(her-)
Gmaj7 Asus4 C/E Cmaj7 D
A♭maj7 B♭sus4 D♭/F D♭maj7 E♭
- i - tance, O Lord.
(her-)
Verse 1
D G D/A Gsus2
E♭ A♭ E♭/B♭ A♭sus2
O LORD, my al - lot - ted por - tion and my cup, you it is who
G/B D/A C/E D C G/D
A♭/C E♭/B♭ D♭/F E♭ D♭ A♭/E♭
hold fast my lot. I set the LORD ev - er be - fore me; with
G/B A/C♯ D Gmaj7 Asus4 A
A♭/C B♭/D E♭ A♭maj7 B♭sus4 B♭
to Refrain
him at my right hand I shall not be dis - turbed.
Verse 2
Gsus2 D/A Gsus2 D Gsus2
A♭sus2 E♭/B♭ A♭sus2 E♭ A♭sus2
There-fore my heart is glad and my soul re - joic - es, my bod - y, too, a - bides in

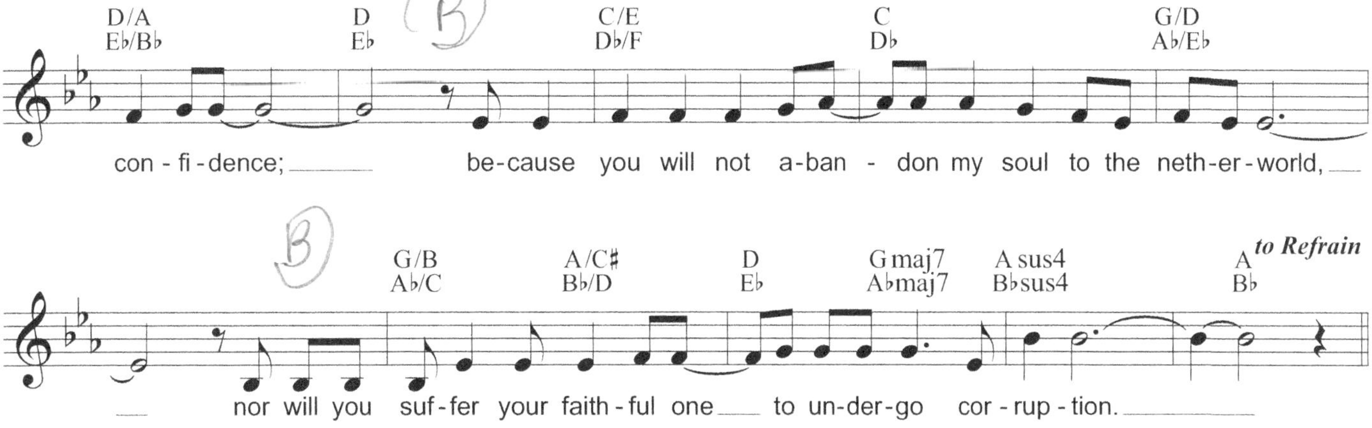
D/A Eb/Bb D Eb C/E Db/F C Db G/D Ab/Eb
con - fi - dence; be-cause you will not a-ban - don my soul to the neth-er-world,
G/B Ab/C A/C♯ Bb/D D Eb Gmaj7 Abmaj7 Asus4 Bbsus4 A Bb
to Refrain
nor will you suf-fer your faith-ful one to un-der-go cor-rup-tion.

Verse 3

Dsus2 Ebsus2 D Eb Gadd9/B Abadd9/C Gmaj7 Abmaj7 A Bb Bm7 Cm7 Bm9/A Cm9/Bb
You will [show me,] show me the path to life,
G Ab D/F♯ Eb/G C/E Db/F G/D Ab/Eb Csus2 Dbsus2
full-ness of joys in your pres-ence, the de-lights at your right hand [for-
G/D Ab/Eb G/B Ab/C G Ab D Eb
to Refrain
ev - er,] for - ev - er.

Gospel Acclamation: Luke 21:36

Acclamation: (Keyboard/SATB) NO. I

(𝅗𝅥 = c. 96)

Capo 1: D Eb A/C♯ Bb/D G/B Ab/C D/A Eb/Bb G Ab D/F♯ Eb/G D/A Eb/Bb A Bb Bm Cm Em Fm D/F♯ Eb/G Gsus2 Absus2
Al - le - lu - ia, al - le - lu - ia, al - le - lu - ia.

Verse: (Cantor) *to Refrain*

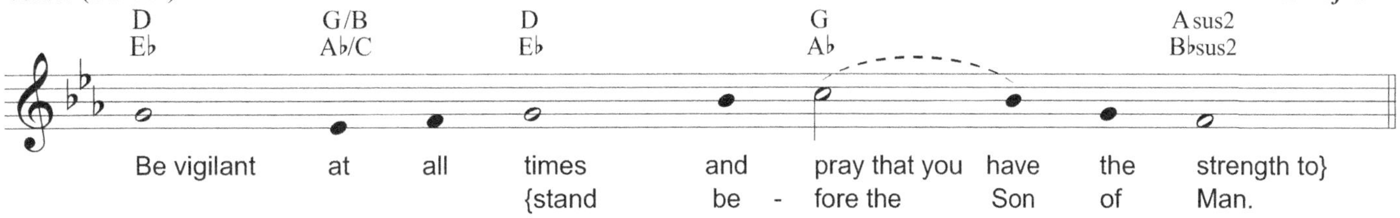
D Eb G/B Ab/C D Eb G Ab Asus2 Bbsus2
Be vigilant at all times and pray that you have the strength to}
{stand be - fore the Son of Man.

Our Lord Jesus Christ, King of the Universe

November 21

(M.M. ♩ = c. 72)

Psalm 93:1, 1-2, 5

REFRAIN
Capo 3: D Em D/G♭ A Bm Bm/A G Em Asus4 A
F Gm F/A C Dm Dm/C B♭ Gm Csus4 C
The Lord is king; he is robed in maj - est-y.
Verse 1
A/C♯ Bm A/C♯ D A/C♯ D
C/E Dm C/E F C/E F
The LORD is king, in splen - dor robed;
Em Am Bm G Em7 Asus4 A
Gm Am Dm B♭ Gm7 Csus4 C
robed is the LORD and girt a - bout with strength.
to Refrain
Verse 2
A/C♯ Bm A/C♯ D A/C♯ D
C/E Dm C/E F C/E F
And he has made the world firm, not to be moved. Your throne stands
Em Am Bm G Em7 Asus4 A
Gm Am Dm B♭ Gm7 Csus4 C
firm from of old; from ev - er - last - ing you are, O LORD.
to Refrain
Verse 3
A/C♯ Bm C/E D A/C♯ D
C/E Dm C/E F C/E F
Your de - crees are wor - thy of trust in - deed;
Em F♯m Bm G Em7 Asus4 A
Gm Am Dm B♭ Gm7 Csus4 C
ho - li - ness be - fits your house, O LORD, for length of days.
to Refrain

Gospel Acclamation: Mark 11:9,10

Acclamation: (Keyboard/SATB) NO. V

(M.M. ♪ = c. 150)

C Dm Am Dm F/A G/B G
Al - le - lu - ia, al - le - lu - ia. Al - le - lu - ia, al - le - lu - ia.

Verse: (Cantor) *to Refrain*

Am G/B F/A F Dm9 G
Blessed is he who comes in the name of the Lord!}
{Bless - ed is the kingdom of our fath - er David that is to come!

Thanksgiving Day

November 25

(M.M. ♩ = c. 78)

REFRAIN [or: Alleluia]

Psalm 113:1-2, 3-4, 5-6, 7-8

Capo 3
Bless - ed be the name, bless - ed be the name,
bless - ed be the name of the Lord for ev - er.
Verse 1
Praise, you ser - vants of the LORD, praise the name of the LORD.
Bless-ed be the name of the LORD both now and for - ev - er.
to Refrain
Verse 2
From the ris - ing to the set - ting of the sun is the
name of the LORD to be praised. High a - bove all na - tions is the
LORD; a - bove the heav - ens is his glo - ry.
to Refrain

For alternate **Responsorial Psalms**, see *Lectionary for the Mass, Second Typical Edition* #945.

Verse 3

Am Cm C E♭ G B♭ Dm Fm C/E E♭/G
Who is like the LORD, our God, who is en - throned on high and

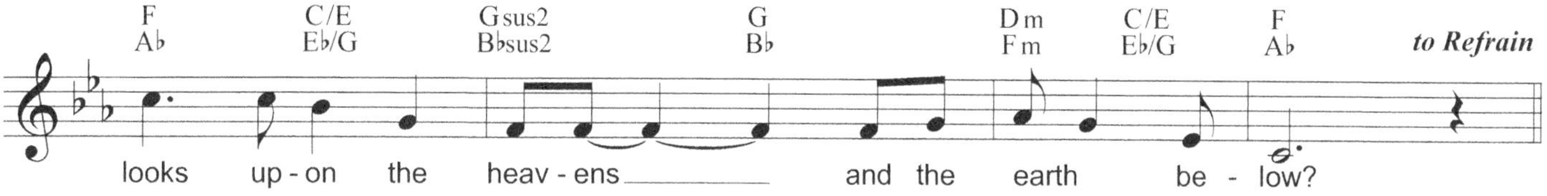
F A♭ C/E E♭/G Gsus2 B♭sus2 G B♭ Dm Fm C/E E♭/G F A♭
to Refrain
looks up - on the heav - ens and the earth be - low?

Verse 4

Am Cm C E♭ G B♭ Dm Fm Am Cm
He rais - es up the low - ly from the dust; from the dung - hill he lifts up the poor to

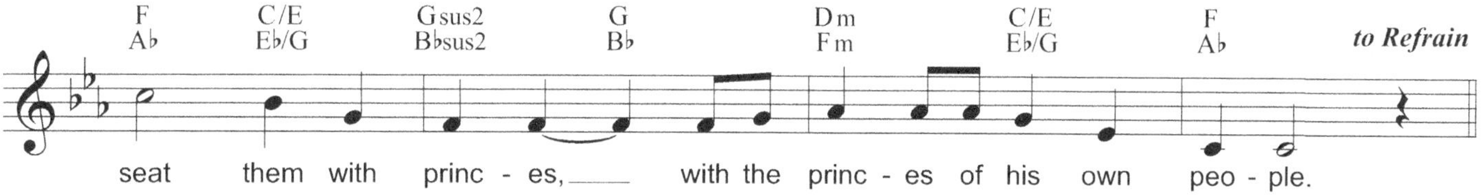
F A♭ C/E E♭/G Gsus2 B♭sus2 G B♭ Dm Fm C/E E♭/G F A♭
to Refrain
seat them with princ - es, with the princ - es of his own peo - ple.

Gospel Acclamation: 1 Thessalonians 5:18

Acclamation: (Keyboard/SATB) NO. II

(M.M. ♩ = c. 130)

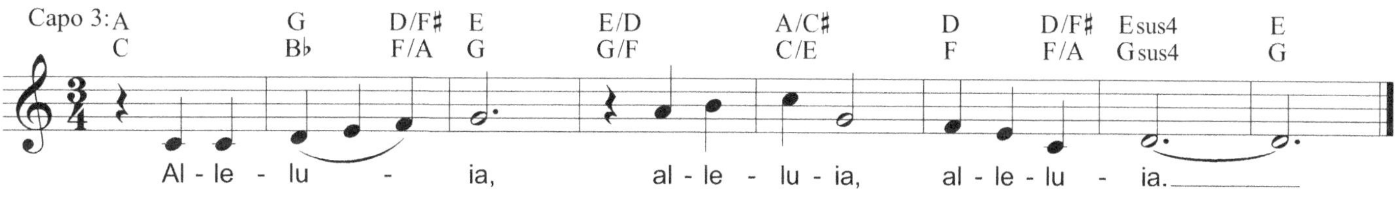
Capo 3: A C G B♭ D/F♯ F/A E G E/D G/F A/C♯ C/E D F D/F♯ F/A Esus4 Gsus4 E G
Al - le - lu - ia, al - le - lu - ia, al - le - lu - ia.

Verse: (Cantor)

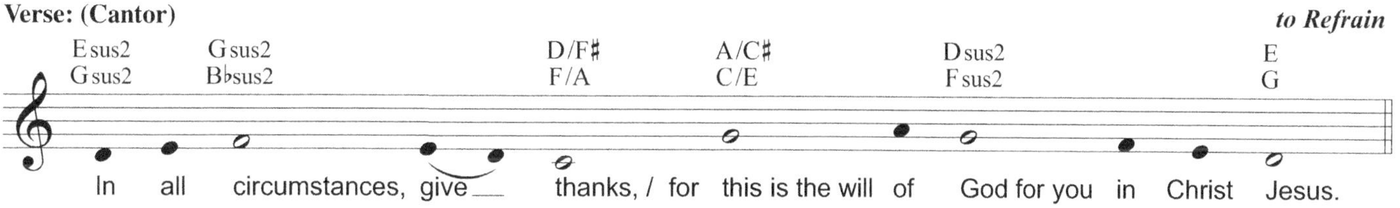
to Refrain
Esus2 Gsus2 Gsus2 B♭sus2 D/F♯ F/A A/C♯ C/E Dsus2 Fsus2 E G
In all circumstances, give thanks, / for this is the will of God for you in Christ Jesus.

For alternate **Gospel Acclamation Verses**, see *Lectionary for the Mass, Second Typical Edition* #946.

Rite of Entrance into the Order of Catechumens

(M.M. ♪ = c. 132)

Psalm 33:4-5, 12-13, 18-19, 20 & 22

REFRAIN

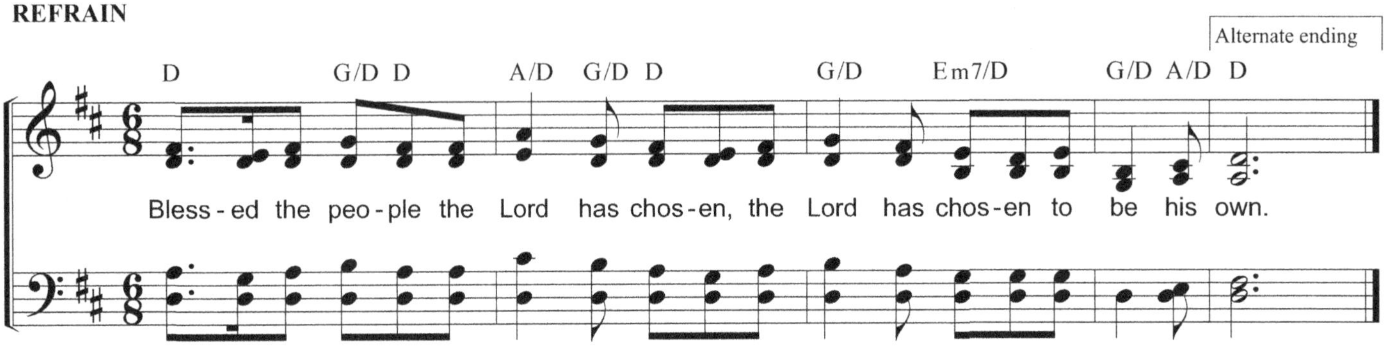
Alternate ending
D G/D D A/D G/D D G/D Em7/D G/D A/D D
Bless-ed the peo-ple the Lord has chos-en, the Lord has chos-en to be his own.

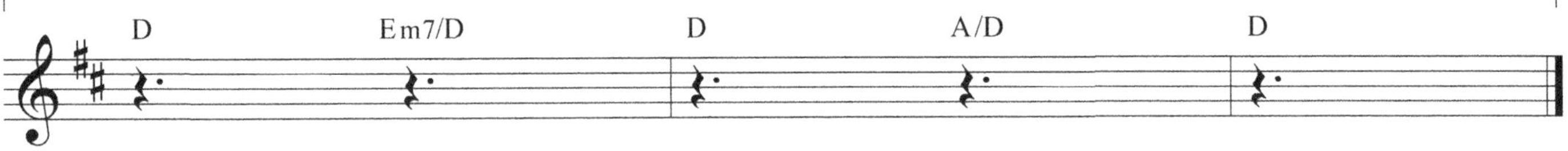
Optional Interlude before Verse 3 & after final Refrain
D Em7/D D A/D D

Verse 1

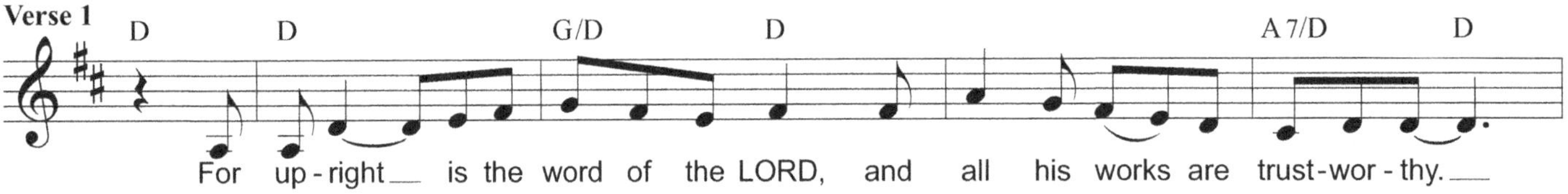
D D G/D D A7/D D
For up-right is the word of the LORD, and all his works are trust-wor-thy.

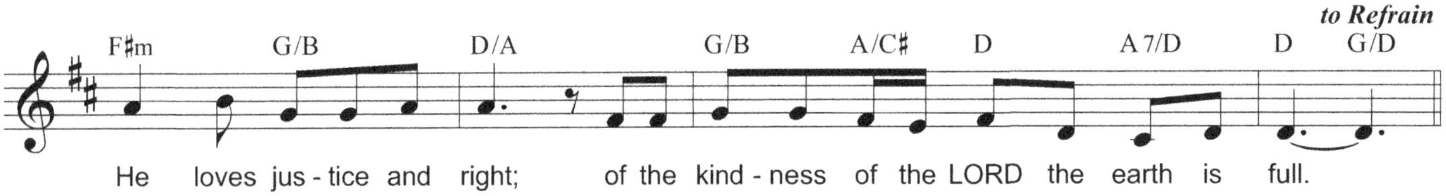
to Refrain
F♯m G/B D/A G/B A/C♯ D A7/D D G/D
He loves jus-tice and right; of the kind-ness of the LORD the earth is full.

Verse 2

D G/D D
Bless-ed the na-tion whose God is the LORD, the peo-ple he has

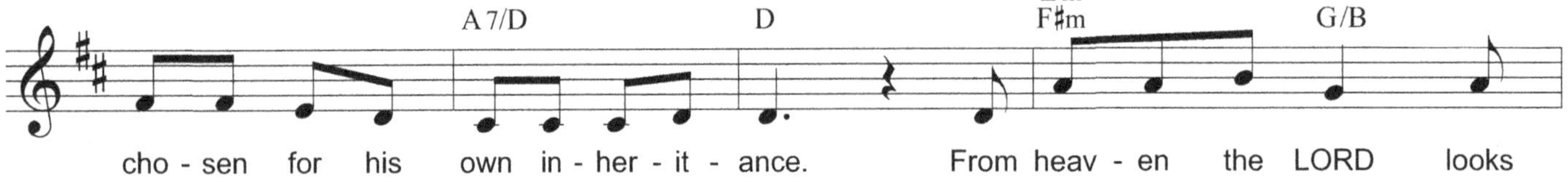
A7/D D Em F♯m G/B
cho-sen for his own in-her-it-ance. From heav-en the LORD looks

to Refrain
D/A G/B A/C♯ D A7/D D G/D
down; he sees all man-kind.

Alternate response: "Lord, let your mercy be on us, as we place our trust in you."

Verse 3
D G/D D
But see, the eyes of the LORD are up - on those who fear him,
A7/D D F♯m G/B
up - on those who hope for his kind - ness, to de - liv - er them from
to Refrain
D/A G/B A/C♯ D A7/D D G/D
death and pre - serve them in spite of fam - ine.
Verse 4
D G/D D A7/D D
Our soul waits for the LORD, who is our help and our shield. May your
to Refrain
F♯m G/B D/A G/B D A7/D D G/D
kind - ness, O LORD, be up - on us who have put our hope in you.

Gospel Acclamation: John 1:41, 17b

Acclamation: (Keyboard/SATB) NO. V

(M.M. ♪ = c. 150)

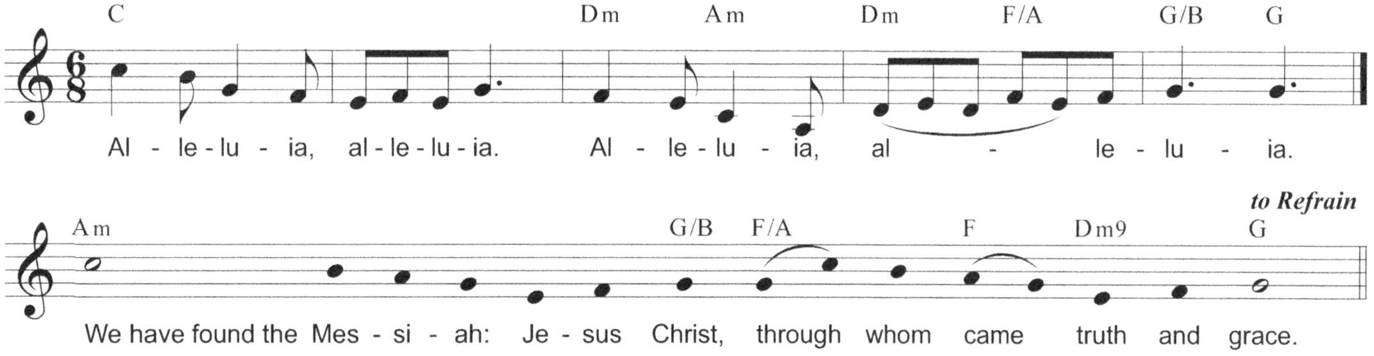
C Dm Am Dm F/A G/B G
Al - le - lu - ia, al - le - lu - ia. Al - le - lu - ia, al - le - lu - ia.
to Refrain
Am G/B F/A F Dm9 G
We have found the Mes - si - ah: Je - sus Christ, through whom came truth and grace.

Selected Psalm for Weddings

(M.M. ♪ = c. 138)
Psalm 128:1-2, 3, 4-5
REFRAIN
Capo 1: A7sus4 D A/D D G A7sus4 D
B♭7sus4 E♭ B♭/E♭ E♭ A♭ B♭7sus4 E♭
Bless-ed are those who fear the Lord. Bless-ed are those who fear the Lord.
Verse 1
D G D/F♯ G Asus2 Asus4
E♭ A♭ E♭/G A♭ B♭sus2 B♭sus4
Bless-ed are you who fear the LORD, who walk in his ways! For you shall
D G Bm Em9 Gmaj7 Asus2
E♭ A♭ Cm Fm9 A♭maj7 B♭sus2
to Refrain
eat the fruit of your hand-i-work; bless-ed shall you be, and fa-vored.
Verse 2
D G D/F♯ G
E♭ A♭ E♭/G A♭
Your wife shall be like a fruit-ful vine in the re-cess-es of your
Asus2 D G Bm Em9 G Asus2
B♭sus2 E♭ A♭ Cm Fm9 A♭ B♭sus2
to Refrain
home; your chil-dren like ol-ive plants a-round your ta-ble.
Verse 3
D G D/F♯ G Asus2 D
E♭ A♭ E♭/G A♭ B♭sus2 E♭
Be-hold, thus is the man bless-ed who fears the LORD. The LORD

Alternate Response: "See how the Lord blesses those who fear him."
For alternate **Responsorial Psalms** for weddings, see *Lectionary for the Mass, Second Typical Edition* #803.

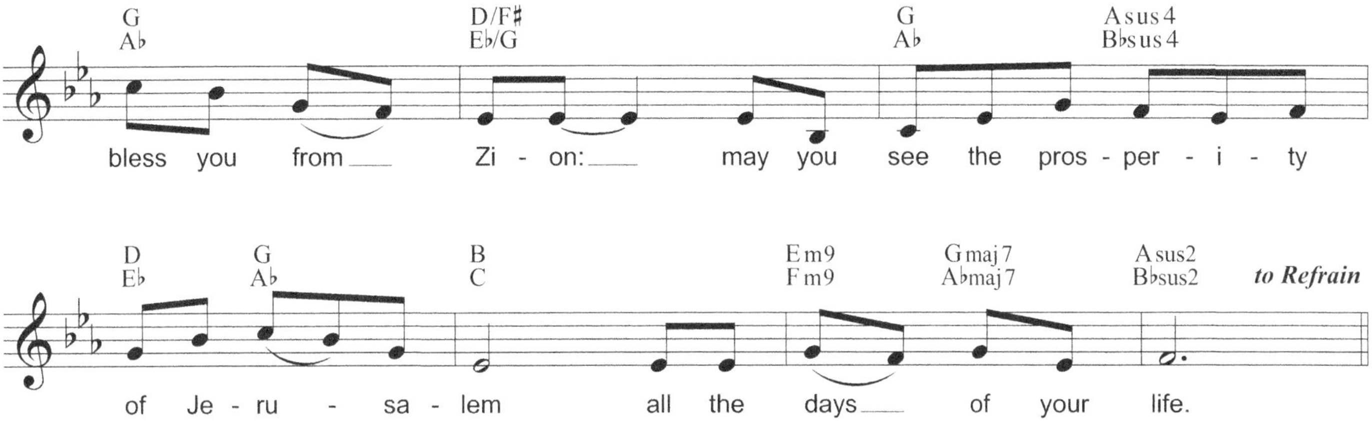
G D/F♯ G Asus4
A♭ E♭/G A♭ B♭sus4
bless you from Zi - on: may you see the pros - per - i - ty
D G B Em9 Gmaj7 Asus2
E♭ A♭ C Fm9 A♭maj7 B♭sus2
to Refrain
of Je - ru - sa - lem all the days of your life.

Selected Psalms for Funerals

(M.M. ♩ = c. 68)
REFRAIN
Psalm 103:8 & 10, 13-14, 15-16, 17-18
Capo 1: D D/C♯ G/B D/A Gsus2 D/F♯ Em7 Asus4
E♭ E♭/D A♭/C E♭/B♭ A♭sus2 E♭/G Fm7 B♭sus4
The Lord is kind and mer-ci-ful. The Lord is kind and mer-ci-ful.
Verse 1
D D/C♯ Bm Bm7/A G D/F♯
E♭ E♭/D Cm Cm7/B♭ A♭ E♭/G
Mer-ci-ful and gra-cious is the LORD, slow to an-ger, and a-bound-ing in
Em7 A Bm F♯m/A G
Fm7 B♭ Cm Gm/B♭ A♭
kind-ness. Not ac-cord-ing to our sins does he deal with us,
D/F♯ Em D/F♯ Gsus2 Asus2
E♭/G Fm E♭/G A♭sus2 B♭sus2
to Refrain
nor does he re-quite us ac-cord-ing to our crimes.
Verse 2
A7sus4 D D/C♯ Bm Bm7/A G
B♭7sus4 E♭ E♭/D Cm Cm7/B♭ A♭
As a fa-ther has com-pas-sion on his chil-dren, so the LORD has com-
D/F♯ Em7 A Bm F♯m/A
E♭/G Fm7 B♭ Cm Gm/B♭
pas-sion on those who fear him. For he knows how we are
G D/F♯ Em D/F♯ Gsus2 Asus2
A♭ E♭/G Fm E♭/G A♭sus2 B♭sus2
to Refrain
formed, he re-mem-bers that we are dust.

Alternate response: "The salvation of the just comes from the Lord."

For alternate **Responsorial Psalms** for funerals, see *Lectionary for the Mass, Second Typical Edition* #1013.

Through composed octavo Ed. 30100716, available at www.ocp.org.

Verse 3
A7sus4 D D/C♯ Bm Bm7/A
B♭7sus4 E♭ E♭/D Cm Cm7/B♭
Man's days are like those of grass; like a
G D/F♯ Em7 A Bm F♯m/A
A♭ E♭/G Fm7 B♭ Cm Gm/B♭
flow-er of the field he blooms; the wind sweeps o-ver him and he is
G D/F♯ Em D/F♯ Gsus2 Asus2
A♭ E♭/G Fm E♭/G A♭sus2 B♭sus2
to Refrain
gone, and his place knows him no more.
Verse 4
A7sus4 D D/C♯ F♯m/A
B♭7sus4 E♭ E♭/D Gm/D
But the kind-ness of the LORD is from e-ter-ni-ty, to e-
Bm Bm7/A G D/F♯ Em7 A
Cm Cm7/B♭ A♭ E♭/G Fm7 B♭
ter-ni-ty toward those who fear him, and his
Bm F♯m/A G D/F♯ Em7 D/F♯
Cm Gm/B♭ A♭ E♭/G Fm7 E♭/G
jus-tice toward chil-dren's chil-dren a-mong those who keep his
Gsus2 A7sus4 Cmaj7 C/E Em7/G A
A♭sus2 B♭7sus4 D♭maj7 D♭/F Fm7/A♭ B♭
to Refrain
cov-e-nant and re-mem-ber to ful-fill his pre-cepts.

Selected Common (Seasonal) Psalm for Ordinary Time

(M.M. 𝅗𝅥 = c. 72)
REFRAIN
Psalm 27:1, 4, 13-14
Capo 3:
The Lord is my light, the Lord is my
light, my light and my sal - va - tion.
Verse 1
The LORD is my light and my sal - va-tion; whom should I fear? The LORD is my
life's ref - uge; of whom should I be a - fraid?
to Refrain
Verse 2
One thing I ask of the LORD; this I seek: to dwell in the
house of the LORD all the days of my life. that I may gaze on the

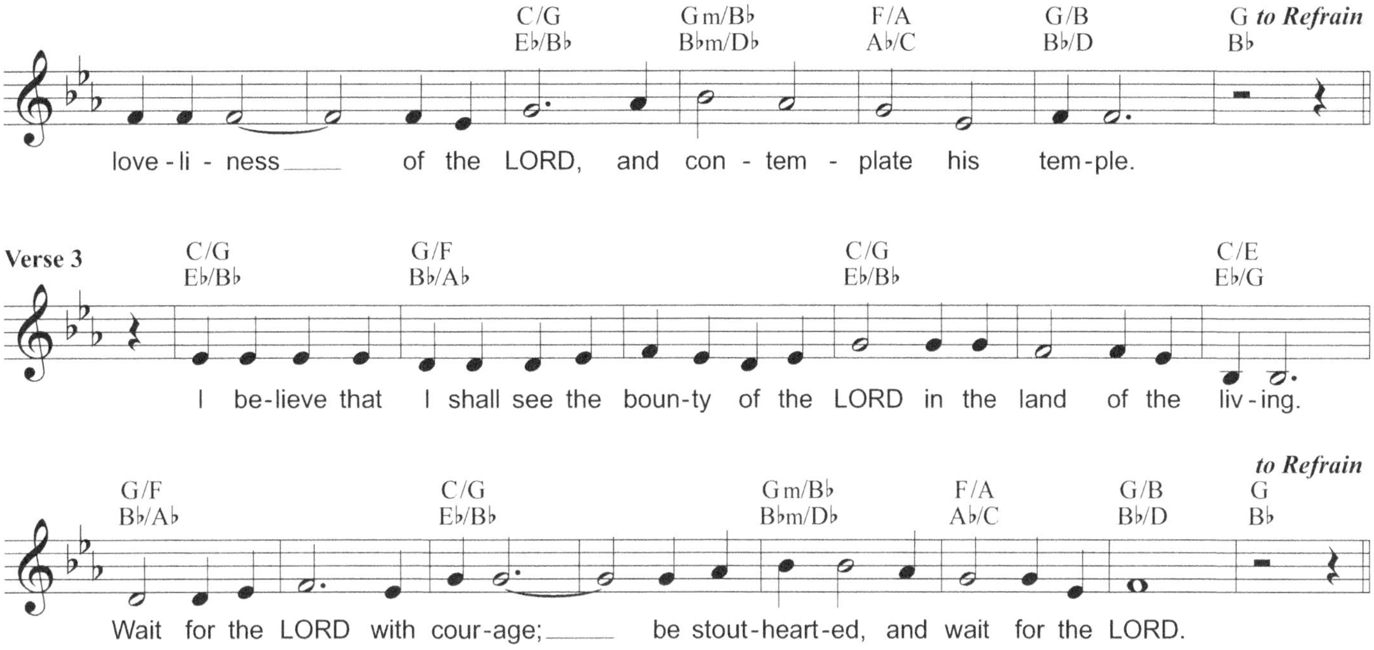
C/G G m/B♭ F/A G/B G to Refrain
E♭/B♭ B♭m/D♭ A♭/C B♭/D B♭
love - li - ness of the LORD, and con - tem - plate his tem-ple.
Verse 3
C/G G/F C/G C/E
E♭/B♭ B♭/A♭ E♭/B♭ E♭/G
I be-lieve that I shall see the boun-ty of the LORD in the land of the liv - ing.
to Refrain
G/F C/G G m/B♭ F/A G/B G
B♭/A♭ E♭/B♭ B♭m/D♭ A♭/C B♭/D B♭
Wait for the LORD with cour-age; be stout-heart-ed, and wait for the LORD.

Made in the USA
Monee, IL
11 October 2020

44511909R00109